Metavista

"In writing this book Martin and Colin have gifted us with a truly substantive text on the Bible in relation to the task of recalibrating the church along missional lines. It is well written, theologically stimulating, meticulously researched, and will no doubt be an authoritative text in its genre. But the best thing about *Metavista* is that is simply great missiology in the Newbigin tradition."

Alan Hirsch, author of *The Forgotten Way* and of *The Shaping of Things To Come.*
He is a founding director of Shapevine.com,
a global forum for engaging in world-changing ideas.

"This very substantial book helps define the missional task and creative opportunity facing the church in cultures which are emerging out of Christendom. Its particular strengths lie in its historical and cultural analysis, its vision of the biblical narrative as a resource to shape culture, and its three-way conversation between Bible, culture and reshaping the church for mission. *Metavista* takes us beyond 'Gospel and Culture' and beyond 'Emerging Church' to put the Bible back at the centre of the conversation."

Graham Cray, Bishop of Maidstone, Chairman of the *Mission-Shaped Church* report.

"With vision, finesse, skillful scholarship and rigorous cultural analysis *Metavista* moves us into uncharted territory of our current context of a massively changing world. In this book the Biblical story frames a re-imagined missional community that has the potential of reshaping the emerging cultures of the 21st century. I know both Colin and Martin well. These are seasoned theologians, historians and leaders of the church who are in touch with the currents of change reshaping Western culture and the church. They are able to offer wise and important insights into where we are and how we may move forward. insights rooted within the biblical imagination. It is refreshing to be encountered by wisdom which is practical, with a passion for the gospel, that has listened to the context. This is essential reading for any Christian committed to the mission of the church."

Alan J Roxburgh, author, speaker

"*Metavista* daringly invites the people of God to delight in emerging views of life and the gospel in our post-Christendom context. Skillfully navigating through the most pressing cultural shifts of our time, Greene and Robinson bring their outstanding scholarship and ecclesial practice together to re-imagine missional community and the counter-cultural life. *Metavista* may well be the first 'must read' of the 21st century for any Christ-follower seeking to embody the Gospel in our global context."

Dwight J. Friesen, Assistant Professor of Practical Theology,
Mars Hill Graduate School, Seattle.

"If you have a taste for the subversive, a passion for the church, a heart for biblical engagement, and an eye on the future; this book is a must-read."

Roy Searle, Northumbria Community and Former President
of the Baptist Union of Great Britain

"'How should Christianity engage with its surrounding culture?' That challenge is as old as the church itself. *Metavista* provides a comprehensive guide to the many ways that the Church has tried to face it, and offers a dynamic and empowering alternative for today's fast-changing world. A 'must read' for anyone wanting to take cultural engagement and mission seriously."

Jason Clark, Sutton Vineyard and Emergent UK

Metavista

*Bible, Church and Mission in an
Age of Imagination*

Colin Greene and Martin Robinson

Authentic

MILTON KEYNES ● COLORADO SPRINGS ● HYDERABAD

Copyright © 2008 Colin Greene and Martin Robinson

14 13 12 11 10 09 08   7 6 5 4 3 2 1

First published 2008 by Authentic Media
9 Holdom Avenue, Bletchley, Milton Keynes, Bucks, MK1 1QR, UK
1820 Jet Stream Drive, Colorado Springs, CO 80921, USA
OM Authentic Media
Medchal Road, Jeedimetla Village, Secunderabad 500 055, A.P., India
www.authenticmedia.co.uk

Authentic Media is a division of IBS-STL UK,
limited by guarantee, with its Registered Office at Kingstown Broadway,
Carlisle, Cumbria CA3 0HA. Registered in England & Wales No. 1216232.
Registered charity 270162

British Library Cataloguing in Publication Data
A catalogue record for this book is available from the British Library

ISBN 13: 978–1–84227–506–1

Photographs on pages xxv and xxvi by permission of PA Photos

Cover Design by fourninezero design.
Printed Management by Adare
Typeset by Waverley Typesetters, Fakenham
Printed and bound in Great Britain by J.H. Haynes & Co., Sparkford

Contents

Dedication   vii

Preface   ix

Introduction   *Colin Greene*   xi

PART ONE   *Colin Greene*

1. Modernity: Legacies that Remain   3
2. Postmodernity: A Matrix of Meanings   25
3. Metavista: Discerning the Rules of Engagement   43
4. Metavista: Naming the Post-postmodern Condition   65

PART TWO   *Colin Greene*

5. Cultural Engagement and the Refiguring of the Scriptures   91
6. Constructing a Biblical Theology for Cultural Engagement   113
7. Metavista: The Political Capital of the Bible in Cultural Engagement   132

PART THREE   *Martin Robinson*

8. Deconstructing the Secular Imagination   153
9. Imagining the Missional Community   168
10. Reimagining a Counter-cultural Life   183

11. Towards a Hermeneutic of Imagination   206
12. Conclusion and Beyond   *Colin Greene*   223

Notes   236
Bibliography   257

Dedication

For my mother Esther Greene (b. 1923–) keeper of the faith and champion of the arts whose experience of both first sparked my imagination.

Colin Greene

To my mother Constance Lilian Robinson (1922–82) whose writing gifts have been a source of joy to me and who has given me much more besides.

Martin Robinson

O man, take care!
What does the deep midnight declare?
"I was asleep –
From a deep dream I woke and swear: –
The world is deep,
Deeper than day had been aware.
Deep is its woe –
Joy – deeper yet than agony:
Woe implores: Go!
But all joy wants eternity –
Wants deep, wants deep eternity."

F. Nietzsche – *Thus Spoke Zarathustra*

Preface

Until September 2007 Dr Colin Greene lived in Seattle and was Professor of Theological and Cultural Studies at Mars Hill Graduate School. After four and a half years' teaching in the United States he has now returned to the UK, where he runs his own theological consultancy and is also involved in theological education.

Dr Martin Robinson lives in Birmingham, England, and is the Director of Together in Mission, an inter-denominational organization seeking to bring fresh vision and leadership to the church.

Before they took up their present positions the authors worked as friends and colleagues for the British and Foreign Bible Society (BFBS) in England. Together with the then chief executive, Mr. Neil Crosbie,[1] and a creative team of people inspired by the same vision, they were largely responsible for constructing a new model of mission based on the notion of radical cultural engagement, which many national church leaders in Britain regarded as vital and central to the future of the church in our time.[2]

This book is largely the fruit of the authors' combined labors and the many years they worked together developing and testing a hypothesis. In their new roles and responsibilities they are continually refining that hypothesis, but they have felt that it is time now to share the results of their long years of research, consultation and collaboration, in the hope that by doing so they might awaken a dream in the hearts and minds of a new generation of Christian thinkers and leaders who understand that mission in some shape or form is inevitable when the centrifugal power and energy of the Christian faith are clearly grasped and understood (Acts 1:8).

Many friends, colleagues and mission initiatives in different parts of the world provide the inspiration and background to this book which seeks to map out crucial aspects of both the theology and praxis of what we call radical or subversive cultural engagement. By nature this is an interdisciplinary venture which has to reckon with the intercultural reality of a globalized world which is no longer dominated by Eurocentric and Anglo-American theological procedures and methodologies.

Over the years we have accrued a debt to many friends, colleagues, church leaders, missiologists and theologians who have helped us formulate both the thesis and the content of this book, but special thanks go to Neil Crosbie, Linsi Simmons, Roy Searle and Chris Sunderland. We are also deeply grateful for the inspirational example of Dan Beeby and Lesslie Newbigin. Both authors owe a huge debt to Mary Publicover, the Research and Information Manager at Together in Mission whose patience and skill in assisting with revision, editing and footnoting has been invaluable.

Colin Greene and Martin Robinson
September 2007

Introduction

What is radical cultural engagement and why is it important? Or: What have Seattle and Birmingham to do with Jerusalem?

"Every age has its own outlook. It is specifically good at seeing certain truths and specifically liable to make certain mistakes. We all, therefore, need the books that will correct the characteristic mistakes of our own period. And that means the old books."

(C.S. Lewis)[1]

It is often noted that the twentieth-century German theologian Emil Brunner once remarked that the church exists by mission as a fire exists by burning. Yet there have been many periods in church history when the nature and design of an appropriate mission strategy was far from clear. We live at just such a time. Old ways of doing things either no longer seem appropriate or do not yield satisfactory results. Accordingly we propose a new way of doing mission which we call *radical cultural engagement*. We broker that subject in this introduction through a deliberate play on Tertullian's often misquoted question, "What has Athens to do with Jerusalem?" We do so to make our case more difficult to advance and justify so that we can place our concerns within the debates, disputes and dispositions that now, more than ever, characterize the history of Christian mission.

Even a casual glance at the fuller context of Tertullian's remarks would appear to suggest that mission which is deliberately aimed at engaging the host culture in any philosophical or reflective sense is a misdirected exercise in futility, indeed, a heretical and hopeless waste of time that stems from the impulse to distort rather than delineate the core of the Christian gospel:

Whence spring those "fables and endless genealogies" and "un-
profitable questions" and "words which spread like cancer"? From
all these, when the apostle [Paul] would restrain us, he expressly
names *philosophy* as that which he would have us be on our guard
against.

What indeed has Athens to do with Jerusalem? What concord is there
between the Academy and the Church? What between heretics and
Christians? Our instruction comes from "the porch of Solomon,"
who had himself taught that "the Lord should be sought in
simplicity of heart." Away with all attempts to produce a mottled
Christianity of Stoic, Platonic and dialectic composition! We want
no curious disputation after possessing Christ Jesus, no inquisition
after enjoying the gospel! With our faith, we desire no further
belief.[2]

What concord is there between the academy and the church, asks
Tertullian, or between heretics and Christians? If indeed it is the
case that there is none, how can a vision of mission as radical
cultural engagement be credibly advanced? Cultural engagement
is nothing new in the history of the church, and unfortunately
most of those agendas have eventuated in cultural assimilation
or accommodation where the prophetic voice of the church has
been silenced in the name of apparently more attractive options.
Did not Karl Barth, probably the greatest theologian of the
twentieth century, revisit the "strange new world of the Bible"
in order to resist that reverence before history and culture which
typified the bourgeois theology of liberal Protestantism? Indeed,
Barth, not unlike Tertullian, tried to expunge philosophy with its
anthropological tendencies from the agenda of theology altogether
in favor of the primacy of the Word of God. This indeed was Barth's
main concern and preoccupation as he turned toward writing the
initial volumes of his *Church Dogmatics*.

So is it not a dangerous strategy, then, to advocate a mission
agenda that both Tertullian and Barth appeared to repudiate?

There is one – and probably only one – way to answer this
kind of question. Context, my friend, context – each generative era
signifies the radical priority of new historical and cultural contexts,
just as our initial quote from C.S. Lewis suggests.

The context in which Tertullian came to faith and the context
that he, probably more than any other Church Father, best

represents, was both premodern and pre-Christendom. It was a church nurtured and purified on the blood of the martyrs. The context in which Karl Barth learned his craft we could call the epistemological imperialism of modernity, and his own massive theological tour de force went some considerable distance toward spiking that particular balloon.[3]

In reality, of course, neither of these great theologians could avoid the confrontation and engagement with their respective cultural contexts. No Christian can. The route they took, however, was to do so on their own terms rather than concede to the terms dictated to them by the cultural mandates that defined their respective eras.

Tertullian became a Christian because he was so struck by the courage and fortitude of ordinary Christian men and women, many of them poor, uneducated slaves, who were fed to the lions as sport for the Graeco-Roman dignitaries whose blood lust was satisfied by that particular kind of grotesque spectacle. His turning toward genuine Christian faith was inspired by the realization that he could no longer ignore the truth for which such ordinary people were prepared to die.

Tertullian embraced the Christian faith in hard times when the church suffered indiscriminate persecution by successive Roman emperors (mainly Nero and Diocletian, of course). Consequently he had no love for the State or the politics of repression and he saw no point in dialogue between the holy Catholic Church and an unholy, corrupt empire. In fact, Tertullian did not have much love for the Catholic Church of his day, either – he regarded it as worldly, lacking in spiritual zeal and compromised in its relations with the State. That is why he became a Montanist later in life and joined the first manifestation in the early Christian church of a rigorous, over-scrupulous charismatic sect.

Tertullian's six-point mission agenda was clear and stark and it had no place for cultural engagement in any shape or form.

(1) Jesus chose twelve disciples to be the teachers of human-kind.

(2) After his resurrection, he ordered the eleven surviving apostles to go and teach all men to be baptized in the name of the Father, the Son and the Holy Spirit.

(3) The eleven preached the faith and founded churches, first in Judea and then throughout the whole world.

(4) From the churches they founded, other churches acquired, and still today continue to acquire, a graft of faith and the seeds of true doctrine.

(5) Hence these churches, too, are considered apostolic, being offshoots of the original apostolic churches.

(6) Since the nature of every object is determined by its origin, every church is apostolic, so long as unity is maintained.[4]

Tertullian was one of the first Church Fathers to embrace fully the doctrine of apostolic succession, and it is easy to see that one of his prime reasons for doing so was to preserve the purity and unity of the church and protect it against pagan influence, control or contamination. That is why there was to be no truck between Athens and Jerusalem, no flirtation with culturally attuned mission agendas. In its stead he advocated a spirited church-planting strategy through which the apostolic mission of the church could be expanded and guided.

There is no doubt that a premodern, pre-Christendom persecuted church still exists in certain parts of the world, particularly where Islamic rule is operative and enforced. Our context in the twenty-first century in the First World, however, is radically different. We shall argue that it is post-Christendom, post-secular, post-colonial and post-individualistic, in no particular order of priority, and therefore post-postmodern. And that "postist" reality requires an entirely new mission agenda that will not be adequately understood through adherence solely to church-planting strategies. Indeed it is a new cultural context where the word cultural takes on a whole new meaning and significance which necessitates that any mission agenda worth its salt simply cannot afford to ignore the importance of cultural engagement and transformation.

The differing mission situations in the UK and the US

In the United Kingdom the specific nature of what is meant by the phrase *cultural engagement* was given renewed focus through the publication in 2001 of Callum Brown's well-researched, intriguing, but (for some) deeply unsettling book *The Death of Christian Britain*.[5] In his book Brown opened the debate about cultural engagement by examining the conventional way sociologists of religion examine the impact a particular faith makes on its surrounding culture and community. He did so by concentrating on the primary roles or functions of religion in a modern democratic state and postulated a number of indicators of success or failure:

(1) Institutional Christianity: Not surprisingly this one, which is the most obvious, is measured in terms of the numerical growth or decline of church attendance in order to gauge the extent of overt religious practice in a particular community, area or nation.

(2) Intellectual Christianity: This is measured in terms of the viability or otherwise of shared structures of belief that bind a particular community together and provide it with a definitive and reasonably coherent Christian worldview.

(3) Functional Christianity: This indicator tries to measure the influence or lack of influence Christianity has on certain areas of public life – usually education, government policy, moral values and social welfare programs.

(4) Diffusive Christianity: This is calculated in terms of the success or lack of success of programmatic activities such as evangelism, social justice and mission-based strategies.

To all of these, and based particularly on insights gained from modern cultural theory, Brown adds a fifth role or function and indicator:

(5) Discursive Christianity: This is measured in terms of the discursive power of the Christian narrative or story to create a common sense of identity or belonging in a particular community or society.

This latter indicator, says Brown, is the decisive factor in determining the health or otherwise of a religion in the context of modern democratic states. Indeed, Brown goes further and claims that this indicator provides the foundation to the other four sociological factors that have been utilized to measure the effect of religion on its host culture and community, and comments:

> For Christianity to have social significance – for it to achieve popular participation, support or even acquiescence – in a democratic society free from state regulation of religious habits, it must have a base of discursivity. Otherwise, it is inconceivable.[6]

Brown's analysis can be deployed as one way of distinguishing modern democratic societies from Islamic theocratic counterparts. In the latter there is no separation of church and state, so all religious allegiances and practices are, in theory, regulated and controlled by the state.[7] Where no such controls pertain, however, then in order for a particular faith to exercise discursive power, some aspect of its basic narrative of salvation and redemption needs to have penetrated crucial areas of contemporary culture, be that the books and magazines people read, the television and movies they watch, or the lifestyle innovations they adopt and value.

Applying Brown's criteria

When Brown's five criteria are applied to try and measure the current health of the Christian religion in Britain and Europe the situation looks very bleak.

(1) *Institutional Christianity*

The depressing statistics have been well rehearsed in countless sociological studies and religious journals. In the past 50 years, mainline historical denominations of every kind have experienced a catastrophic numerical decline in terms of church attendance and active participation in church life and ministry, so much so that it is calculated that if this trend continues, some denominations will actually go out of business by the middle of this century.

There are some interesting exceptions to this general trend of steady numerical decline, notably mainly among the black-led churches, the so-called independent non-denominational churches, and (in Britain) the Baptist Church. As we shall see in chapters eight and nine, the situation throughout Europe is more varied and complex than this; nevertheless, it still conforms to the general pattern of decline.

(2) Intellectual Christianity

In terms of intellectual influence Christianity has again been steadily waning as Europe becomes increasingly multicultural, pluralist and diverse in religious affiliation. Furthermore, the critique of religion undertaken by Feuerbach, Marx, Freud and Nietzsche has penetrated the cultural mores of the intelligentsia in Europe in ways that few people have recognized.[8] While converts to Islam and Buddhism continue to increase, some previously mainline denominations, such as the Methodists, are in a perilous state of decline.

(3) Functional Christianity

In regard to functional Christianity, however, there has been a moderately significant renaissance of the church's influence on public life in Britain, particularly in the areas of education and social welfare programs, and much more so in the United States.[9]

(4) Diffusive Christianity

When we attend to the effectiveness of diffusive Christianity the evidence again is not encouraging. In the 1990s all the mainline Christian denominations, including the Roman Catholics, united around the call for a decade of evangelism. Apart from the notable success of the Alpha program and a sizeable influx of new ordinands and candidates for ministry, there is strikingly little evidence that Christianity had any significant effect on the wider cultural context in the 1990s.[10]

(5) Discursive Christianity

The title of Brown's book, *The Death of Christian Britain*, is well chosen. His diagnosis of the state of Christianity in Britain was based on the observation that when it comes to discursive Christianity the churches appear to have no agenda or understanding of mission in terms of cultural engagement whatsoever. In fact, since the 1960s popular culture and church culture have been moving more or less in opposite directions.

The empirical center of *Death* is a fascinating examination of the period between 1850 and 1950, which Brown refers to as "the last great Puritan age." His analysis leads him to contend that the theory of secularization based on the notion that the influence of Christianity had been in steady decline in Europe ever since the industrial revolution is a complete myth.[11] In fact, during the period 1850–1950 church attendance in Britain was still relatively high and the church held its own in all of the indicators we have looked at, mainly because the evangelical narrative of redemption and sanctification had indeed penetrated the cultural mores and corporate psyche of large numbers of people in Britain, particularly women. (This contention will be examined in further detail in chapter 8.) Among women there was a widespread belief that a church-going husband makes for a better husband, a better father and the likelihood of a higher family income.

A good indicator of the validity of Brown's conclusions was the surprising success of the Billy Graham crusades in Britain during the 1950s, where in both England and Scotland millions either attended crusade events or watched Graham preach on television. However, says Brown, since the moral and lifestyle revolutions of the 1960s, which has most affected women, the discursive power of the Christian narrative of conversion has been steadily losing ground and is now almost completely vanquished in terms of moral and public significance in Britain, which is why we are experiencing the death of Christian Britain.[12]

Brown's book sparked off a lively debate, but as with any text it is possible to read his analysis in a number of different ways.

For some, while they were grateful for the analysis, their response was to suggest that it could well be possible to reverse these depressing trends and so put the church back on the map in what was once Christian Britain. Here the role of cultural engagement in Brown's analysis is effectively displaced; rather, it was claimed that mission-minded churches need to continue to work at making their services and church buildings more attractive and more seeker-sensitive and design alternative forms of being church.[13] Similarly, seminaries need to train up good preachers, apologists and evangelists and so equip new leaders to spearhead an energetic church-planting agenda. At the same time, churches and parachurch organizations should put aside time and money to support a Christian moral reform agenda in public life. At the youth end of the religious market it is imperative that the churches rebuild the equivalent of the American Young Life program or other similar programs. When and if all this is put in place, then the churches in Britain and Europe will start reversing these depressing trends, just as the churches in many parts of North America have demonstrated.

We opposed this latter view, and suggested that such well-meaning reformers had, in fact, missed the whole point of Brown's book. What he was describing in terms of cultural context was the move from a situation where the remnants of Christendom were still in place to a wholly post-Christendom situation where the church was in a totally new mission situation. In such a situation a reversal mentality, a back-to-Christendom crusade, simply would not work. What the church in Europe had to accept was that as far as the First World is concerned, we were now in a decidedly post-Christendom, postmodern situation, and that required the abandonment of the reversal model and the embracing of a dispersal or *diaspora* mission agenda such as we find in the book of Acts.

Is it still the case, however, that in terms of this analysis the situation in the United States is quite exceptional? The Christian religion in America seems to some to be extraordinarily alive and vibrant – indeed experiencing, in recent years, something of a revival in regard to all the sociological indicators Brown put forward. Could it be, therefore, as some sociologists of religion contend, that in regard to the rest of the world it is Europe that represents a special case of decline and moribund faith?[14]

In many parts of North America church attendance is still surprisingly high and so-called civil religion, where the office of the minister and pastor is required to bless many aspects of civil life, is still viewed as important to the social and moral fabric of society.[15] Intellectually America still has a semblance of being a Christian nation. Despite the widespread religious pluralism and multiculturalism that also typify modern America, the Christian worldview, which in the US always had dispensationalist leanings, is still widely adhered to in many parts of the US.

Similarly, the marriage of an increasingly fundamentalist Christian right with an equally rightwing republicanism has thrust a Christian moral agenda of sorts back into public life. Add to that the megachurch phenomenon, where programmatic evangelism and mission-based agendas do appear to have more success in the US than in Europe. Indeed, this might well be the case because the US worldview was born out of a curious mixture of the discursive power of the evangelical story of conversion and Enlightenment rationalism.

In short, so the argument goes, there are many active Christians in the worlds of business, sport, movies, art and contemporary music making a real impact on popular culture. Consequently, many churches and church leaders in America still behave as if their country is largely an exception to the rule in terms of the decline of Christian influence in the West. Indeed, some contemporary sociologists of religion make this very point – America, they claim, is still happily within its own version of Christendom and there is every indication that it will remain so.[16]

It is our belief, however, that this apparent state of affairs is a dangerous illusion and that unfortunately many churches and church leaders in the US are being taken in and snared by this seductive ideology.[17] Contemporary American culture – indeed, much contemporary American church life – is, in fact, deeply and profoundly secularized and to practice an ostrich mentality in regard to that fact, preferring instead to live in the glory days of the past, is to make no contribution at all to the obvious need for a renewal of "societal imagination" in the US.[18] On the other hand, what is worse, and in fact more prevalent, is the widespread phenomenon of churches absurdly accommodated to the entertainment, celebrity status, and prosperity gospel agenda dictated by our consumer society which in the United States has been turned into something of an art form!

There is no doubt that, as in the 1950s in Britain, the remnants of Christendom are still all around us in the US, but they are just that – remnants, and they are rapidly disappearing, and churches and theology schools that do not gear up to meet the new post-Christendom situation are the ones that are going to be left behind.[19] In a post-Christendom, postmodern situation reversal strategies simply will not work, because the very fabric of the host culture has fundamentally changed.

Nor will it help to go back to a pre-Christendom avoidance mentality and act as if the church and culture are like chalk and cheese, never to be confused and never to be brought together in a process of cross-fertilization.

We contend, therefore, that in our current context in the First World there is an urgent and absolutely crucial need to develop dispersal mission strategies that have radical and subversive cultural engagement as their cutting edge.

What, then, *is* radical cultural engagement?

In our work with the BFBS (British and Foreign Bible Society) it took us eight years to develop an experimental model of mission as cultural engagement that eventually gained the support of most of the leaders of all the mainline Christian denominations, including the Roman Catholic Church and some of the non-denominational church affiliations.[20] The cultural hermeneutics that lay behind this model of mission can be illustrated by three interlocking circles (Figure 1).

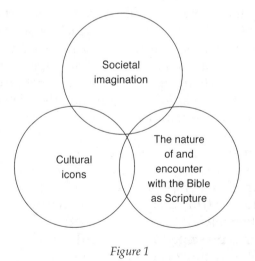

Figure 1

In terms of Figure 1 it would not be unfair to say that the Bible Society movement worldwide has, since its inception, concentrated most of its activities in the circle labeled "The nature of and encounter with the Bible as Scripture." In other words, the Bible Societies understood their core endeavors in terms of two primary activities: the distribution of the Scriptures in a language people could understand and at a price they could afford, and by implication, the translation of the Scriptures into the many languages that accompanied the missionary advance of Christianity, particularly in the eighteenth and nineteenth centuries.[21]

The British and Foreign Bible Society gained its name as the founding Bible Society inaugurated as a charity in 1804. The social context from which it drew inspiration and nourishment was that confluence of evangelical revivalism associated with John and Charles Wesley and George Whitefield, and the radical social and political action undertaken by William Wilberforce and the Clapham Sect. Some have argued that this was the last significant period when the Christian faith actually penetrated the social mores of popular culture in Britain and it was this cultural achievement which, as Callum Brown has suggested, lasted well into the twentieth century.

Revisiting that context, we discovered the importance of what is represented by the top circle and which we labeled "societal imagination."[22] That is, the distribution and translation of the Scriptures was not an end in itself, but an important and crucial means to radically changing the societal imagination of the British nation. This is what Lesslie Newbigin and others later termed the Bible or the Christian faith as "public truth."[23] Culture changes when public opinion changes and public opinion is reliant on public discourses that are orientated toward creating a healthy and flourishing society. Public discourses change when a culture's social imagination is impacted by a new vision or conviction of what constitutes a truly human and ethical way of life, indeed, a new orientation toward the common good.

The factor represented by the third circle was born out of reflection on the nature of culture understood in the postmodern sense as a semiotic system or a system of signification and meaning based on the referential import of the sign.[24] In a postmodern culture, however, signification is a deeply iconic activity. It can be described in terms of linguistic or semantic theory, but it is mediated through iconic personalities and structures that are deeply enmeshed in the public psyche of communities, societies and cultures.[25] It is, however, not easy to identify and isolate such iconic structures within any given society or culture, because they change over time and are often resistant to critical analysis. Iconic personalities such as sports and media stars are easier to detect, but their personality status is dependent on the iconic structure they represent and the disillusion of a supporting iconic structure inevitably contributes to the rapid rise and fall of celebrity icons in contemporary society.[26]

We will investigate the nature of iconic structures in contemporary culture in more depth in chapter 3. At this stage, however, it is sufficient to indicate that a cultural system is a function of the interaction of all three circles. All cultures look to primordial myths and stories for their religious orientation and at times (more dangerously) their legitimation, and for Western culture that has always been the Judaeo-Christian faith. Similarly, the interaction of that religious orientation with the social imagination of a particular people group is constitutive of their core identity and the construction of iconic matrixes that both preserve and mediate that identity to successive generations. The perennial struggle in the relationship between religious narratives and cultures is the tendency for one to collapse into the other. The domestication of the religious story for the sake of "culture-religion" which endorses the political and social status quo not only took place in Nazi Germany; it is also currently a feature of much of American church life.

A further refinement of this model was to address the question, "Which aspects of contemporary culture are most amenable to iconic activity?" Based on the sociological analysis that there are certain core areas within a given culture that mediate change we opted for four interconnecting cultural indices that are instrumental to change in modern democratic societies, namely politics, the media, education and the arts.

These four areas can be best represented by two inverted triangles (Figure 2). The feeding frenzy happens along the Politics-Media axis. An election campaign dramatically illustrates the power of the media in contemporary society for political influence and control, both good and ill. Many of the issues generated are more spin than substance, more heat than light, more sound bite

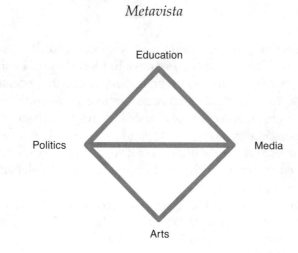

Figure 2

than serious political dialogue; nevertheless, it is along this axis that a lot of the debate about the future well-being of society is focussed.

If that change is to be lasting, however, it must also impact the areas of the arts and education. We provide two examples, one from America and one from Britain, that illustrate how spontaneous campaign initiatives can be generated when all four areas are impacted by one single event or series of events. It is a tribute to the enduring iconic status of the photograph (Figure 3, p. xxv) that everyone, regardless of generational status, recognizes it as the media/arts icon that virtually ended the Vietnam War. Once this picture hit the television screens of the American people it quickly generated a huge resistance movement to the bombing policy of the Johnson administration in Vietnam and convinced the American public that the only sensible remedy to the Vietnam conflict was a quick and dignified exit.

Much less widely known, but in similar vein, is the photograph represented by Figure 4 (p. xxvi). This media image caught the imagination of the British public and generated an ecological campaign to end the dumping of redundant oil platforms in the Atlantic Ocean even though Shell oil had dutifully emptied the platform of all residual toxins.

Figure 3

Our work was heavily influenced by the missiological thinking and strategy spearheaded by Bishop Lesslie Newbigin, Dr Dan Beeby and The Gospel and our Culture movement. Indeed, we worked in partnership with them for a number of years.[27] However, what was new in our work was the fact that we took aspects of that theology of cultural engagement plus our own thinking and crafted it into a practical hypothesis which we sought to test and refine through successive campaigning activities. No one that we were aware of at that time had moved the whole debate generated by Lesslie Newbigin's work into the area of practical theology, or what Aristotle referred to as *phronesis*, practical wisdom. In that sense we did not think of our work in terms of overt evangelistic practice or indeed as a form of Christian apologetics. It was, for us, a dialogical hermeneutical activity where we deliberately tested the thesis that the Christian faith could function as public truth in

Figure 4

our contemporary pluralist postmodern context. Neither did we try and reinvent the wheel, recognizing that other organizations, individuals and corporate enterprises would be involved in similar activities. Accordingly we tried to identify some of the most obvious of these and work in partnership with them.[28] Similarly, we built a research and development team that endeavored to find, support and utilize, where possible, some of the intellectual capital that was beginning to emerge in Britain at that time.

We want to emphasize again that this was a hypothesis, one that we tested in a number of significant ways and refined over the years. Arguably we were never able to complete our work or, for that matter, generate enough funding to promote enough campaigning activity. Further work requires to be undertaken, as such models constantly need to be adapted, adjusted and refined as new data and insights become available. In this book we want to concentrate our efforts on describing in much more detail the cultural, missional, theological and ecclesiological contexts that propelled us in this particular direction.

Defining *culture*

At this stage it is imperative that we come clean, so to speak, and define more precisely exactly how we understand the vexed term *culture*.

The study of human cultures first appeared within the context of German Romanticism and maintained a decidedly aesthetic flavor. Culture was understood largely in terms of "high" culture and the cultural goods produced within the worlds of music, literature and the arts. For some sociologists and cultural theorists, for instance Theodore Adorno, this is still the way culture is understood.[29] In a postmodern culture, however, distinctions between "high" and "low" culture have largely imploded. We have already indicated that we have some sympathy with the postmodern cultural theorists who understand cultures in terms of semiotic systems and symbols that generate shared systems of belief, shared values and particular worldviews among specific groups of people. We do not, however, think this is a sufficiently comprehensive view of the nature of culture, which has also to do with power arrangements, institutional entities, and symbolic and iconic cultural structures.

Accordingly, we propose to understand culture largely in terms of narratology.

To use Paul Ricoeur's suggestive terminology, cultures are already prefigured, configured and reconfigured in the narratives and stories that express their corporate intentionality.[30] We tell stories about ourselves when we are asked to do so; consequently, cultural and symbolic activity is inscribed within powerful stories and narratives that define something of that culture's internal psyche.[31]

We are also, of course, well aware that globalization and the almost ubiquitous presence of free-market global economics are no longer limited to the First World but are recurring features of the social, cultural and religious life of Africa, the Middle East, Southeast Asia, Latin America and the former Soviet empire.[32] Fundamentalist Islam continues to resist the influence of the West, even though there is a lot of evidence to suggest that that fundamentalism is still strikingly influenced by the very modernity it seeks to overthrow.[33] In more moderate Islamic nations, however, the same changes are taking place both internally and through alliances with other Islamic and non-Islamic countries.

This global reality is well attested to by Indian missiologist Vinoth Ramachandra:

> In our technology- and market-driven environment, the real theological challenges are being faced by our children and by Christians who are at the cutting edge of scientific and medical research, or who are engaging with the new artistic media thrown up by the communications revolution, or who are caught up in the complex arena of economic modeling and social policy, who are asking questions of a profound theological character that professional theologians (and church leaders) need to address.[34]

Outline of the book

Here follows a brief outline of the book and an explanation of how it has been set out.

Part one

In part one we seek to explore the notion of culture as a narrative identity, starting with modernity and postmodernity, because more so than any other cultural episodes in human history both are cultural constructs based on different cultural narratives. In each case we use a signifier or a cultural artifact to illustrate this reality.

The story of modernity has been told in many different ways, most recently by Jean-François Lyotard as the mastery of the metanarratives in his seminal book *The Postmodern Condition: A Report on the Condition of Knowledge*. We choose to tell the story slightly differently, referring to it as "Modernity: Legacies that Last." We do so by highlighting three particular publishing achievements that unleashed the primary ideas of the modernity project over a seventy-year period. However, modernity is still very much with us in many parts of the world and it is arguable that free-market capitalism is still the greatest vestige of the modernity project, that which Fredric Jameson concluded is part of the logic of late capitalism.[35] It is our contention that this story needs to be told in a more robust and hard-edged fashion, because the will to dominate and a cultural theory of aggression still lie at the heart of this particular project,[36] which has radically infiltrated certain conservative and republican political programs that are not only operative in our world today but continue to be funded by the same conservative, self-interested power brokers within multinational capitalism.

The story of postmodernity as a "matrix of meanings" trades on the phenomenal success and genuine originality of the movie blockbuster *The Matrix*, first released at Easter 1999. That same originality was not maintained in the two sequels that followed the original. Instead, the temptation to explore computer-generated cinematic special effects all but overwhelmed the intriguing philosophical, epistemological and theological components of the original story line. The polyphonic and fragmentary nature of contemporary cultures means that premodernity, modernity, postmodernity and post-postmodernity, or what we designate by the signifier *metavista*, which we will explain in a moment, co-exist. They are all cultural spaces within a fabric of evolving cultural patterns and indices and arguably the United States has yet fully to embrace the acerbic deconstructionalist agenda of postmodernity, just as it has yet to move fully beyond the false securities of Christendom.

(1) *Metavista*

The most problematic story to recognize and recite is one which has not yet fully announced its arrival and is indeed parasitical upon more clearly understood and comprehended narratives. Thus we have chosen a signifier that speaks not from the supposedly legitimating foundations of a metanarrative or a hurriedly revamped metaphysic, but from a relatively unclaimed space or "clearing" (to use Heidegger's suggestive phrase) – so, therefore, a *meta-"space"* or *meta-"vista."* We will attempt to illustrate what we mean by this term with reference to the remarkable and virtually unnoticed story of what used to be, and often still is, called "disability" as an example of what we believe could, and probably will, happen in our time and in the not too distant future (chapter 3).

This tentatively emerging "clearing" where "Being" once again disguises itself has, in our view, now subsumed postmodernity within its metaframework and therefore requires a truly global perspective. The contours of this new world regime are only just coming into view and indeed appear fragile and tentative – and yes, we would agree, not yet fully apparent.

So why attempt to tell the story in that case?

Simply because it remains an imaginative possibility and the future belongs to those who will tell stories that reimagine our present possibilities and so contribute to changes in our present cultural topography. It is not our wish to take such possibilities and simply "throw them down in the world without an explanation" (to quote Heidegger again). The story we tell is a dialogical possibility and it will depend on other, more gifted storytellers pursing these matters further. It is for this reason that our story comes replete with explanation (chapter 4), because if it is truly a global reality it will be upon us soon enough.

Part two

Part two looks at the role the Bible could play in such a situation if we can imaginatively re-enter its narratival space. It is our contention that the hegemony of the historical-critical paradigm, obsessed as it is with the "world behind the text," plus the general malaise that beset the role of the Bible, Bible reading and Bible telling in a Christendom context, has made it nearly impossible for many to grapple with this issue seriously and convincingly. Accordingly, for most Christians in the First World the Bible remains a closed book, a Pandora's Box of isolated and unrelated proof texts, or – what is worse – an individualistic invitation to hang out with a cool dude called Jesus. There have to be better reasons for reading, performing and reciting the Scriptures than these.

Part three

Part three looks at the role the church plays as the interpretive community, those who are the contemporary readers of the biblical story, who, in so doing, reconfigure the original story and, indeed, their own place within that ongoing drama. In this way, as Gerard Loughlin suggests, God reads his own story.[37]

It is our conviction that to see the issues in this way is also to reimagine the role, place and significance of the church in contemporary society. If we do not know how to be part of the biblical story, then we also do not know how to "be" church. "Going to" church is a Christendom activity; "being" church is an ecumenical post-Christendom possibility. We will leave the important discussion of the role of the imagination to later in our study, but suffice to admit at this stage that epitaphs like the Dark Ages, the Age of Reason, the Age of Criticism and now, as we suggest, the Age of Imagination, are mere heuristic devises. If they catch something of the spirit of the age they do so only partially and often belatedly. This means that we do not ascribe to an essentialist view of human cultures as if you could describe the essence of modernity or postmodernity in a few well-rehearsed sound bites. Cultures are not great ideas in the mind of God that consequently have some transcendental validity; they are practical disciplines, amorphous belief systems, ever-changing frameworks of meaning and significance, negotiated compromises between past verities and future possibilities, and it is for that reason that we remain agnostic about the language of worldviews. There are no isolated worldviews in the twenty-first century, only ways of being and living in an increasingly global urban village that just happens to be the way we do things around here and we are glad you do it differently!

What does seem to us incontestable, however, is our contention that the contemporary Christian church has been for some time beset by a profound failure of the imagination. There are some as yet inconclusive signs that this may be changing, and so it is in an effort to fuel that imaginative exercise that we offer this book to the wider public.

Part One

1

Modernity: Legacies that Remain

*"There is probably no more telling index by which a cultural ethos
can be evaluated than the social system it has produced; it is in the
political arena that various understandings of the meaning of human
existence find expression. This is especially true of the culture of
modernity with 'emancipation' as its dominant theme."*

(John Thornhill)[1]

The 1997 award-winning film *The Apostle* tells the remarkable story
of itinerant evangelist and popular preacher Eulis "Sonny" Dewey.
A truly inspirational and gripping performance by Robert Duvall
captures the enigma of a gifted individual who has two sides to his
character: one that embraces the raw passion and stirring rhetoric
of a small-time Southern boy truly committed to a life of service
and witness to his personal Lord and Savior, Jesus Christ, and
the other that reveals a flawed and vulnerable human being who
reacts with stunning violence to the reality of his wife's adultery
with an associate pastor. Sonny captures our imagination and our
sympathy because his personal character and career are caught
in the dialectical tension between captivity to a crime of passion
and a ministry of freedom and emancipation to ordinary, poor,
upstanding, Christian people.

The equally remarkable and imaginative story of modernity
unfolds in a similar manner. At its center is the liberating
heartbeat of a socio-political movement of emancipation for
hardworking, down-to-earth, good people. In its soul, however,
there is a rebellious energy that has easily turned emancipation
into captivity, progress into idolatry, and the inherent worth of
the individual into totalitarian ideology. To capture the essence

of the modernity story we have to keep this dialectical tension constantly before us.

Two remarkable books by Robert Bellah and associates have sought to do just that as they diagnose the impact of modernity upon its most illustrative *enfant terrible*, the United States of America.[2] The writers analyze constitutive changes in American social and political life that exhibit this dialectical character and yet, at the same time, have led to making the US the greatest superpower and economic producer and consumer in the world today. Again and again, however, the writers circle round what they view as the fundamental problem at the heart of modern America:

> Perhaps the crucial change in American life has been that we have moved from the local life of the nineteenth century – in which economic and social relationships were visible and, however imperfectly, morally integrated as parts of a larger common life – to a society vastly more interrelated and integrated economically, technically and functionally. Yet this is a society in which the individual can only rarely and with difficulty understand himself and his activities as interrelated in morally meaningful ways with those of other, different Americans.[3]

These are not superficial alterations to the fabric of American life and the "habits of the heart" that define its citizenry; rather, they are fundamental changes that go all the way down to the substratum of modern America's core value system. They are also the vestiges or the legacy of a sea change in our thinking about, and understanding of, how the world actually works that took place in Europe more than a century before the economic and political ripples of this vast cultural upheaval eventually hit the American shores.

We call this cultural experiment "the modern world," or "modernity," or the "scientific and technological project."[4] The vast majority of us in the world today have never known anything else; this is our narrative, our story, to which we once referred as the Enlightenment, or the Age of Reason.

Now, as already indicated, we are not so sure.[5] Wherever and however we make our home in today's global village, modernity is either already there or has moved on ahead of us. It is this economic, socio-political, intellectual, philosophical and historical cultural revolution that we once thought of as the greatest movement of emancipation in human history which has now entered a new stage of its development, and despite the protestations and deconstructive strategies of the postmoderns, it shows no sign, as yet, of terminal exhaustion.

We will attempt to provide our own version of the modernity story and we will tell it differently from the way others do, no doubt because (as with all grand stories) perspective, or a point of view, is itself part of the story.

Of one thing, however, we are absolutely certain: to tell the modernity story as if we have somehow passed through it and left this project behind is a grave and a dangerous mistake. Jeffrey Stout, in his important book *Democracy and Tradition*, charts the course whereby both the postmodern radicals and the premodern traditionalists appear to be in danger of making this unfortunate error:

> Postmodernism is apocalyptic in tone. It prepares the way for something radically new – something, utterly beyond modernity, which has hitherto appeared, if at all, only at the margins or in the fissures of official Western culture. Traditionalism, on the contrary, tends toward nostalgia. It is trying to find its way back to premodern traditions in the hope of reconstructing and defending them anew. The difference between the two is often summed up in a question like the one MacIntyre poses halfway through *After Virtue*: "Nietzsche or Aristotle?" It is as if our troubled journey beyond modernity had finally brought us all, after much strife and destruction, to the same crossroad, where we must turn either right or left, certain only that modernity itself lies in ruin behind us.[6]

Stout argues that there are two reactionary movements to modernity that are simultaneously contesting its emancipatory rhetoric. One tries to get behind modernity to premodern traditions that have been buried by the landslide of new knowledge modernity has thrust upon us; the other, however, seeks to move beyond modernity by unearthing other radical traditions that will eventually, they assert, overthrow it. Philosophers, ethicists and theologians tend to tell the modernity story in one or other of these ways because it is the contemporary state of the knowledge industry, which we will look at more closely in our next chapter, that most concerns them.

Again, however, as Stout also indicates, the modernity project simply can not be reduced to one particular fashion of thought or intellectual discourse, because all cultures were more complex and variegated than such a view suggests.[7] Similarly, what the traditionalists and the postmoderns who refer to modernity in the past tense appear to underestimate is the sheer size of the internal combustion engine that fuels modernity's voracious appetite for prosperity and success.

The story of modernity used to be told as the rise of the natural sciences, or the emergence of republican democracy, or the secularization of society, or the historization of humanity or the inevitability of social progress. The first two descriptors are partially correct and the latter three have simply outlived their usefulness. More recently the story has been told as the mastery of the metanarratives, which we will look at in more detail in chapter 2.[8] But if such a description is also taken to mean that modernity is now exhausted, then this seems to us simply to fly in the face of the facts. If we may put it this way: modernity has always had higher aspirations than any of these descriptors makes clear. In fact, one could say that since 1989 modernity's greatest ideas have coalesced in such a way that the modern world is now burning more high-octane information fuel than ever before.

It is also the case that most civilizations or cultural transformations revolve around a few key ideas, strategies, or changes in how people view the world and their place in that particular drama, which, in turn, coalesce into a powerful narrative or story that ushers in considerable social changes, often over a relatively short period of time. This is not to reduce cultural change to a history-of-ideas project, which is manifestly inadequate. It is, however, to maintain without any apology that ideas, and particularly big ideas, are important and that they are often responsible for vast changes in society for both good and ill. As Maynard Keynes once remarked, "Sooner or later it is ideas, not vested interest, which are dangerous for good or evil."[9] In regard to the modern era those key ideas emerged through the end of the eighteenth century to the middle of the nineteenth, roughly between 1775 and 1850, and were disseminated by three books – two that became primary texts for understanding the evolution of modernity and one that became a publishing sensation of its time: Adam Smith's *The Wealth of Nations* (1776), Thomas Paine's *The Rights of Man* (1791), and Robert Chalmers's *Vestiges of the Natural History of Creation* (1844).

Adam Smith and the "invisible hand" of the market

In 1776, at a time when the basic rules of economics were barely understood, Adam Smith (1723–90) published his remarkable book *An Inquiry into the Nature and Causes of the Wealth of Nations*. Smith, a shrewd, brilliant and generous-minded Scot, had spent many a long year witnessing the futile economics of mercantilism that granted subsidies and monopolies to merchants and farmers alike to protect them from "unfair competition," which, at the same time, was intended to halt free trade and the introduction of labor-saving machinery. The *Wealth of Nations* became the textbook of modern economic theory, probing deftly into the role of self-interest in promoting wealth, the significance of the division of labor, the function of the markets and the international implications of *laissez-faire* economics.[10] Smith's jaundiced attitude to government intervention, tariffs and protectionist guilds was occasioned by the examples of free trade and economic expansion he saw going on in many other nations around the world at that time. He is most remembered for his belief in the "invisible hand" of the market which, he believed, was self-regulating and required no other restrictions or incentives:

> Every individual necessarily labors to render the annual revenue of the society as great as he can. He generally indeed neither intends to promote the public interest, nor knows how much he is promoting it. He intends only his own gain, and he is in this, as in many other cases, led by an invisible hand to promote an end which was no part of his intention. By pursuing his own interest he frequently promotes that of the society more effectually than when he really intends to promote it. I have never known much good done by those who affected to trade for the public good.[11]

It has sometimes been noted that Smith's advocacy of the principle of benign self-interest seemed to contradict his previous emphasis on empathy as the primary organ of morality in his book *The Theory of Moral Sentiments* (1759).[12] Be that as it may, *Wealth of the Nations* outlined in persuasive manner the basic tenets of free-market capitalism which, for many, still hold true today.

The apparent victory of capitalist economics over its Marxist and communist counterparts in 1989 has been accompanied by a renewed emphasis on the apparent inviolability of the free market. It is still generally accepted, not just by economists, but also by politicians, the media, opinion-formers and the ordinary citizenry, that unregulated self-interest working along side unbridled market forces will promote national wealth, alleviate poverty and increase public welfare.

Few economists would dispute the centrality of Adam Smith's ideas to modern economic theory. Indeed, there is a direct line of descent from Smith through Thomas Malthus, David Ricardo and Karl Marx, and, in the twentieth century, John Maynard Keynes and Milton Friedman. *The Wealth of Nations* was as important to the social and economic life of the eighteenth and nineteenth centuries as was Newton's *Principia* to our understanding of the cosmos. But whereas Newtonian physics and cosmology have now largely been superseded by quantum physics and Einstein's theory of general relativity, such is not the case in regard to the abiding legacy of Adam Smith in the realm of modern economics. The belief in the "invisible hand" of free-market forces is still the cornerstone of multinational capitalism and more than any other idea has been responsible for generating the wealth-creating impetus of the modern consumerist society.[13]

Thomas Paine on rights, responsibilities and democratic freedoms

In 1791 Thomas Paine, the indomitable intellectual, adventurer and pamphleteer, published *The Rights of Man*. Ostensibly written as a riposte to Edmund Burke's *Reflections on the Revolution in France*, this book went on to become one of the founding documents of the American Declaration of Independence and indeed of modern democratic culture.[14] Like Smith, Paine took aim and fired both barrels of his sarcastic rhetoric at what was once thought to be a divinely instigated natural order of how things were intended to be in the world. Equivalent to the supposed natural order of trade barriers and restrictions (mercantilism) was the natural order of hierarchical status and inherited position in society which ultimately derived from the theory of the divine right of kings. The nobility, it was argued, had rights relative to their preordained position in society, and of course the further down the ladder you go the fewer rights and responsibilities there are to dole out to everyone. Accordingly the well-being of society was supposed to depend upon such entitlement and deference to those in authority. It was the violation of this prescribed order of society that Burke most objected to in what he regarded as the horrific excesses of the French Revolution:

> We fear God; we look up with awe to kings, with affections to parliaments, with duty to magistrates, with reverence to priests, and with respect to nobility. Why? Because when such ideas are brought before our minds, it is natural to be so affected.[15]

An integral part of the natural ordering of society is to defer to the authority which such people are granted by God and which constitutes their dignity and their responsibility to rule according to their prescribed vocation. A firm believer in the complete corruption of human nature, Burke could see no way of keeping the poverty-stricken masses in control other than through the beneficent rule of the nobility.

Whereas Burke thought in terms of governance through the divine right of kings, the accumulated wisdom and dignity of the nobility and the indispensability of such a hierarchical ordering of society, Paine saw only the justification of tyranny, the inevitable misuse of power, and corruption through privilege and entitlement, all of which, he asserted, were opposed to the natural rights of freedom, equality, security and property attributed to human beings through nothing other than being human. He pours scorn on Burke's notion of inherited power and wisdom:

> Notwithstanding the nonsense, for it deserves no better name, that Mr. Burke has asserted about hereditary rights, and hereditary succession, and that a Nation has not a right to form a Government of itself; it happened to fall in his way to give some account of what Government is. "Government," says he, "is a contrivance of human wisdom ... Admitting that government is a contrivance of human

wisdom, it must necessarily follow, that hereditary succession, and hereditary rights (as they are called), can make no part of it, because it is impossible to make wisdom hereditary."[16]

In place of hereditary rights Paine asserts the inherent rights of human beings, which became the basis of the charter for republican democratic government:

(1) Men are born, and always continue, free and equal in respect of their rights. Civil distinctions, therefore, can be founded only on public utility.

(2) The end of all political associations is the preservation of the natural and imprescriptible rights of man; and these rights are liberty, property, security, and resistance of oppression.

(3) The nation is essentially the source of all sovereignty; nor can any individual, or any body of men, be entitled to any authority which is not expressly derived from it.[17]

The obvious similarity between these disparate notions of human rights and the "self-evident truths" enshrined in the American Declaration of Independence is clearly not a historical accident, for both the formularies of the latter and Paine drew a lot of their inspiration and language from John Locke's *Second Treatise of Government*. Like Locke, Paine understood the purpose of government as being to protect the ineradicable rights of every human being, rights which are theirs by dint of birth and nature, not of status or privilege.[18] All institutions which do not benefit the individual and the nation are both illegitimate and dispensable, whether that institution is the monarchy, the nobility or indeed the military establishment.

Not surprisingly, the publication of *The Rights of Man* and the views expressed therein were regarded by the powers that be in Britain as both seditious and highly dangerous. Paine consequently fled to France, where he was immediately elected a member of the National Convention.

Paine, again like Smith, had been converted to Deism and his later publications on the topic of religion tarnished his image and eventually led to his demise.[19] Nevertheless, he remained in the eyes of Thomas Jefferson, George Washington and many of the formularies of the Declaration of Independence one of the revered exponents and representatives of modern liberal democracy.

Both Alasdair MacIntyre and Stanley Hauerwas in their various writings have repudiated the rhetoric of natural rights and of liberal democracy as largely morally incoherent and philosophically untenable in favor of older ethical traditions.[20] For the former that means the tradition of Aristotelian virtues and for the latter the subversive ethics of the gospel story.[21] Jeffrey Stout, on the other hand, with the aid of Whitman, Dewey and Ellison and the American pragmatic tradition, wants to retrieve some of this discourse as the basis for a reform of democratic ideals that will not only guide us in the struggle against international terrorism, but also uphold the exigencies of democratic culture which, he believes, is under threat in the world, today more so than ever.[22]

Most postmoderns question whether there is such a thing as a universal human nature, natural law or a common morality upon which such democratic ideals can be founded; and indeed, such notions are becoming more and more difficult to defend. What is clear, however, is that those who enjoy the perceived benefits of liberal democracy are extremely unlikely to give up either the belief in, or the political practice of, this form of governance. Indeed, the present incumbent in the Oval office seems determined to ride the wave of Huntington's clash of civilizations rhetoric, claiming that the protection and practice of democracy over and against ruthless dictatorships and Islamic theocracy is the basic ideological struggle of the twenty-first century. Of this we can be sure, however: liberal democracy – the government *of* the people *by* the people and *for* the people, inextricably linked to the espousal of basic human rights – is one of the great ideas of the modernity project which is now being put to use in ways not previously foreseen.

Robert Chalmers and the story of evolution

In 1844, in the midst of Victorian Britain, a book was published that is often seen as the natural forerunner to Darwin's *On the Origin of Species by Means of Natural Selection* (1859). The book, *Vestiges of the Natural History of Creation*, was published anonymously and almost immediately became a publishing sensation that continued to outsell Darwin's latter volume well into the early twentieth century. Only 40 years later, after his death, was it revealed that the writer was the eccentric but prolific Scottish author Robert Chalmers (1802–71). The twelfth edition of *Vestiges* was released in 1884. In the midst of a dysfunctional economy and unpopular political changes, *Vestiges* held more than 100,000 readers spellbound by its grand tale of development and the progress of creation. From interstellar gas clouds to the formation of stars and planets to the successive geological ages of the earth and eventually on to the spiritual destiny of humankind, *Vestiges* was the only evolution book around during the 1840s and 1850s.

The book achieved notoriety not merely because of its popularity but for the invective it drew from both the church and the academy. Even Benjamin Disraeli, the popular novelist and future prime minister, felt compelled to satirize this publishing sensation. A scene from the third novel of his *Young England* trilogy describes Tancred's drawing room conversation with an enthusiastic female admirer of a new book called *Revelations of Chaos*. She exclaims, "First we were nothing, and then we were something, and then we were something else!" Evolutionary theory had indeed achieved street credibility!

> As gripping as a popular novel, *Vestiges* combined all the current scientific theories in fields ranging from astronomy and geology to psychology and economics. The book was banned, it was damned, and it was hailed as the gospel for a new age. This is where our own public controversies about evolution began.[23]

Darwin later accepted that *Vestiges* was the natural precursor to his own scientific investigations, but at the height of the controversy occasioned by the publication of this book he felt compelled to delay the publication of *The Origin of Species* for a number of years.

What was it about *Vestiges* that really caught the public attention and imagination of Victorian Britain?

It is not sufficient to claim that it was simply the novel notion of evolutionary development in itself, because, as Darwin was also soon to discover, it was this new evolutionary science that was vilified by the scientific establishment and condemned as heretical by the religious traditionalists. Chambers was able to avoid some of this critique because he kept the idea of the divine superintendence of the evolutionary process intact, although he was notably cavalier over the fate of weaker species. Darwin, of course, dispensed with divine providence all together (although not in terms of his own personal beliefs) and introduced the altogether more troubling ideas of random selection and the survival of the fittest. It was the introduction of these two refinements on Chalmers's existing thesis that so stuck in the craw of orthodox believers and occasioned the disastrous debates and conflicts between science and religion orchestrated by "Darwin's bulldog," Thomas Henry Huxley (1825–95).[24]

What is often forgotten amidst all the hysteria that ensued from this conflict between science and religion, however, is the observation that, immersed in the sub-text of this debate, glittered two of the great enduring ideas of the modernity project, namely the notions of *interconnectivity* and *innovation*. To view the whole created process as a spectacular journey from inanimate matter to self-conscious human beings was to view either God's creative activity or a random process of evolutionary development as essentially highly innovative and leading to ever higher levels of social interconnectivity. Both ideas also appeared in Hegel's philosophy of historical development and the social Darwinism of August Comte.

Unfortunately, what took place in nineteenth-century England is being repeated in twenty-first-century America as the evolutionists and the creationists square up against one another yet again.

However, both are apparently still totally missing the point. The theory of evolution, like the various cosmological theories about the eventual fate of the universe, remains just that – an as yet insufficiently substantiated theory. While the notion of a six-day creation is equally unsubstantiated and a lot more scientifically suspect, what has stayed high on the agenda of public imagination is the fundamental notion that everything from the first atom to the human brain is interconnected and susceptible to the highest degree of developmental innovation. Indeed, biologists and geneticists nowadays are claiming that the human brain is evolving at an unprecedented rate to cope with the rapid advances and innovations of modern technology.

These then, are the great books and ideas that inspired the modernity project. In economics it was the notion of enormous wealth creation and the alleviation of systemic poverty through free trade guided and expanded simply by the invisible hand of the international markets. In politics the idea of democratic freedoms as the inalienable rights of every human being and the basis of governance in, through and for the people. In science it was the belief that all life from its inanimate forms to the spiritual destiny of humanity are interconnected, still evolving through innovative dynamic processes regulated by scientific laws and principles.

Not all of these ideas were necessarily revolutionary or even new. Democratic government, for instance, went back to the pre-Socratics and Plato's Dialogues. At this moment in history, however, these creative ideas came together to form a stirring emancipation narrative that caught the public imagination and led irrevocably to fundamental changes in the way people experienced the world. To "indwell the world" (Michael Polanyi's suggestive phrase)[25] no longer meant to be bound inevitably to the accepted social order instituted by God and maintained by the authority of the aristocracy. Neither did it mean to accept one's appointed lot in life which, for most, was one of grueling poverty, hardship and suffering. Nor did it mean to view religion and the church as the only safe refuge from a harsh and mercurial world that did not appear to operate according to any particular inbuilt order.

Old verities were indeed being challenged and new entre-preneurial, productive and potentially lucrative possibilities were opening up which contributed to the rise of the middle classes and led to vast demographic changes and the diversification of society in general. The sociological achievement of the Enlightenment was the rise of the new bourgeoisie, and it was among this new class of rich merchants, bankers and industrialists that the narrative of emancipation was most venerated.

Add to this the revolution in philosophy and the knowledge industry initiated by Descartes, Kant, Hume and Locke fervently advocating that certainty, truth and knowledge were largely hardwired into the cognitive apparatus of the human subject and it is clear what was taking place. No wonder so many of the promulgators of these new ideas were deists, because in all of this the previously admired divine order of things was being deconstructed and banished to the fringes of society – indeed, to a place that few of the so-called "free thinkers" of this period really wanted to return, a private sequestered place called religion.

Religion was by no means uninformed about these changes in its fortunes; in fact, some devotees of the religious life welcomed them. But many more vehemently opposed these views, believing that the modern era was fast becoming godless and atheistic.

It was no accident that at the same time as these fundamental changes in the way people understood the world were taking place, evangelical fervor in the form of the Wesley brothers and George Whitefield exploded, later accompanied by the social reform movements inspired by William Wilberforce's antislavery campaign and the work of the Clapham Sect. As we shall see, however, despite these protestations, initially modernity and Christendom formed an alliance because each needed the other to survive, particularly to further the colonial adventure in Africa and South East Asia in which both were then heavily invested.

From emancipation narrative to imperialistic metanarrative

The story of this shift may well be told as the story of globalization in two episodes.

Globalization – part one

When great ideas enter the discourse and common parlance of innovators, entrepreneurs, change agents and key influencers in society, and when these ideas begin to form a convincing story of progress and emancipation that is also manifested in cost-effective labor-saving devices and new technologies, then societies and cultures begin to change rapidly as well. The change did not come about simply because of the move from a largely agrarian economy to industrialization, or the appearance of heavy manufacturing industry, or the widespread availability of fossil fuels that initiated the first stage of globalization; more than all of these it was the reduced cost of transportation that allowed commerce, business, finance and technological innovation to become international and global possibilities.

And behind all of this lay the rise of the British Empire. From the 1800s to the start of the First World War, the lack of international trade restrictions and embargoes, the mass manufacturing of utility goods and the invention of the steam engine, the telegraph and eventually the telephone and the internal combustion engine allowed Britain to emerge as the dominant world power. Colonization and free trade encouraged financiers in Britain to invest heavily in international markets. Thomas Friedman notes that on the agenda for the first national congress of the TUC in Manchester in 1868 was: "The need to deal with competition from the Asian colonies" and "the need to match the educational and training standards of the United States and Germany."[26]

However, two world wars, the Russian revolution and the Great Depression of the 1930s brought this first impressive era of globalization to a virtual halt. Furthermore, after the end of the Second World War the world divided both physically and ideologically between international capitalism and centralized communism.

The Cold War ushered in a much more demarcated and controlled international system that lasted roughly from 1945 to 1989. With it came new trade embargoes, huge financial investment in defense, fiercely guarded national borders, and restrictions on immigration, travel and the sharing of technology and ideas. The symbol of the Cold War was the Wall, or the Iron Curtain, which became a powerful iconic metaphor of how the world actually behaved.

What the Wall did not stop, however, was the emergence of another world power with coastlines that bordered both the Atlantic and Pacific Oceans, a vast population, and a voracious appetite for international trade, economic prosperity and, again, significantly reduced transport costs. Friedman describes this situation well:

> [T]his new era of globalization is also different politically from that of the 1900s. That earlier era was dominated by British power, the British pound and the British navy. Today's era is dominated by American power, American culture, the American dollar and the American navy. American power after World War II deliberately set out to forge an open international trading system to stimulate employment and counterbalance Soviet communism. It was America that drove the creation of the International Monetary Fund, the General Agreement on Tariffs and Trade (GATT) and a host of other institutions for opening markets and fostering trade around

the world. And it was the American fleet that kept the sea lanes open for these open markets to easily connect. So when the Information Revolution flowered in the 1980s – and made it possible for so many people to act globally, communicate globally, travel globally and sell globally – it flowered into a global power structure that encouraged and enhanced all these trends and made it very costly for any country to buck them. [27]

Friedman alerts us to the dialectic of cultural and social movements, although he does not give sufficient attention to this reality himself.

Globalization accompanied by the rise of a dominant empire easily turns emancipation rhetoric into an imperialistic metanarrative that seeks to universalize the perceived benefits that the empire most cherishes. With the first era of globalization the British Empire cherished hopes and aspirations of global expansion as well as inventing most of the necessary technology to accomplish this objective. With the second era of globalization it has been equally hard at times to distinguish between the rapid technological changes taking place in the world and the ideology of Americanization and consumerism. The culture wars that are now taking place in the world, particularly between radical Islam and the West, are evidence that Americanization or Westernization is perceived as a totalitarian metanarrative that readily extinguishes the hopes and aspirations of other less secular and technologically motivated societies. The problem here, of course, is that Islam cherishes its own totalitarian ideals:

> Islam also has traditionally had aspirations to universal dominance. Islam has always expected world history to issue – by God's design and human effort – in the *umma*, the universal success of Islam, the universal Islamic state, accommodating no other forms of belief or life.[28]

Saudi Arabia and Iran are national manifestations or anticipations of this universal victory and as such they help to fuel the rhetoric of the fundamentalists. In effect, the argument goes that we have two imperialistic metanarratives, Americanization and Islam, contesting the human space occupied by a pluralism of religious beliefs and nationalities.[29]

The vision of the end of time articulated in Revelation 7 and 21 does, in fact, welcome a plurality and diversity of races, nations and beliefs, and so is better able to express the hopes of the world as it actually is and hopefully will remain.

Globalization – part two

Friedman's key idea in his most recent books (*The Lexus and the Olive Tree* and *The World is Flat*) is that what is new about the world post-1989 and the collapse of Soviet-led communism is the rapid explosion of a new stage of globalization which he does not see as synonymous with Americanization, but which is, nevertheless, truly turning the world into an international market place like never before. His thesis is similar in many ways to that of Francis Fukuyama in his book *The End of History and the Last Man* – that the real ideological struggle that has marked the emergence of the modern world was not that between Kierkegaard and Nietzsche or between Kant and Hegel, but the one between Adam Smith and Karl Marx. Accordingly the end of history is marked by the victory of free-market capitalism and liberal democracy over its Marxist-communist alternative.

Friedman also acknowledges the importance of some other thinkers who have sought to describe the world post-1989 in terms of one central idea. Among these is Paul M. Kennedy, author of the impressive *The Rise and Fall of the Great Powers: Economic Change and Military Conflict from 1500 to 2000*. Kennedy's incisive analysis of the emergence and then the collapse of the Spanish, French and British Empires, due mainly to their over-reaching themselves economically, politically and militarily, led him to conclude that the American Empire was heading in the same direction. Friedman believes that the relative decline of American worldwide influence in the 1980s was simply due to the US having to gear up for the next stage of rapid globalization, something it did ahead of most other world powers, yet from which it is now reaping the obvious benefits.

The continued resilience of the American economy and the US's continued dominance in world affairs would bear out this analysis. It is also the case, however, that America's present military capacity is sorely stretched in Iraq, Afghanistan and some 37 other nations in the world and the defense budget is continuing to rise at an alarming rate. As we will see in chapter 4, the theory that empires inevitably overstep their economic and military capabilities is well evidenced by history. In that sense the rise of Indo-Chinese countries with their respective huge and cheap labor markets, as well as the continued expansion and economic success of the new Europe, are formidable competitors to continued American dominance in the world.

Obviously the work of Robert D. Kaplan and Samuel P. Huntington in their book *The Clash of Civilizations and the Remaking of World Order* also has to be taken on board. Again, Friedman believes that their analysis is just too bleak:

> I believe both Kaplan and Huntington vastly underestimated how the power of states, the lure of global markets, the diffusion of technology, the rise of networks and the spread of global norms could trump their black-and-white (mostly black) projections.[30]

Clearly, however, the present stand-off between America and (to a certain extent) Europe, and an increasingly militant Islam in the Middle East, Indonesia and North Africa would suggest that there is a clash of civilizations of sorts going on in the world today. Paul Tillich once remarked that historically Christianity was the only world religion that had allowed itself to go through the fires of criticism that engulfed it during the Enlightenment. What emerged, he believed, was a more chastened Christian religion that now knew how to adjust to the exigencies of the modern world. There are many who believe Islam will have to do the same if it is really to come to terms with the West and its undiluted faith in intellectual freedom, liberal democracy, religious pluralism and inalienable human rights for both males and females. On the other hand, Tillich's view represents for others the essence of liberal democracy that can see no other political future for the world than the continued extension of democratic freedoms, now of course ironically instigated in the Middle East by imperialistic coercion rather than by persuasion.

There are those who believe that Friedman's reading of the world post-1989 as essentially the spread of a new and rapid stage of globalization is too superficial and optimistic. He appears to return much too conveniently to the emancipation narrative without taking adequate account of its transmigration into an imperialistic metanarrative that many believe threatens the future of the world as much as radical Islam. What we have derived from Friedman's analysis, however, is the fascinating manner in which the key ideas of modernity have now moved into another mode of joint operation, although Friedman never states it in quite this way. That reality seems to be genuinely new and worthy of considerable attention; however, the question whether or not this new phase in the development of global capitalism can actually stop the sort of clash of civilizations to which Huntington and Kaplan elude, remains a genuinely contentious issue.

In a new book the Harvard School[31] has issued a new manifesto for the twenty-first century which promulgates a thesis not dissimilar to the one we are exploring in this book. They are convinced that cultural values and aspirations manifested in democratic government and strong economies are the chief factor for international change and development. This factor has been largely ignored by anthropologists and economists in the past 20 years, but the impressive collection of contributors are largely convinced that culture truly matters and now must be the central issue in tackling underdevelopment and underachievement, particularly in the Two-Thirds World.

From Wall to Web and Metavista

If the iconic symbol of the Cold War was the Wall, then there is no doubt that Friedman is correct when he suggests that the iconic symbol of this new era of globalization is the Web. The revolution in information technology, particularly the internet, which is wholly democratic and controlled by no global power, has ushered in the reality of integrated global markets, nation states, and new technologies like never before. The key tenets of this new process of globalization are, firstly, *free-market capitalism* unleashed as an ever extending financial network that endeavors to create more and more efficiency in manufacturing, production and communications through the use of intriguing new developments in technology; secondly, alongside this economic reality, an equally expanding communications network represented by the *interconnectivity* of the worldwide web; and thirdly, the ever-increasing capacity of the microchip and constant *innovation in technology*.

Friedman describes these developments as the three new democratizations: the democratization of *technology*, the democratization of *finance* and the democratization of *information*.[32]

In effect the reality of democracy and increased individual freedoms is no longer an *ideological contest* in politics as it was in the eighteenth and nineteenth centuries; it is an *economic and financial reality* based on the ready availability, to everyone, of vast amounts of information. The internet breaks down the old financial, economic and national hierarchies that used to control the global markets, and threatens the continued dominance of Americanization. The new dotcom industries are thriving, wealth creation is taking place like never before, and international travel and communication has never been so swift or easy.

This new reality of international globalization clearly means that, as in any economic system, there are going to be both winners and losers.[33]

Cultural change and transition are also now going on more quickly than ever before, in the midst of which it is possible to discern the indistinct but nevertheless emerging culture of the post-postmodern – what we refer to as the new "metavista" culture of innovation and imagination. This newly emerging cultural space is also a truly global phenomenon because it is not simply, or even mainly, a philosophical or an ideas project. Metavista is also an economic and socio-political reality that is forming into a new narrative of liberation. Indeed, it is an imaginative story that could, if we had the will, leave behind both a flawed narrative of emancipation and that narrative's migration to an imperialistic metanarrative, in the process also uncovering one of the greatest narratives of dispossession ever to tarnish the face of human history, a narrative of dispossession and betrayal that modernity both created and has tried hard to forget.

But more of that later.

Modernity and the domination of reason

At the heart of the modernity experiment has been a love affair with the supposedly neutral and ideologically untainted power of human reason. Indeed, there is some truth in the assertion that modernity replaced the divine trinity of Father, Son and Holy Spirit with a humanistic and individualistic equivalent of subject, ego and reason. Kant's mantra, "Enlightenment is the emergence of man from immaturity that he himself is responsible for. Immaturity is the incapacity to use one's own intelligence without the guidance of another person,"[34] exemplifies how individualistic, rationalistic and just plain wrong were some aspects of this new emancipation movement.

Not surprisingly, this obsession with what became known as *instrumental reason* created some misgivings about the whole enterprise. Nietzsche was the first to link the exercise of reason with the will to power. His particular Dionysian worldview enculturalized reason as but one way human beings mold the world to reflect their own desires and preferences. He rejected idealism and the valorization of the philosophy of subjectivity that went with it in favor of a materialistic philosophy of the will to power.

The renowned nineteenth-century sociologist of religion Max Weber was the next significant thinker to raise other objections to the unfettered exercise of reason in modern society. He saw how

> uncontrolled rationalization could turn into a form of bureaucratic and institutional domination, in which the bureaucratic elites and institutions justify their power and authority on the grounds of superior knowledge and by claiming that their power embodies the claims of reason itself.[35]

The most sustained critique of the socio-political and cultural results of over-rationalization came, however, in the twentieth century from the Frankfurt School of Critical Theory. M. Horkheimer and T.W. Adorno, in the *Dialectic of Enlightenment*, analyzed how the capitalist economy, Enlightenment instrumental reason and technology united to create bureaucratic and institutionalized systems that acted as a form of mass indoctrination and domination. In that sense the emancipatory ideals of the Enlightenment – progress through wealth-creation, democratic freedoms, and technological interconnectivity and innovation – had turned into their very opposite, ensuring a system of mass control through the hegemony of instrumental reason. The dialectic of the Enlightenment was indeed a two-edged sword that created a new system of hierarchy based on bureaucratic institutionalization and oppressive social control mechanisms.

Similar serious concerns were voiced by Martin Heidegger and Jacques Ellul in their respective ruminations on the totalitarian influence of technology in modern society that served mainly the interests of the new capitalist elite.[36]

None of these thinkers were rejecting modernity per se, and most of them were not offering viable or convincing alternatives; what they were discerning was the process whereby the great ideas of modernity could be corralled into systems of ideological control and coercion:

> Thus, capitalist modernity is, in effect, presented in much critical theory as a self-reproducing and stabilizing system of commodity production and exploitation under the domination of capital. No alternative politics other than individual resistance is posited by Horkheimer and Adorno; consequently an adequate politics remains a problem with critical theory to this day.[37]

As we shall see in our next chapter, the same complaint can be laid at the door of those postmoderns who make very similarly observations about the modern capitalist system but provide very few genuine political alternatives. Adorno's later work carried on in the same vein, but he particularly isolated idealist philosophy as one of the major contributors to modernity's totalizing obsessions. The whole foundationalist exercise of *prima philosophie* from Descartes through Kant, Hegel, Husserl to Heidegger that sought to locate the foundations of knowledge in some esoteric aspect of human/divine subjectivity or philosophy of Being, he viewed as a philosophy of rage that exhibited a hatred of the other, the particular and the diverse.[38] Not surprisingly, the totalizing tendencies of idealist philosophy sought to subsume, capture or assimilate the other within its own grandiose, all-encompassing philosophical systems. Such totalitarian idealist cravings inscribed within the intentional fabric of reason easily produced its equally totalitarian and fascist political equivalents such as Hitler's National Socialism and Stalin's Gulag archipelagoes. For Adorno, philosophy cannot overstep itself in this way – there simply are no grand ontological blueprints or totalizing systems that can rationally grasp the cosmos of all that exists; indeed, philosophies that attempt such a task are mere veils and distortions.[39]

The attempt by Horkeimer and Adorno to limit the pretentious illusions and ideological tendencies of the capitalist economy aided and abetted by instrumental reason were in some sense challenged and counterbalanced by the reforming perspectives of another representative of the Frankfurt School, Jürgen Habermas.

Habermas exhibits the reforming tendency within modernity that seeks to rehabilitate the emancipatory logic of the modern project by rejecting the emphasis on instrumental rationalism while constructing a new theory of communicative rationality in its place. He concentrates his attention on what he believes are the inherently democratic and liberating aspects of human speech, intersubjective communication and consensus-driven rationality. He believes that in this way we can salvage the emancipatory ideals of modernity and at the same time resist the colonization of the "life-world" by the media and consumer-driven culture industries.[40]

The obvious question now needs to be faced: Do we similarly see the emancipatory ideals of the Enlightenment as crucial public values that can be stripped of their ideological contamination and rehabilitated in a new progressive world order?

We agree with Adorno rather than Habermas in respect of what we discern are the aggressive and terrorizing tendencies of modernity's great ideas and emancipation narrative to produce empires that always demonstrate voracious appetites for economic, military and political control and domination. We agree that there is a dialectical dimension to the modernity project, which means that although economic progress and wealth creation, democratic freedoms and human rights, as well as scientific and technological innovation, do not necessarily have to follow this particular path, the fact is that they invariably do. As Nietzsche observed, the will to power still resides at the heart of the modernity story and it still remains wedded to an erroneous philosophy of individualistic, aggressive subjectivity that Habermas's theory of communicative action has done little to dislodge or dismantle. It is this aggressive philosophy of subjectivity wedded to political and economic opportunism that the postmoderns have tried most systematically to eradicate. It is this project that we must now address.

2

Postmodernity:
A Matrix of Meanings

"Vacant metaphors, eroded figures of speech, inhabit our vocabulary and grammar. They are caught, tenaciously, in the scaffolding and recesses of our common parlance. There they rattle around like old rags and ghosts in the attic. This is the reason why rational men and women, particularly in the scientific and technological realities of the West, still refer to 'God'."

(George Steiner)[1]

In his book *Postmodernism for Beginners* Richard Appignanesi suggests that the postmodern is something unavoidable. His candid assessment is that the "modern is always historically at war with what comes immediately before it" and is, therefore "always post-something."[2] Zygmunt Bauman arrives at a very similar conclusion:

> All in all, postmodernity can be seen as restoring to the world what modernity, presumptuously, had taken away; as a *re-enchantment* of the world that modernity had tried hard to *disenchant*.[3]

If we accept, for the time being, Bauman's essentially positive assessment of the arrival of postmodernity – which is by no means shared by all the advocates, devotees and critics of the postmodern – the question arises: So when and where did this so-called re-enchantment begin?

Postmodernity first began to announce its tentative arrival on the cultural scene in the avant-garde artistic and literary circles of the late 1950s and early 1960s. It was associated with an anti-modernist movement that sought to move away from the non-representational self-reflexive literature and art of that period and rehabilitate narrative and representational practices back into the human sciences. It should never be forgotten that postmodernity, not unlike Romanticism, originated within the humanities as a new aesthetic that began to challenge previously accepted practices and procedures. As such it moved quickly from art and literature to architecture and then into the visual arts, particularly photography, the media and film.[4]

There have been a number of candidates for the archetypical postmodern movie. The 1970s futuristic thriller *Bladerunner* was, for a while, many film critics' first choice with *True Stories*, *Diva* and *The Draughtsman's Contract* proving worthy competitors for second prize. However, probably no film has, as yet, blended the artistic, philosophical, epistemological and religious elements of postmodernity as successfully as the Wachowski brothers' cyberpunk cinematic blockbuster, *The Matrix* – now, of course, a three-part thriller where parts two and three never quite matched the imaginative brilliance of the first film. *The Matrix*, with its relentlessly focussed trio, Neo, Morpheus and Trinity, happily mixes philosophical conundrums and stunning special effects with the martial arts. Travelling along a philosophical trajectory that began with Plato, reappeared in the sixteenth century with Descartes, moved through Nietzsche to typically postmodern philosophers such as Jean-François Lyotard and Jean Baudrillard, *The Matrix* spins out a great story that is carefully crafted to undermine our unprepossessing faith in common sense reality. As Colin McGinn, Professor of Philosophy at Rutgers University, New Jersey, notes:

> Philosophical purists may weep and gnash their teeth, but the fact is that movies are the most powerful cultural influence we have today. Nor is there anything unintelligent about the way the makers of the film handle the philosophy. It seems to have been made expressly to explore the issues of how appearance relates to reality, how knowledge is possible, and what we would lose if we entered a permanent dream world – as well as how to dodge bullets, blow up predatory machines and dress apocalyptically.[5]

The Matrix also reinvents religion, updating the Messiah story for the twenty-first century. Neo, played by Keanu Reeves, is the handsome, cool, yet charismatic Christ figure, unsure of himself at first but gradually maturing into his divinity. He performs miracles, fights against and exorcises evil in the form of the sinister Agents, and eventually wins the world back from the grip of the machines and the illusory power of the computer-generated simulation, the Matrix. Morpheus is a strongly prophetic John the Baptist; Cypher (surely a play on, and synonym for, *Lucifer*) is the treacherous Judas; and Trinity is the female personification of the Spirit who at the end of the first film resurrects Neo from the dead. Again, as McGinn comments:

> This is the New Testament story for people raised on video games, *Star Wars*, and extreme fighting. Jesus Christ with cool shades and a beltful of guns. I am not saying this is a good way to recast the central characters of Christianity, but it's hard to deny its cultural impact.[6]

In a postmodern world there is no denying the return of powerful narrative storytelling, but it is storytelling that unashamedly draws from a plethora of sources. In the process reality ceases to be what we have always believed everywhere at all times and becomes, instead, a culturally constructed pastiche or simulation of what we imagine the world could really be like and our precarious place in it.[7]

There is a real sense, therefore, in which postmodernity can be regarded as essentially a new aesthetic that originated within the artistic world but then moved out to invade the rational and cognitive domains in the 1970s and 1980s and finally the economic and political ones in the 1990s. In short, the postmodern world has been heavily aestheticized, and many would claim, therefore, that if you want to understand the popular culture of the present world, it is at the level of the aesthetic that you should begin, rather than at the level of the philosophical or epistemological.

The postmodern as a new aesthetic

The privileging of the aesthetic in contemporary culture goes hand in hand (as indeed *The Matrix* makes clear) with an anti-foundational stance in philosophy and cultural theory. It is, however, also closely linked with the expansion of consumerism that has been such a dominant feature of modern life since the latter part of the eighteenth century. As Mike Featherstone explains:

It draws on tendencies in consumer culture which favour the aestheticization of life, the assumption that the aesthetic life is the ethically good life and that there is no human nature or self, with the goal of life an endless pursuit of new experiences, values and vocabularies.[8]

The history of consumerism is, indeed, a fascinating story. It has it roots in that great flowering of bourgeois culture that was a distinctive feature of late eighteenth-century and early nineteenth-century European life. It is also closely associated with the way large urban centers ceased to be simply industrial organs of production but developed into centers of aesthetic enjoyment. There is a direct line of descent from the department stores and shopping arcades of nineteenth-century London and Paris to the aestheticized commodity-driven macrospaces of contemporary shopping malls which are now a distinct feature of every major city in the world.

The rapid expansion of the early capitalistic exchange mechanisms into a process whereby commodities and production goods ceased to be utility items or, indeed, even luxury goods, but increasingly became aestheticized items associated with fashionable brand identities, is a distinctive feature of the development of consumerism from the nineteenth to the twenty-first century.

After the devastation of the First World War, consumerism was manipulated in the 1930s by the new public relations and advertising industries, particularly in the US. The ever increasing production of consumer goods was less and less orientated to commodity use or exchange value but was adapted, instead, to appeal more and more to our desires and, increasingly in the later part of the twentieth century, to our fantasies. In the process commodities become fetishes like items associated with lifestyle priorities, group identities, technological innovations and subversive elements within popular culture that resist the status quo. Previously we may have visited the great art galleries, the Sorbonne, the National Gallery, or the Tate Modern to indulge our aesthetic tastes. Now we redesign our living room or the garden, make sure our dress code is dictated by certain brand identities, or express our sense of who and what we are through the cars we buy, the music we listen to and the food we eat. The cultural intermediaries of this insidious process are the new bourgeoisie, the educated middle classes who have perfected "the necessary dispositions and sensibilities that would make them more open to emotional exploration, aesthetic experience and the aesthetisation of life."[9]

It is the all persuasive nature of consumerism as the new political economy of the rich capitalist countries in the world that led Mark Poster to suggest "the possibility that consumption had become the chief basis of the social order and its internal classifications."[10] In other words, as Jean Baudrillard indicated, consumerism has moved through a number of crucial stages and has now become a sophisticated and essentially coded system of meaning dominated by the value of the sign. Increasingly, lifestyle advertising, direct and indirect marketing and television commercials are orientated less and less to products and commodities, and more and more to what they signify. As such, consumerism plays with our aspirations, deliberately clouds the boundaries between reality and fantasy, and so constructs "a classification system that codes behaviour and groups."[11]

It is the coded nature of these subliminal and deeply persuasive messages that began to occupy Baudrillard's attention between 1968 and 1980 as the media became the new power broker in the world of the hyper-real.[12] Baudrillard suggested that we don't realize "how much of the current indoctrination into systematic and organized consumption is the equivalent and the extension, in the twentieth century, of the great indoctrination of rural populations into industrial labor, which occurred throughout the nineteenth century."[13] It is at this point that we draw close to the sinister and disturbing account of reality that undergirds *The Matrix*. Under the pressure of consumerism's system of ubiquitous signs and the relentless manipulation of our subconscious desires by the media, the relationship between commodities and their sign value implodes entirely. More and more we become hooked on the media-induced or consumer-driven simulation.[14]

Consumerism has consequently moved through three crucial stages. The first takes us from the Renaissance to the Industrial Revolution, in which value was entirely "natural," i.e. grounded in real products and commodities. The second was that of the industrial era where value was commercial, based largely on exchange value. According to Baudrillard we have now entered the so-called third order of simulacra (a representation or image of an object or value system without the substance or significance of the original), which is located entirely in the differential value of the sign. As such it is controlled by the code and ruthlessly manipulated by the media, particularly the electronic media. We are now bombarded with information that continually distorts our perception of reality, indeed deconstructs the real and replaces it with the hyper-real, a sophisticated simulation that masquerades as a form of social control.[15]

The *Truman Show* has indeed arrived. It is not simply that we can manipulate or duplicate the real. We actually *displace* the real, so that distinctions between what is real and what is not no longer apply; indeed, they become empty and superfluous.[16] Advertising, consumerism and any form of media-based communication can be insiduously based on disinformation that increasingly makes the simulacra the only reality we recognize.

A less sinister, but no less persuasive, account of the wholesale effects of consumerism on contemporary culture is that offered by Scott Lash.[17] Modernity, Lash claimed, privileged discursive signification. It was oriented to the word rather than to the image, discursive meaning, formalism and representation in the arts. In other words, it existed under the sensibility of the *ego*, creating an essentially rationalistic view of culture based on the distinction or distance between the artistic object and the audience or, in the philosophical sense, the dichotomy between subject and object.[18] Postmodernity, on the other hand, is almost wholly orientated to figural signification. It gives priority to the visual and is highly dismissive of all formalism, excessive rationalism and didacticism. It is much more interested in the sensuous impact of art rather than in its inherent or discursive meaning, so it collapses the distance between the artistic object and the audience, immersing the spectator in a flow of sensation and energy that operates under the "sensibility of the id."[19]

Susan Sontag's discourses on erotic consumerism and Lash's notion of figural signification link postmodernity with a radical theory of desire – desires which are frequently not humanly befriending but often technologically agitated and manipulated. In postmodern consumerism, Descartes's thinking ego has receded in favour of Freud's desiring libido. Freud translated Nietzsche's materialistic will to power into flows of libidinal energy or desire. Gilles Deleuze, Felix Guattari[20] and Jean-François Lyotard[21] have applied Freud's psychoanalytic theory beyond the realm of the individual to embrace new forms of cultural practice. What characterizes the postmodern consumer is his or her involvement with an ever expanding net of essentially unstable and transitory libidinal energies, or flows, that are highly viseral and iconic and penetrate the subliminal levels of human desire and motivation:

> The effect on the consumer, the spectator, the "public," is equally by means of the unconscious. The flows of libido embodied in the book, painting, or piece of music produce forces that give rise to "sensation" when they strike the bodies of consumers, through the now polyvalent eye or ear.[22]

Postmodern lifestyles that are highly attuned to consumerism give preference to the body over the mind, the id over the ego, the image over the word, the sensuous over the cognitive, the aesthetic over the rational, the symbolic and iconic over the utilitarian and practical. So while consumerism quickly orientated itself to the phenomenon of human desire, it has, in the course of its development, given rise to a radical aestheticization of social and cultural forms of living that has both intentionally and unintentionally subverted the domination of the ego and the inflation of the rational that characterized the ethos of modernity. It is this accompanying crisis in the knowledge industry that we must now examine.

Postmodernity and the end of representation

To return to *The Matrix*: this film deliberately plays with – indeed subverts – our normal conceptions of what we mean by reality, continually raising epistemological problems in regard to how we experience and cognitively map what is real. The nightmare scenario that *The Matrix* raises is that first postulated by René Descartes (1596–1650): How do we know that our experience of the world might not, in fact, be a gigantic hoax? Suppose we are being deceived by an omnipotent malevolent genus who continually manipulates our experience so that what we think is reality is, in fact, a matrix-like simulation?

What Morpheus and his associates eventually discover is that the world is controlled by machines that have installed humans in pods that simulate lifelike experiences without the usual cognitive processes being activated by external stimuli. Consequently, our experience is a simulated illusion and in reality our bodies are batteries supplying the machines with essential energy. When Neo takes the reality pill, is eventually unplugged from the Matrix and wakes up from his dream world, Morpheus's chilling remark, "Welcome to the real world," is carefully crafted to disturb our own common sense sensibilities and make us wonder whether or not we might be the victims of a similar colossal act of epistemological trickery.

The Matrix also raises a more subtle epistemological conundrum: What, in fact, is the value of knowledge? What would be so wrong with living in a dream or fantasy world, as long as we remained blissfully ignorant of our existential dilemma? It was Nietzsche, after all, who remarked that there is no pre-ordained harmony between knowledge and happiness. Neither is it the case, as *The Matrix* postulates, that gaining access to knowledge will promote the greatest happiness for the greatest number! In fact, quite the reverse is the case. Cypher decides that living in the illusory world where a steak still tastes like a real steak is preferable to the unhappiness of continually having to risk his life heroically in the fight against the machines. In that sense he is archetypically postmodern, because in the end experience and good sensations – even those based on illusion – take priority over the search for truth and right knowledge.

Descartes, of course, resolved his epistemological conundrum by doubting everything until he arrived at the apparently unassailable Archimedean epistemological core of reality: "I think, therefore I am."[23] So even when he is caught in the existential dilemma of not knowing what is real he is aware of himself as a self-conscious thinking being. He perceives that his grasp on reality goes via a rational, thinking ego or self that apparently gains epistemic assess to the world through the cognitive apparatus of the mind.[24]

Immanuel Kant took more or less the same route in his search for indubitable knowledge and epistemological certainty. He divided the world into *nomena* (things as they exist in themselves, which we cannot know) and *phenomena* (things as they appear to us and so form the basis of our experience of the world). He then further bolsters the epistemological security of the thinking, rational subject by defining the nature of the cognitive apparatus that enables us to make sense of the world around us. The human mind is apparently arrayed with a cognitive grid called the *apriori* categories of thought – concepts such as space, time and causation, for instance, that sort out the jumble of external stimuli that continually bombard our senses, so transforming our experience of the world into a coherent rational entity. In other words, it is the combination of a self-conscious individual self and a rational thinking ego that allows us to accurately represent the world as it is through clear and distinct ideas.[25]

To date very few, if any, postmodern philosophers have believed this account of how things are in the real world and all have therefore sought alternative explanations. No one contests that we actually know things or experience reality in some shape or form; it is just that the foundations upon which that certainty of true knowledge was based have been discarded or reinterpreted as a social construct and therefore prone to ideological self-delusion.

Three accounts of the basis of knowledge

Not surprisingly, therefore, *The Matrix* offers a number of different accounts of how and why knowledge might be possible and why the search for truth, certainty and knowledge might be inherently profitable, i.e. valuable in itself. There are at least three versions of the knowledge industry implied in *The Matrix* storyline and each takes its inspiration from three different postmodern thinkers.

Richard Rorty and American pragmatism

The first, as represented by Cypher, is the easiest to deal with and originates with the laid-back American pragmatism of Richard Rorty. Following Nietzsche, Rorty takes a long, hard look at the representational epistemology of modernity and concludes that it is simply an example of asking the wrong sort of questions and arriving at the wrong sort of answers! The notion that the concepts of the mind can actually mirror reality and so represent the world as it actually is, is simply that – an unsubstantiated notion or a metaphor which expressed the particular Enlightenment penchant for manipulating the world for our own purposes. It is but an example of epistemological hubris that provided the flourishing knowledge industry of Descartes, Kant and Hegel, and in Britain Hume and Locke, with the illusory assurance that they had provided indubitable foundations to our knowledge of ourselves and the world around us. In reality, as Neitzsche claimed, it simply reflects a particular society's or culture's will to power, the inherent desire of a particular group of people to succeed. If we think our thoughts and ideas actually represent the world as it really is then such apparent knowledge will inevitably help to bolster and advance that particular society's best interest.[26]

Rorty's solution to all of this is to claim that as far as the successful realisation of liberal democracy is concerned we really don't need the various philosophies of self-consciousness to which the Enlightenment gave birth; nor do we need Nietzsche's (or Lyotard's, for that matter) various attempts to puncture the respective epistemological balloons of the foundationalist philosophers of the Enlightenment. He claims this whole philosophical trajectory was

> just a side-show, something which an isolated order of priests devoted themselves to for a few hundred years, something which did not make much difference to the successes and failures of European countries in realizing the hopes formulated by the Enlightenment.[27]

And what was the nature of those real hopes? To free ourselves from the constraints of feudalism and establish a new basis to society founded on the democratic freedoms of the individual. We have no need of epistemological foundations to this venture based on a universal self-consciousness that anchors such notions as moral choice, rational freedom and human dignity in the apparatus of our own self-reflexivity. Rather, we require simply the pragmatic ability to accept that each society and community utilizes certain epistemological procedures and language games to remain true to its own institutions and cultural practices, which in Rorty's case is that of bourgeois liberal democracy! So on this basis Cypher was perfectly at liberty to opt out of the reality equation, because it served his own best interests to do so and there was no underlying moral justification that said he should seek out the truth and remain with his companions. Life at the end of the day is what you choose to make it, and if good vibrations and pleasant experiences are what really matters, then forget the futile search for epistemological and moral certainties, because they just don't exist. Life is just a gamble and it doesn't matter much how you place the bets. So that is the pragmatic option that many people in a postmodern world prefer to embrace. The truth is that truth is what you make it and there is no external legitimation or moral re-evalution of the search for truth other than what a particular group of people prefer to believe about themselves and the world they inhabit at that particular point in time.

There are two other postmodern philosophers whose connection to *The Matrix* storyline is more obvious. The first is one of the most well-known of postmodern thinkers, Jean-François Lyotard.

Jean-François Lyotard and incredulity toward metanarratives

Lyotard first came to prominence with the publication of one of the most seminal texts of postmodernity, The *Postmodern Condition: A Report on Knowledge* (1979), in which he coined the phrase "incredulity toward metanarratives" in connection with postmodernity.

Lyotard's complaint against the scientific pretentions of modernity is that the expositors of this Enlightenment tradition continually exemplified a disparaging bias toward narrative and other socially conditioned forms of knowledge in the name of some supposedly objective scientific rationality that allowed us to arrive at a coherent account of how things really are in the world around us.

The irony of all this, however, is that science is itself exposed as an ideological discipline that relies on certain hidden metanarratives of legitimization to bolster its foundational claims to knowledge. The whole knowledge industry so carefully constructed from the seventeenth to the nineteenth century relies on two fundamental philosophical discourses or legitimating grand stories to support its claims that knowledge is both possible and a moral imperative for those engaged in its heuristic endeavors.

The first is the old, well-worn doctrine of human progress. The natural and human sciences, it is claimed, aid and abet the emancipatory forward march of civilisation. The more knowledge we gain about ourselves and the world around us the more progress we make in securing a good and decent future for the generations that follow.

The second is a more subtle philosophical story that originated with Hegel and the Romantics and sees the search for knowledge as a feature of the odyssey of the divine Spirit to lose itself and find itself in the other – "the other" being the whole history of humanity and our pursuit of knowledge in and for its own sake.[28]

What postmodernity exemplifies is incredulity toward these particular metanarritives which renders science simply a series of pragmatic disciplines devoid of epistemological foundations and so based on the principle of performance. What matters most is how such disciplines perform in the academy in terms of offering a tenable and convincing explanation of the nature of the world around us.

So Lyotard's target, like Rorty's, is any notion that there are transcendent universal principles or moral imperatives that undergird the pursuit of knowledge. The Enlightenment produced two such grand narratives of legitimation. The first was a political one that viewed history as a process of emancipation and progress based on the moral principle of universal freedom; the second was a philosophical story that viewed science as the realisation of the divine Reason and therefore based on the principle of universal knowledge. Any attempt to rehabilitate such democratic ideals, such as Jürgen Habermas's notion of a consensus-driven communicative rationality,[29] is, says Lyotard, doomed to failure because it always falls back on the now discredited metanarrative of emancipation. Instead we must accept that no consensus is possible – or, for that matter, to be desired; rather it is *dissensus* that opens up the path to truth and knowledge because it relies on "an ever increasing awareness of the contingent and localized – the unstable – nature of all norms for representing the world."[30]

This is, indeed, the world postulated in *The Matrix*, where science and technology have no emancipatory logic at all, but have led to a nightmare scenario of domination, control and ruthless exploitation. The very machines created by humans in the pursuit of freedom, progress and knowledge have wrested control of the world out of their hands and imposed an erroneous representation of day to day reality upon them. The only chance of liberation is to accept this and engage in an agonistic, localized destabilizing of the status quo. The real is, at the end of the day, a construct which mirrors either our desires for control and domination or our deeper awareness that there may be some more egalitarian utopian alternative.

Jean Baudrillard's dystopia

The third philosophical alternative that lies behind *The Matrix* is one to which we have already referred. It is the dystopian vision offered by Jean Baudrillard's ruminations on the destructive power of hyper-reality.

The Matrix postulates two complementary apocalyptic scenarios. The first is that the political economy of capitalism, aided and abetted by technology, led inexorably to the commodification of everything – including, of course, human beings, who are now no more that battery fuel for the machines. The second is that the machines achieve all this through a sophisticated cybernetic control system that simulates everyday reality.

Both scenarios come straight from Baudrillard. In his highly influential *Simulacra et Simulation*[31] Baudrillard links the "neo-capitalist cybernetic order that aims now at total control with contemporary structures of communication, that is the media."[32] It is the media that has now invaded and destroyed both public and private space through a constant bombardment with information that actually inhibits rather than helps communication. It is the power of the new information technologies apparent in advertising, marketing, television and the internet to simulate the real and so create the hyper-real which, in turn, simply collapses all distinctions between the real and the simulacra. Internet chat rooms, virtual reality games, Big Brother television shows and the like all dislodge us from reality and get us hooked on the reproduced hyper-real. The effect, again as in *The Matrix*, is a form of mass saturation or disinformation that manipulates the masses into a kind of inoculated inertia which is ultimately socially implosive.[33]

The Matrix postulates only two forms of human community. The first is a simulation of the modern city, where the masses move through the daily routine of work, family and leisure totally unaware of their bondage to a sophisticated cybernectic system of control. The second is the chosen few who have been unplugged from the system and now search for a messiah who will break the power of the Matrix.

The politics of direct action

It should be no surprise to us that certain radical political groups who have simply given up on the normal processes of political representation and are committed, instead, to subversive and often violent forms of direct action, find some inspiration from *The Matrix*. This is, after all, the political situation *The Matrix* postulates. If the system is the enemy, then democracy is an illusion, and those engaged in it are hopelessly unaware of the ideological nature of political power. The alternative, as exhibited by those who systematically attack what they believe is the ideological power base represented by the G8 economic summit, is violent direct action. If it simply is the case that there are no legitimating foundations, whether epistemological, philosophical or moral, to what we know about ourselves and the world, then the same applies to how we try to govern ourselves and society in general. If politics can find no justifiable theoretical foundations in the discourses of either Marxism or capitalism, then ultimately politics is about who holds power and how it is used. There are many postmodern thinkers who have welcomed this observation, believing it will ultimately lead to a much more heterogeneous form of political democracy:

> To embrace politics in a postmodern sense is to place a stake on contingency, on the insight that power, no matter how grounded in "reality," how seemingly bound to "material" necessity, is up for grabs, movable and therefore removable.[34]

Consequently, postmodern politics is a "radically contingent arena of imagination, strategy and creative manoeuvre"[35] that could lead to all sorts of new forms of political representation. The difficulty, of course, is how we get any political project off the ground in a postmodern world if politics is ultimately devoid of any moral or philosophical foundations.

Probably the most well-known and most often quoted political commentatory on the postmodern is Ernesto Laclau and Chantal Mouffe's *Hegemony and Socialist Strategy: Towards a Radical Democratic Politics*. Laclau and Mouffe are happy to continue the postmodern "abandonment of the myth of foundations," while at the same time claiming that this does not seriously undermine the Enlightenment agenda of freedom and equality for all. In the place of the universalized human subject that formed the basis of the social contract theory of Jean-Jacques Rousseau and John Locke they argue for a radical democracy of difference.

In similar fashion they reject the foundations of classical Marxism with its materialistic and historicist depiction of human identity as purely a function of production and the class struggle. Taking into account the post-structuralist insights of Jacques Derrida and Michel Foucault they contend that human identity is inherently relational and cannot be a product of one economic indicator. Rather, human identity is open to "a multiplicity of discourses which in turn operates from a multiplicity of power bases and produces a multiplicity of subject positions."[36] Consequently, radical democracy acknowledges the heterogenous, the plural, the emergence of different forms of rationality, openness to the diversity of human identity, the proliferation of divergent fields of human discourses and the never finalized nature of emancipatory politics.

How, then, do we decide which political agenda is legitimate and which is to be rejected? Here both Laclau and Mouffe, like Alasdair MacIntyre,[37] turn to the role of tradition in mediating social, moral and political options to contemporary citizens. They claim that it is possible

> to distinguish between the just and the unjust, the legitimate and the unlegitimate, but this can only be done from within a given tradition, with the help of standards that this tradition provides; in fact, there is no point of view external to all tradition from which one can offer a universal judgement.[38]

The problem here is that the political tradition they want to uphold is based on universal judgements concerning the inherent right of each individual to freedom, equality and the pursuit of happiness. To seek to salvage such emancipatory virtues by immersing them in a radical politics of difference leads to the obvious questions: So just how far can this difference and the plurality of discourses extend? Can liberal democracy co-exist, for instance, with radical Islamic fundamentalism? The perpetrators of what is now euphemistically referred to as 9/11 obviously didn't think so. So far the different political and religious traditions that have produced the Israeli–Palestinian conflict or the ethnic conflict in Sri Lanka and all the bloodshed associated with these disputes have shown no evidence of being able to co-exist happily, but have resorted again and again to the politics of direct action and terror.

Other postmodern political theorists, such as Best and Kellner, who similarily want to reject foundationalism, or the quasi-foundationalism of Jürgen Habermas, recognize that the problem of legitimisation simply won't go away, nor can it be solved by resorting to the language of tradition. Rather, they say, "a just society requires establishing certain universal rights like equality, rule by law, freedom, and democratic participation."[39]

The assertion that these so-called "universal norms" are not based on universal epistemological or moral principles, but are the direct result of "historical struggle," solves nothing. Al-Qaeda, Hamas, Hezbolla and other such Islamic terror groups believe they are involved in a justifiable historical struggle to end the ideological and militarist dominance of the West enshrined in the state of Israel and the imperialism of the US, and so replace the hopeless emancipatory pretentions of liberal democracy with the authoritarianism of Islamic teaching and law. Here is the nub of the issue: once the legitimating foundations of liberal democracy that supposedly guarantee freedom and equality for all are rejected, then it is but a short step to claim democracy is a political ideology that justifies the economic and militarist imperialism of the US or the West. If this is the real state of affairs then, as in *The Matrix*, there are only two genuine political alternatives: either submit to ideological control or get involved in the politics of direct action.

Reinventing religion for the twenty-first century

The Matrix, however, is not a political satire, nor is it a film that glorifies or tries to legitimize terror, violence and subversion. Both the philosophical search for truth and the politics of direct action are based on a utopian vision that comes not from the world of philosophy, politics or cultural theory but from religion.

Many have been quick to describe *The Matrix* as an updated version of the Jesus story. It is no surprise that the movie was released on Easter weekend and both *The Matrix* and the sequel, *Matrix Reloaded*, contain many obvious allusions to Christianity. The central character in both films is obviously a kind of messianic deliverer who gradually becomes more and more aware of his divine powers. *Neo* is an anagram for *One*; in Greek *neo* means "new," and at the end of the first film Neo enters into a new, resurrected existence where his divine powers are extended both inside and outside the Matrix.

Even the apparently innocuous name Thomas Anderson has clear Christian parallels. Like doubting Thomas, Neo is plagued with doubts about the reality of the Matrix and his own abilities to undermine it. The surname Anderson derives from the Greek root *andr-*, meaning "man," and so has clear links, etymologically, with the Christological descriptor, Son of Man. After Neo gives Choi the illegal software (hidden, incidentally, in a copy of Baudrillard's *Simulation and Simulacra*), Choi remarks, "Hallelujah, You're my savior, man, my own personal Jesus Christ."[40]

Neo's messianic vocation has clear echoes of the original story: a special calling, an intimate relationship with a Father figure, and his own particular virgin birth. When Neo takes the reality pill, he wakes up in a womb-like vat of liquid, where he is quickly unplugged from umbilical-cord-like cables and slides down a tube that is clearly representative of the birth canal. Neo later willingly sacrifices his life to save Morpheus and is raised to life again in Room 303 by Trinity's kiss. After his restoration to new life he is arrayed with new powers that symbolize his full entry into the divine. Just as Jesus ascended in bodily form to heaven, so in the final scene Neo flies through the sky, which is also reminiscent of the Superman movies.

Intriguingly disguised biblical references are also part of the film's appeal to Christians. The last remaining city is called Zion, synonymous in Judaism and Christianity with the heavenly Jerusalem. When Neo enters the Nebuchadnezzar for the first time, the camera rests on the model number of the ship: Mark III No. 11.

Mark 3:11 reads, "Whenever the unclean spirits saw him, they fell down before him and shouted, 'You are the Son of God!'"

So is this apparent obsession with the classical messiah figure that may or may not be the Son of the living God a vacant metaphor, an eroded figure of speech, as the quote from George Steiner at the beginning of this chapter suggests?

There is no doubt that religion has been extended a new work visa among the diverse discourses of postmodernity. No longer relegated to the private sphere or designated as mere private belief, religion has emerged from the shadows of modernity to become an important feature on the postmodern landscape. *The Matrix*, however, in the spirit of postmodern syncreticism, draws from many religious sources. The Wachowski brothers are clear about this: "It's not just a Judaeo-Christian myth; it also plays into the search for the reincarnation of the Buddha." [41] So Christian themes, the Taoist traditions and the oracles of Greek mythology all meld together to form a postmodern pastiche of religious possibilities equivalent in many ways to the postmodern preference for individualized spirituality over and against organized religion.

In the world of *The Matrix* religious beliefs and practices are essential in the fight against the machines and in preserving genuine human identity. In that sense the film delivers a prophetic message that could well be essential to our survival as we move into a new post-postmodern era. Postmodernity does not as yet know where to position religion in terms of the search for the common good. On the other hand, so called, "foundational" religious narratives not only legitimate certain codes of behaviour, they also regulate them. They depend, however, as we will shortly explain for their survival on a "fiduciary framework" that mediates a sense of core identity to its practitioners and the cultures which they nurture and control. The success of Christendom in protecting and preserving Christian culture in the West in both its ecclesial and political senses until the later stages of the Enlightenment bears witness to this reality. It is time now to explore the nature of such fiduciary frameworks because they provide a way out of the postmodern impasse of no legitimating foundations to knowledge, ethical and political practice and, indeed, religious belief.

3

Metavista: Discerning the Rules of Engagement

"All cultures are, inherently, negotiated compromises between the already established and the imaginatively possible ... Cultures in their very nature are marked by contests for control over conceptions of reality. In any culture, there are both canonical versions of how things really are and should be and countervailing visions of what is alternatively possible. What is alternatively possible comprises both what seems desirable or beguiling, and what seems disastrous and horrifying. The statues and conventions and authorities and orthodoxies of a culture are always in a dialectical relationship with contrarian myths, dissenting fictions, and (most important of all) the restless powers of the human imagination."

(A.G. Amsterdam and J. Bruner)[1]

The cultural sojourn from one era to another, to which Walter Brueggemann refers, is not without considerable cost. Nor, for that matter, does it happen quickly or even sequentially. The gradual transition from the medieval world dominated by the theological and philosophical worldview of St Thomas Aquinas went via the Renaissance's love affair with the world of ancient Greece and the Reformers' return to the world of the Bible and probably embraced a period extending from the middle of the fourteenth century to the late seventeenth century. Historically, to move forward, it appears, one has to reappropriate, rediscover or re-enter some basic aspect of the world of the past. In that sense the post-critical always has some affinities with the pre-critical, as the theological movement currently referred to as "radical orthodoxy" is endeavoring to demonstrate.[2]

Previously in human history it took generations, and during the Christendom era, constant renegotiations between the scientific community and the church, before the likes of Galileo, Copernicus,

Francis Bacon, Isaac Newton or Albert Einstein could emerge and simply reimagine the world as it was then understood. In our time new discoveries in the areas of cosmology, physics, molecular biology and genetics happen much more rapidly and without any necessary stand-off between the scientific community and the religious authorities. In that sense we now live in a time where the previous divisions between faith and reason, fact and value, private and public, high and low culture, science and religion – distinctions so beloved by modernity – no longer apply. The collapse of these previous distinctions has made us all heirs of a new age of imagination, indeed an age where the possibility of reimagining our own story opens up exciting possibilities for those who were previously categorized as the marginalized and the dispossessed. The following is an example of one such inspiring transformational story.

The story of disability

To celebrate the International Year of Disabled People in 1981, Rehabilitation International (RI) held a congress on disability in Winnipeg, Canada. Like so many care organizations in the field of disability, RI was an organization comprising mainly non-disabled professionals who worked in the area of disability awareness. There were 3,000 delegates at the congress, but only 200 were disabled. The minority of disabled participants made a request that the representation of disabled people on the Board should increase to 50 percent. This apparently reasonable request was refused. What happened next was nothing short of extraordinary. The disabled minority left the hall, met together in another room and started their own organization, called Disabled Peoples' International (DPI). The following is a personal account of this experience from a disabled South African social worker:

> I think until then disability for me was definitely a personal thing, and it was a tragedy; it was something you felt sad about; it wasn't in any kind of way something that was exciting. Winnipeg for me changed all that. There were all these professional carers giving their papers about what they were doing to help disabled people. And there were disabled people confronting them head-on, asking pertinent

questions and exposing the complete inadequacy of services for disabled people. On a daily basis they produced a newsletter during the conference that satirized the speakers from the previous day. It was exciting and positive.[3]

What DPI contended was that organizations concerned with disability should be run *by* disabled people *for* disabled people. A new public relations strap line emerged: "Nothing about us without us," and the previously disunited and disempowered disability movement emerged from the shadows into public awareness.

McCloughry and Morris explain that what transpired at this congress was a shift in emphasis as far as disability was concerned from a medical to a social model, a shift that turned people's awareness of disability away from a medical diagnosis that viewed disabled people as patients with a problem to the notion of disabled people as normal citizens with rights. The authors explain the differences between the two contrary attitudes:

> The medical model located disability in the individual; the social model in society. The medical model focussed on the individual's need to adjust to society; the social model on the need of society to adjust to the presence of disabled people. The medical model saw people as patients; the social model as citizens. The medical model saw disability as deficit; the social model saw it as diversity. The medical model saw the priority as cure; the social model saw it as social change. The medical model saw disability as professionally defined; the social model as self-defined. The medical model said, "This is my diagnosis"; the social model said, "This is my life." The medical model used science; the social model used politics. The medical model was maintained by non-disabled people; the social model by people with disabilities.[4]

What had in fact transpired as far as the issue of disability was concerned was a social revolution brought about by an imaginative reappraisal, on the part of disabled people themselves, of what it looked and felt like to be a disabled person. Over the past 25 years or so this quiet revolution has gained momentum, emerging into a worldwide movement that has completely transformed the way disability is viewed, discussed and experienced in contemporary culture.

Let us be more specific about the radical nature of this complete transformation. Thirty years ago all the following factors pertained if you suffered the misfortune of being a disabled person:

1. People with disabilities were largely invisible. Most public buildings, social amenities, walkways and other public access routes simply did not cater for people in wheelchairs, or indeed for people with any other forms of disability. Not surprisingly, disabled people were consequently confined to their homes, hospitals or other specially designed institutions.

2. Disabled people were marginalized from the mainstream of society, effectively rendering them invisible within society. And any group that is invisible is usually also mis-represented, particularly in the areas of education, health care, and access to the media and the arts. There is often little sympathy for, or awareness of, their particular plight, and such groups aren't recognized as significant members of society who can contribute to the common good.

3. Disabled people were disempowered. Those with disabilities simply did not have access to the normal avenues of power, the political pressure groups or the pervasive influence of the media, all of which can bring about significant changes of attitude and behavior in contemporary society.

4. Finally, disabled people were effectively silenced. A group that is largely invisible, marginalized and disempowered is also inevitably silenced. No matter how much such a group may try to campaign for recognition of their particular rights and unique situation of disadvantage, they are not heard; they are overwhelmed, instead, by the critical mass of apathy and indifference toward them that is a cancer at the heart of modern democracies.

It is a tribute to the work of the DPI and other disabled peoples charities and representatives that this situation has completely changed – very rapidly:

1. Disabled people are no longer invisible when the world-famous British Broadcasting Company (BBC) can introduce

its main features of an evening with a clip that has become euphemistically renowned as the "wheelchair dancers." Here is what the producer of this feature had to say:

> This [the promotional ident featuring the disabled basketball players] was part of a portfolio of idents which covered the diversity of our audience and is aiming to explore the universal theme of rhythm, dance and movement through different activities, moods and world cultures. From the power and grace of a Brazilian dance to the raw energy of a festival, from the high elegance of ballet to the speed and agility of basketball players.[5]

In other words, precisely what the DPI intended, had taken place. The media helped to move our awareness of disability away from the medical model that views disability as a deficit to a social model where disability is part of the diversity of peoples and cultures we want to celebrate. Ironically, this shift in consciousness appears to have taken place due to the ingenuity of disabled athletes and sports personalities who have demonstrated that the world of professional sport and athletics is not nearly as inimical to disability as society previously imagined. The athletic accomplishments of disabled sportsmen and sportswomen are often staggering to behold and such amazing achievements continually destabilize the binary opposition that was previously enshrined in the terms *able-bodied* and *handicapped*.

2. Disabled people are no longer marginalized when organizations like VisAble People exist as modeling agencies for disabled people[6] or when an organization like JobAbility can tenaciously promote equal opportunities for disabled people in the workplace. JobAbility organization recently deployed a movie advertising campaign written and directed by, and starring, Ricky Gervais (of *BBC Office* fame) which relentlessly utilizes irony to expose the prejudices toward disabled people which unfortunately still exist in our contemporary society.

3. Disabled people are no longer disempowered when they can change the whole nature of the discourse that used to designate or signify just what disability actually means. In

this regard, as we have already indicated, the arts can play a central role. So, for instance, the English-born artist and sculptor Mark Quinn (1964), made eight life-sized nude statues, which were displayed in the Victoria and Albert Museum during the year 2000 in a hall that was already displaying many famous classical sculptures such as Canova's *the three graces*. His figures were of four men and four women, each deprived of one or more limbs by birth, illness or accident. Quinn used the sitters' names, emphasizing that they represent real individuals, not mythical figures. For many, walking around that sculpture hall was a new and fascinating experience as classical ideas of beauty, heroism and perfection as these relate to the human form were deliberately destabilized, displaced and decentered.

4. Disabled people are no longer silenced when a number of separate charities for the disabled, epitomizing a spirit of co-operation, can set up a Disability Rights Commission (DRC) which campaigns for the genuine needs and rights of disabled people within contemporary society. The charter for the DRC clearly articulates the issues they seek to address:

> Attitudes to disabled people have changed significantly during this century. From seeing disabled people as the passive recipients of charity, society has come to recognize the legitimate demands for disabled people to have equal rights. However, traditional preconceptions and long held prejudices still prevail. Barriers that prevent full participation in society confront disabled people every day of their lives. Activities that the rest of society takes for granted are denied to many disabled people. The Disability Discrimination Act 1995 (DDA) marked an important step forward. But there are gaps and weaknesses in the Act which mean that disabled people continue to be denied comprehensive and enforceable civil rights. Whilst legislation in itself cannot force a change in attitudes, it can provide certain rights and lay down a framework that will encourage and hasten a change in culture.[6]

5. Finally, disabled persons are no longer discouraged, demotivated and dispirited when the DRC can sponsor a groundbreaking short film called *Talk*, which portrays a society where people without disabilities are the pitied minority

and disabled people live full, active and happy lives. The film was part of a campaign called *Actions Speak Louder than Words* which was specifically designed to impact leaders and key influencers from the worlds of business, sport, entertainment and the media.[7]

As the DRC makes clear, an enormous amount of hard work and campaigning still needs to take place before ignorance, prejudice and unhelpful stereotyping are overcome in regard to contemporary attitudes toward disability. What has already been achieved, however, adds up to a complete reimagining of how disabled people live, move and co-exist in our world today.

What has been described above is not merely a chronicle of how just and appropriate rights for the disabled have been established; it is a remarkable example of how a particular people group was able to reimagine their situation and tell another powerful story about their hopes and aspirations. It is a credible and challenging example of how radical cultural engagement and cultural change were instigated and deliberately disseminated in a way that irrevocably altered the cultural mores and practices of democratic societies in their embrace and welcome of disabled persons.

It is possible to delineate even further the "rules of engagement" that generated such a social transformation and to view them as hermeneutical indicators of success in the process of reimagining the stories particular communities and indeed cultures seek to recount. We will do so by underlining the factors that define the nature of the cultural transition we are presently experiencing, that which we have called "metavista", the age of imagination, because at its core lies the ability to effect dramatic change from the bottom up, rather than (as the privileged custodians of the knowledge industry had previously opined was necessary) from the top down.

Stories can and should be retold and reinterpreted

As previously indicated, one crucial aspect of postmodernism has been the rediscovery of the place and power of narrative, not just in contemporary storytelling but also in codifying and encrypting what has been referred to as narratival worldviews.[8] For too long modernity's obsession with deductive, scientific, instrumental reason held us in the grip of grand universal theories or metanarratives that carefully disguised their own philosophical and political foundations and ideological legitimization. One reason the film industry has experienced a renaissance over the past 30 years is that local heroes and local stories provide illustrations of the process of meaning-making essential to cultural transformation. And this is an important point: this renaissance has not taken place simply because of more advanced technological innovation, but because of a cultural shift in our appreciation and understanding of the function of narrative in our own lives and those of others.

Fiduciary frameworks

To date postmodernity has been unable to provide us with a satisfying or legitimating account of why local stories are any more credible and authentic than the universal theories and archetypal myths we once found determinative of human existence and therefore believable. It is not sufficient just to say that all stories are tradition-specific and so inevitably reflect previously held, fallible, philosophical, religious and politically motivated beliefs, opinions and knowledge.[9] Tradition cannot function as this kind of catchall, epoch-framing repository of all that is true, certain and wise and therefore still worth believing. We need a more robust, credible and ultimately satisfying theory of knowledge than this, which, surprising as it may seem, we can find in Michael Polanyi's notion of fiduciary frameworks. Traditions (religious or otherwise) are, after all, only one aspect of a *fiduciary framework* that seeks to articulate, ratify and perform a vision of the true, the good, the just and the beautiful, and which, in turn, is also a much more comprehensive notion of legitimization:

> We must now recognize belief once more as the source of all knowledge. Tacit assent and intellectual passions, the sharing of an idiom and of a cultural heritage, affiliation to a like-minded community: such are the impulses which shape our vision of the nature of things on which we rely for our mastery of things. No intelligence, however critical or original, can operate outside such a fiduciary framework.[10]

A fiduciary framework operates exactly as Victoria Harrison suggests in her interesting article on Hilary Putnam:[11] "(1) All knowledge begins in a set of antecedent beliefs about the world; no knowledge can exist without some prior belief. (2) Because objectivity is always relative to a conceptual scheme, objectivity is not the same as neutrality. 'The objects really exist, but … one requires a conceptual scheme appropriate to identifying the object in question.' (3) Because method depends strongly on the object of knowledge, no one method is valid for all forms of inquiry. (4) Rationality is analogical, not identical, across the intellectual disciplines. (5) Some subjective belief stance is the precondition for obtaining knowledge in any field."

Harrison's last point is similar to what Graham Ward means by "a standpoint." Drawing on the work of Sandra Harding (*Whose Science? Whose Knowledge*, 1991), and Nancy Hartstock (*Feminist Standpoint Revisited and Other Essays*, 1998) he writes:

> Standpoints are constituted through identifications and engagements with reflective practices that have a history and certain organized centres of association. One can speak of "becoming" a feminist, a priest, a socialist. Being born female does not imply one is a feminist and similarly being a Christian does not imply one is a priest and being political does not imply one is a socialist … A standpoint can only issue on the basis of a tradition of public visibility and an association, recognized publicly, of those who identify themselves as continuing that tradition.[12]

The power of retold stories

Before Immanuel Kant (in the name of the supposed limits of human reason) constructed his epistemological roadblocks between knowledge, morality and aesthetics (or the true, the good and the beautiful), and in the process reduced religion to practical morality, all three notions would previously have been understood in terms of the acquisition of practical wisdom. Certainly Aristotle Augustine and Aquinas would have been amazed at the suggestion that personal knowledge or certainty of belief could be reduced to that which was either scientifically ratifiable, mathematically indubitable, historically reliable or philosophically incontestable. For all of these precritical thinkers, what we believe is that on which we are prepared to stake our lives, so it must include not only the knowable, but also the ethically justifiable, the aesthetically pleasing and the personally applicable.[13]

To allow for the continued appropriation of the knowable, the ethical, the aesthetic and the practical, stories have to be continually retold and reinterpreted, because every retelling, reconfiguration and reappropriation creates a new story. Stories are not advanced and extended merely to ensure the maintenance of tradition (because tradition is, after all, just the living faith of the dead, as opposed to tradition*alism*, which is the dead faith of the living); on the contrary, what is ultimately at stake is the possibility of either human flourishing or a descent into barbarism, both of which we have experienced in recent times.

To return to our example of disability: for as long as society was aware of the phenomenon of disability it represented that phenomenon by telling a story of deficit and deficiency. Not surprisingly, society's response to its own story was to medically institutionalize rather than to socially embrace and celebrate. As one leading disability rights campaigner put it:

> Our disability frightens people. They don't want to think that this is something that could happen to them. So we become separated from common humanity, treated as fundamentally different and alien. Having put up clear barriers between us and the non-disabled, people hide their fear and discomfort by turning us into objects of pity, comforting themselves by their own kindness and generosity.[14]

It was precisely this patronizing story of disability, which turned disabled persons into hapless victims and misfits, that the DRC and the International Disability Movement set out to contest and overturn. To succeed they needed to articulate and perform another story, one in which disabled people in all their creativity and courage are recognized and welcomed as full participating members of democratic society.

It is just this kind of innovative and imaginative re-telling of central defining stories to which the prophetic tradition of ancient Israel bears witness. As a number of important and significant exegetes have recently reminded us, the choice for Israel was always to decide whether the people of God would live by their own

olitical narratives or imbibe the
rding and persuasive) narratives
as either to go the hard way of
ng the covenant people of God,
ipire" instead. Unfortunately,
back and ultimately leads to
ind political exile.

synagogue, reads from Isaiah
ilfilled that very day, and then
i new way (Luke 4:14–30), he
y of Israel to his hearers. He
ι, the good and the beautiful,
story believe in the ultimate
) they care for the widow, the
sort to bribes or usury, nor do
g the story from the vantage
g servant of God who will
vay that reinterprets Israel's
suffering and political and
virtually none of his hearers
ieen, hence the diversity of

urch has told and retold
g story, one that is now being enthusiastically
upheld and retold by the religious right in the US. It is for many
a fundamental story, a powerful and expansionist story. It is a
Christendom story, but this time devoid of its original context of
mission, witness and service. We will examine this story in much
more detail in chapter 4 – sufficient at this stage to recognize that
the story has become an imperialistic metanarrative that seeks
to hold on illegitimately to the old ways of power and religious
legitimization. It is, in fact, the age-old story of empire and idolatry.
To overturn this propaganda myth the church requires a new
"fiduciary framework" that abandons erroneous Enlightenment
categories of certitude and Christendom models of power. The
church is being called to reimagine itself, to find a way to articulate
its central defining story among the "metavista" refugees who
no longer believe that the church ecumenical and catholic today
is being sustained by a credible vision of the true, the good and

the beautiful. Where are the contemporary prophets, artists and storytellers who can retell our defining story with vigor, passion and persuasiveness?

Ideologies can and should be subverted

Everyone loves a good story, and often whole communities and nations are constructed around such compelling social narratives. Storytelling in and for itself is consequently an important human artistic activity.[16] Good storytelling, however, often operates at a more subliminal level with a hidden code or veiled deconstructionalist agenda designed to unsettle and ultimately subvert ideologies. Brian Walsh and Sylvia Keesmaat have recently contended that this is exactly what Paul is doing in his letter to the Colossians, while N.T. Wright has made a persuasive case that more or less the same thing is happening in Romans and Philippians.[17] In all three letters the cultural context is that of the infamous pax romana, replete with imperial cult, military might and the promise of socio-economic prosperity. Consequently, when Paul proclaims the crucified Jesus as the only *Kyrios* he is specifically denying that Caesar should be understood as such and therefore loyalty to the emperor and the Roman Empire is replaced by allegiance to Jesus and the community of disciples of whom he is the head. Walsh and Keesmaat locate the language of fruitfulness deployed by Paul in Colossians within the context of the socio-economic narrative proclaimed by the upholders of the Roman imperial system:

> If the empire encodes in the imagery of everyday life – on public arches, statues and buildings – the claim that Rome and its emperor are the beneficent provider and guarantor of all fruitfulness, how can a claim that the "gospel" is bearing fruit "in the whole world" be heard as anything less than a challenge to this imperial fruitfulness? Especially if we remember that the word *gospel* (*evangelion*) is the very same term that the empire reserves for announcements of military success and pronouncements from the emperor, doesn't it become clear that there is something deeply subversive in what Paul is saying here? Whose gospel is the source of a fruitfulness that will last and sustain the world – the gospel of Caesar or the gospel of Jesus?[18]

As we have become much more aware of the socio-political and cultural situation of the Roman Empire that paradoxically both aided, abetted and disrupted the growth of the early Christian church, so, like the prophets of postmodernity, we have become much more alert to the corrosive toxins of ideology. However, the difficulty with the concept of ideology, pervasive as it is in modern cultural theory, is its long-time association with the masters of suspicion, Nietzsche, Marx and Freud. In their case, ideology is seen entirely as a pernicious distortion of narratives and stories due to the presence all the way down, as it were, of vested interests and power politics, which is also the way ideology is largely understood by Michel Foucault and Jacques Derrida. Karl Marx believed ideological self-interest could be exposed through objective scientific theory and thereby revealed himself as an exponent of Enlightenment scientism.

Paul Ricoeur, on the other hand, abandons such out-moded scientism in favor of a hermeneutical perspective. Accordingly he infers that all founding narratives and stories that shape cultural identity are prone to a surplus, or "overvalue," of meaning because they require the support of their citizenry.[19] In that sense, such stories tend to lean toward ideological distortion and the concealment of vested interest.

Dan Stiver provides us with an interesting example of this. He notes that:

> George Washington's crossing of the Delaware River in the Revolutionary War is a story told from the American perspective that has left a permanent imprint on the American self-understanding of a beleaguered, underdog nation striving to overcome great odds with "Yankee ingenuity."[20]

It is the same practical ingenuity that is now often called upon to support the spread of liberal democracy to other nations that are not entirely persuaded by this normative ideal. But this time it is no longer an underdog nation that the narrative supports but the ideological reality of empire that can no longer disguise its own powerful self-interest in such expansionist ventures. The sociological reality of power and powerful vested self-interest has become a decisive factor in much biblical interpretation nowadays, ever since Norman Gottwald's groundbreaking book, *The Tribes of Yahweh* (1979).[21] Vested self-interest is a pertinent feature of all social institutions, including the church and the academy. Only constant vigilance on the part of those who retell their founding narratives can protect us from ideological self-delusion.

I return again to the story of disability. Sometime in the past 30 to 40 years someone, or some group, at sometime in some place subverted a dominant ideology. In so doing they exposed rampant self-interest at the heart of the medical profession and broke the power structures that rendered disabled people second-class citizens. In the process a new structure of rights, responsibilities and obligations was established. More to the point, a new discourse was invented based on the notion that *humanness* is not synonymous with *able-bodied*. The terminology of being "handicapped" was completely subverted and abandoned and is now quite rightly rendered politically incorrect. The connection between the media, the arts, education and politics in this process has already been highlighted. The story also illustrates how discourses change when certain signifiers cease to have any legitimate meaning. The word *disability* has experienced a continual destabilization, a deliberate suspension and deferral of meaning. It is no longer a medical term that clearly delineates, disenfranchises and stigmatizes a recognizable group of people.

The same is true, in essence, in the psychiatric world with regard to how homosexuality was previously defined, i.e. in terms of sexual dysfunctionality.

The world we live in is mediated to us through the intentionality and functionality of language and the discourses language constructs. To subvert a particular discourse, vested self-interest has to be exposed and the binary opposition implied in such terms as *able-bodied* and *disabled* deconstructed.

Power is no longer hegemonic and should be redistributed

This theme crops up again and again in the extensive writings of Michel Foucault.[22] Foucault, of course, takes his cue from Nietzsche, for whom the will to power was the central governing aspect of his particular Dionysian dystopia. In the *Genealogy of Morals* Nietzsche asserts that morality, and, indeed, certain theories about human subjectivity, are merely ways in which we internalize social control. Accordingly, Foucault sets about exposing such social systems of control as located in the so-called emancipatory discourses of the Enlightenment and the reified human subject upon whom all this philosophical rhetoric is based:

> One has to dispense with the constituent subject, and to get rid of the subject itself, that's to say, to arrive at an analysis which can account for the constitution of the subject within a historical framework.[23]

Foucault asserts that power in a postmodern society is no longer hegemonic based on now defunct systems of control such as the divine right of kings or Marxist economic theory. Instead, power is heteronymous, highly dispersed, decentered, indeterminate, a purely structural phenomena never controlled by human subjects; indeed,

> never have there existed more centers of power ... more circular contacts and linkages ... more sites where the intensity of pleasures and the persistency of power catch hold, only to spread elsewhere.[24]

As others have noted, however, Foucault's analysis of power in a postmodern society is fragmentary, contradictory and unconvincing. He avoids Baudrillard's thesis that it is the mass media and cybernetic communication systems that are the new power brokers of a society hooked on the hyper-real. Similarly, he seems unwilling to take seriously Fredric Jameson's thesis that the logic of late capitalism is bound up with the totalizing power of free-market economics. Foucault's attempt to dissolve the personal self in a mesh of historical and indeterminate forces means that he fails to grasp the importance of narrative theory in regard to both self-identity and the immersion of the self in wider frameworks of power and meaning. Indeed,

> Whatever new light this perspective sheds in its emphasis that power operates in a diffuse force-field of relations of subjugation and struggle, it occludes the extent to which power is still controlled and administered by specific and identifiable agents in positions of economic and political power, such as members of corporate

executive boards, bankers, the mass media, political lobbyists, land developers, or zealous outlaws in the Pentagon and White House.[25]

Given Ricoeur's concern to develop the philosophical and hermeneutical important of the embodied, narrative and interpersonal self it is surprising that he appears to have so little to say about the distribution of power within such identity narratives. There are plenty of biblical examples to hand if he had wanted to pursue them. So, for instance, when Nathan the prophet went to King David and confronted him over the murder of Bathsheba's husband Uriah, he did so by telling him a parable about the misuse of power (2 Sam. 12). David was rightly incensed and demanded to know who this perpetrator of injustice was. Nathan then turned the tables on the king, saying *he* was the man concerned because he had done the same when he and Joab conspired to kill Uriah to conceal David's adultery with Bathsheba. In effect Nathan had successfully subverted a particular ideology that maintained that kings can do what they want with their subjects as long as they think they can get away with it. He also reminded David that his identity as the king of Israel was secure only as long as it was maintained by Yahweh (2 Sam. 12:7–9). Nathan's next words to David were to inform him that power in his kingdom was about to be redistributed in a way that would make him a victim of warring factions within his own family (2 Sam. 12:11–12).

In our disability example it was the revolt on the part of disabled people at the Winnipeg conference that wrested power out of the hands of the medical and care professionals and returned it to disabled people themselves. Disability consequently ceased to be classified in terms of personal tragedy and became (for some at least) a genuine empowerment exercise in social transformation.

Similarly, when the communist empire collapsed in Europe in 1989 it was because the ideology of Stalinist–Leninist totalitarianism and the ruthlessly imposed rhetoric of the victorious proletariat had become both unsustainable and hopelessly implausible. The result was the wholesale collapse of a hegemonic hierarchical power system based on social control and institutionalized terror. The situation now in the former Soviet empire is still an experiment in the redistribution of power as many relatively new sovereign states seek to take their place in a new, modernized Europe.

In a postmodern society power no longer resides in old institutions such as the monarchy, the judiciary, the church, or, indeed, parliament. Just where power is actually institutionalized and maintained is not easy to discern, because the dispersal of power cites, as Foucault contended, is going on all the time.

The dispersal of power in the Christian story

In the Christian story the divine agent who is continually involved in the redistribution of power is the Holy Spirit, as the gospels and Acts make abundantly clear. So, for instance, the importance of the gospel accounts of Jesus' baptism lies in the fact that Jesus' identity is there defined in terms of divinely mediated Sonship (i.e. through the descent of the Spirit) that incorporates the hopes and aspirations of Israel. Jesus is then taken by the Spirit into the wilderness, where three very specific temptations introduce us to three equally different power discourses that would have driven a wedge between Jesus the Son and that which he represents, i.e. the nation of Israel. Similarly, when Jesus sets his face toward Jerusalem, that representational status brokers a devastating confrontation between himself and the religious and political representatives of second-temple Judaism. The implicit question in the text cannot be avoided: With whom did God-given power and authority reside? Was it with the Scribes and the Sanhedrin or the Herodians and other representatives of Caesar? Or was it with this Spirit-filled, troublesome prophet from Nazareth who had previously spent most of his time in the Galilean villages with the marginalized, the disabled and the dispossessed?

Personal and cultural identities are fluid and can be reimagined

The importance of Paul Ricoeur to contemporary philosophy and discourse theory is in no small measure due to his extensive, thorough and compelling investigations into the nature of narrative. Throughout all of his work he reminds us that we are inherently situated selves. Our identity is fluid and changes because we possess a history through time, we indwell a number of different narratives, indeed we are at best co-authors of our own story, because our story interlocks with the stories of others and because events, challenges, suffering and tragedies come our way that we neither invited nor foresaw.[26] Ricoeur agrees with Merleau Ponty that we are "condemned to meaning"[27] and with Heidegger that we project our story into the future. In that sense we are projects continually in search of meaning and significance.

Ricoeur uses the term *emplotment* to designate personal identity as that which is embedded or "emploted" in an un-finished story.[28] In similar manner Heidegger emphasized the nature of care as the way we constantly negotiate our "emploted" destinies. He believed we anticipate the end of our story, our own death, in order to give expression to this phenomenon of care and so assuage the existential anxiety that is the inevitable fate of "everydayness" or *dasein*.[29] Ricoeur replaces Heidegger's existential language with that of hermeneutics and narrative. The hermeneutical self is constantly maneuvering through the reality of emplotment in order to extract meaning from the stories and narratives we indwell. We do not possess such narratives; they possess us. Accordingly, our story is already prefigured by the stories of others before we make our own particular dramatic entry into the world. Through time we learn the skill of configuration as we seek to bring some scarlet thread of meaning to the seemingly discontinuous, heterogeneous and disrupted reality or our lives. As our personal narratives expand through time and collide with those of others and with the wider cultural story of which we are part we learn to reconfigure our story in accordance with the superabundance of subject matter to hand. Like our conscious lives, which are the tip of the iceberg of a vast subterranean subconscious process of living and learning, so our narratives are always burdened by a surfeit or surplus of meaning. Not surprisingly, then, every new configuration or retelling is also a reconfiguration: a new boundary of meaning is set, a new interpretation is offered. Each interpretation is in part a historical and fictive story because imaginative interpretation owes no ontological debts and can, consequently, do no other. When it comes to imagination there is always a certain amount of self-invention and self-interpretation.

Cultural narratives similarly mediate meaning and significance to those who peruse their reconfigurations. For instance, Zgmunt

Bauman notes how modernity located a narrative self-identity in the producer/explorer configuration that accompanied the rapid expansion of modernity in terms of both new territories and macro-economics. He contrasts that narrative identity with the sensation-seeker/gatherer configuration of postmodernity where the individual self is often transposed into nothing more than an avatar of desire continually seeking either good or bad vibrations.[30]

It was Karl Marx who said that no age sets itself aims and objectives it cannot achieve, and the same is true for our cultural narrative identities. We achieve that for which we strive, and for modern consumers that may, at times, be nothing more than simply consuming ourselves to death.[31]

The terms *handicapped* and *disabled* previously locked a particular group of people into an identity and surveillance system determined by the medical profession. It took no account of the fact that personal identity is fluid and functions not according to the iron law of medical determinism but according to the mediated contingency of narrative frameworks of meaning. Neither our freedom nor our power as situated subjects can be wholly inscribed within surveillance discourses.

The movie *The Magdalene Sisters*, winner at the Venice Film Festival in 1993, compellingly recounts how in the 1950s and 1960s the Roman Catholic Church in Ireland became one such surveillance system, incarcerating an estimated 30,000 young women in penal institutions, supposedly for sexual misdemeanors, of which many were innocent. Similar surveillance systems that brutalize and terrorize women exist in modern fundamentalist Islamic states.[32]

It is a travesty of the nature of human identity when so much Christian discourse and language turns out to be just one more surveillance system. Terms like *born again, saved, Spirit-filled, blessed* and *anointed* cease to be the language of liberation and become, instead, the entry signifiers of a surveillance system that brooks no dissent on behalf of the "inmates." The smash and grab theology that accompanies such discourse is, in fact, as Dietrich Bonhoeffer suggested, just another form of cheap grace.[33]

Narratives are potentially both liberating and lethal. We have referred already to the redistribution of power that took place after David's adultery with Bathsheba. The subsequent feud between Ammon and Absalom went via the terrifying violation of another woman, the rape of Tamar, sister of Absalom and the king's daughter. When Absalom contrived to have Ammon killed he may have expunged his sister's shame, but he achieved nothing that reconstructed her particular story and narrative around a Jewish cultural theology of virtue.

Movements and broad-based coalitions can and should be generated

Surveillance systems are notoriously fragile when they are confronted by broad-based coalitions of people that form a movement for renewal and ultimately liberation, as happened in Europe in 1989, in India when British rule was opposed by Mahatma Gandhi, and in South Africa when the Apartheid regime was faced with the worldwide movement to free Nelson Mandela. In more recent times it was such people power movements that demanded the end to the Milosovich reign of tyranny in Serbia and the end of ethnic strife in the Ukraine. It took William Wilberforce over 20 years to get a bill banning slavery through the British parliament. His eventual success depended in no small measure on the ability of friends and associates to help generate a broad-based people movement and church coalitions that became more and more vociferous in their support of Wilberforce's political campaign.

Norman Gottwald's thesis that the book of Joshua did not describe an invasion from outside the territory of Canaan but documented a broad-based people movement of discontent among the already situated overtaxed peasants against the urban privileged elites who grew wealthy off the surplus income is, to be sure, based on Marxist sociological analysis of the text.[34] But while much of Gottwald's thesis is open to dispute, his contention that the shaping of Israel as a nation took place not on the plane of disembodied ideas but amidst the material conditions of economic threat and the misuse of power, has received widespread support in OT studies – such is the "embeddedness" of narratives in the "everydayness" of socio-political cultural change and upheaval. People movements are essential to such a process, as our example of the disability movement aptly illustrates.

Arguably the reason the Christian church has steadily lost ground among modern day cultured despisers of religion is that it has tenaciously hung on to the vestiges of Christendom rather than become a broad-based ecumenical coalition and people movement. It is only the latter that can replicate the *Diaspora* mission strategies of the book of Acts and so thrive in a post-postmodern context.

Outcomes cannot be predicted

The DRC could not have predicted what has happened to the issue of disability in the past 20 years or so. Our own attempts to design a model that sought to bring the Christian faith back into public dialogue as a partner in the engagement for public truth relied on a 30- to 40-year agenda. Pioneers, like prophets, grow old, hence the reason they feel the need to publish their thinking! And without movements and coalitions, outcomes become very meager indeed. Archbishop Desmond Tutu once remarked while being interviewed on BBC radio: "My advice to anyone who wants to run an oppressive regime would be to ban the Bible, because once that book is in people's hands then the liberation cat is out of the bag!"

Arguably this was Martin Luther's experience as well, although his own deep personal equivocation over the peasants' revolt showed that he, too, had no way of predicting the outcomes of his own particular biblical liberation movement.

And so we could go on adducing more evidence – the civil rights movement that gathered momentum as Martin Luther King preached his particular vision of the kingdom of God; the drop-the-debt campaigns which have mushroomed into the "Make poverty history" movement ... All these were and are reliant on broad-based coalitions and people movements that democratic governments simply cannot afford to ignore or stigmatize.

These, then, are the rules of engagement when it comes to cultural transformation. Without them there can be no retelling of public narratives of faith; and without such a reconfiguration of our stories we remain trapped in the vicissitudes of the past. We become the victims of our own diluted histories that cease to have public credibility. Indeed, as one contemporary missiologist has suggested, the only other option for the Christian church has been to grow idle and fatuous amidst the lengthening shadows of Christendom.[35] It is time to think again. It is time to allow Christian imagination to rethink our current stereotypical agendas and to liberate us to walk the road to Emmaus once again.

But before we try and do that we must take full cognizance of, and endeavor to describe for ourselves, the nature of the terrain we are now transversing or soon will be compelled to transverse.

4

Metavista: Naming the Post-postmodern Condition

"Back in the middle of the 20th century, we honored Kierkegaard as the 'father of Existentialism,' whereas today a good many 'postmodernists' number him among their prime progenitors. Kierkegaard is the whistle-blower, the bleeding individual being chewed up by the Philosophical System who first shouts 'Enough! Somebody get me out of here!' Out of the 19th century, out of World History, out of Absolute Philosophy! Kierkegaard was being driven mad by all this Reason, suffocating from all this Absolute Knowledge. Like the author of the Letter to the Romans, his brilliant and caustic pseudonymous authors do not think that the world makes sense, or that human beings could lift themselves up by the bootstraps of their own Philosophical Reason, or that the soundness of the Moral Law would make us whole."

(John Caputo)[1]

It is surely an interesting irony that in the twenty-first century we are all now indebted to Kierkegaard, the erstwhile whistleblower on all the grand philosophical systems that sought a totalizing vision of universal truth. Against all of this sprawling, gargantuan theory Kierkegaard sought to protect the sanctity of the individual. Kierkegaard could see that absolutism of any form did not bode well for the individual. The same was true of Jesus' message about the coming kingdom. The rule of God can take adequate care of the spiritual and material needs of the individual, as the Lord's Prayer indicates, but it will do so within a socio-political and theological vision of shalom, or interpersonal wholeness and social harmony, that refuses to pit the individual over and against the System. It is to the likes of Kierkegaard, Nietzsche and Heidegger that we owe a particular debt. Not simply because they were the prophets of postmodernity, but because – to their cost – they refused to live amidst the vestiges of a number of vast crumbling philosophical and theological systems. One was metaphysics, another was Christendom. In the nineteenth and early twentieth century Christendom took three huge philosophical hits and in the middle of the twentieth century a number of significant theologians and sociologists also turned their guns on this particular project. And yet Christendom still lingers on. Why? That is not an easy question to answer. As befits our particular methodology we will attempt to do so by telling another story.

Metavista – welcome to the post-Christendom world

The film *Capote* (2005), like all retellings of what are purported to be real, historical events, recounts the disturbing story of celebrated American author Truman Capote, whose book *In Cold Blood* became a classic of recent American literature. The film portrays Capote as an effeminate, alcoholic narcissist who befriends two sociopaths responsible for the murder of an entire family in Holcomb, Kansas. Truman's motive for doing so was to enable him to research and explore the lives, loves and obsessions of these individuals who committed such a heinous crime. In the process, to use Ricoeur's language, Truman becomes "emploted" in, or intrudes into, the story of the two killers. As his desire – indeed desperation – to write the book intensifies, so his own role in the fate of the killers becomes more and more calculating and disturbing. *In Cold Blood* made Capote the most famous man in the US for a time, but he never completed another full novel and died on 26 August 1984 from complications arising from alcoholism and multiple drug intoxication.[2]

Although the analogy is not totally adequate we could say Christendom began in similar fashion as the Christian faith moved from being a persecuted and despised sect to becoming the first great world religion. When Constantine recognized in the Christian faith the socio-political and religious glue that could hold his tottering empire together, Christianity became implicated in the plot of its previous killers, the once unholy Roman Empire. In the process Christianity grew accustomed to this newfound fame and majority status, made peace with the rulers, and intruded more and more into their particular stories:

[The church moved] from being a small, persecuted minority to being a large and influential organization; it changed from harassed sect to oppressor of sects; every link between Christianity and Judaism was severed; an intimate relationship between throne and altar evolved; membership of the church became a matter of course; the office of the believer was largely forgotten; the dogma was conclusively fixed and finalized; the church had adjusted to the long postponement of Christ's return; the apocalyptic missionary movement of the primitive church gave way to the expansion of Christendom.[3]

In its original form, with the help of Constantine, Licinius and Justinian, Christianity simply had to learn how to rule wisely, justly and compassionately. That was the original context of mission and witness that for a time justified the Christendom settlement. It did so through two political projects: the dual authority of church and empire, both of which, it was hoped, should express the rule of Christ.[4] In that sense the rule of Christ was understood as similar to that of the Emperor – it included both spiritual and temporal power and authority, but was also differentiated as two different *forms* of the same rule. This political project was given theological and ecclesiological warranty through the innovative deliberations of Augustine on the validity of a Christianized empire.[5]

The spread of Christendom in both its Western and Eastern forms continued unabated until Byzantium orthodoxy eventually gave way, in 1453, to the expansion of Islam. (It is ironic that in the twenty-first century the same religious standoff is going on again in Turkey and North Africa.) The success of this impressive history writing project was the ability of the Christian religion, through powerful vested self-interest, to reconfigure the fate of the empire and eventually to contribute to its downfall. But that is to anticipate.

From the end of the fourth century onwards, while people on the European edges of Christendom were being converted well into the early Middle Ages, and while submerged pagan, Jewish and Muslim faiths precluded a universal victory of the Christian religion, the church continued to dominate Europe and, from the 16th century, its colonies in the New World.[6]

The problem with the theology of the two authorities, church and emperor, was that empire inevitably became the great millenarian replacement to genuine Christian eschatology, which had always looked to the rule of Christ and his kingdom, not to that of patriarch, pope or emperor. In that sense imperial theology inevitably overstepped its own capabilities:

> It has often been supposed that in the long run this messianic, imperial claim overtaxed Byzantium's political and military potentials and, as religious factor, brought about the collapse of this first Christian empire. Christian triumphalism destroyed itself, because the Christian emperors themselves were unable, even in human terms, to fulfill the expectations of a world-wide Christian empire.[7]

For a while, however, orthodoxy transferred this imperial theology from Constantinople to Moscow, where the church and tsar held sway until the fall of the third Rome in 1917 due to the onslaught of the Bolsheviks and the rise of communism. In the West, the equally triumphalist autocracy of pope and empire became increasingly corrupt and politicized until the "disgrace of the papacy" in the fourteenth century, the ravages of the bubonic plague and the agitation of the proto-Protestants, John Wycliffe (1330–84) and John Hus (1372–1415) prepared the way for the advent of the Reformers. As others have noted, the theological principles of the Reformation – *sola scriptura, sola gratia, sola fidei* – were inherently anti-establishment, but neither Luther nor Calvin, nor the later Reformers, were prepared to advance down this dangerous road of social reform, which was the logical outcome of their own revolutionary teaching.[8] The wars of religion that followed in the wake of the Reformation decimated Europe and effectively ended the political and religious reign of the one, holy, catholic and apostolic church. Yet Christendom survived, although now walking with a limp. As Hall puts it:

> Neither imperial commands, nor councils, nor wars could piece together the humpty-dumpty of Christendom after the 16th century, and the establishments that now had to be worked out on the basis of national identities, international alliances, and the religious choices of the ruling elites were never able to overcome the great ambiguity lodged in the fact that they were now establishments – plural![9]

In its Protestant form Christianity experimented for a while with a number of variations of this marriage of throne and altar, now more respectably referred to as church and state. The radical Reformation at least had the courage to abandon the Christendom experiment altogether, while the Counter-Reformation and the Council of Trent endeavored to resuscitate Christendom arrangements through new alliances with successive popes and governments.

Hall is theoretically correct; practically, however, religious pluralism served Christendom well as Christianity became implicated in yet another expansionist – and, some would claim, imperialistic – adventure, the eighteenth- and nineteenth-century missionary movement that brought Christianity to Africa and Southeast Asia.[10] It should never be forgotten that Christendom survives and does well where it shrewdly invests in the political capital of another cultural narrative, as happened in Europe from the fourth to the middle of the twentieth century.[11]

In the nineteenth century both Kierkegaard and Nietzsche raged against the suffocating mediocrity, the blind herd instinct, the corruption and hypocrisy, the insubstantiality and the fundamental implausibility of Christendom.[12] Heidegger was less virulent in his condemnation, but saw in the death of metaphysics the end of the ontotheology that also supported the Christendom project, although he also followed Franz Overbeck in making a distinction between the essence of Christianity or "Christianness" and its actual historical manifestations in the church and theology: "(A) confrontation with Christendom is absolutely not in any way an attack against what is Christian, any more than a critique of theology is necessarily a critique of faith, whose interpretation theology is said to be."[13]

In the twentieth century, after two world wars and the horrors of the holocaust, Christendom ran out of steam although surprisingly few theologians or church leaders noticed this fact. Dietrich Bonhoeffer, on the other hand, predicted its demise and waited expectantly for the emergence of "religionless" Christianity.[14] In the middle of the twentieth century a number of liberal theologians misread Bonhoeffer's tantalizing ruminations from his prison cell embracing a form of secular theology while at the same time still paradoxically investing in Christendom.[15] In so doing they inadvertently excavated the ground under their own feet, because the last theological vestige of Christendom is the liberal–evangelical standoff, both ends of which trace their origins to dangerous liaisons with modernity, as we will indicate in chapter 6. In the twenty-first century Christendom is dead – we have only yet to arrange the funeral. The problem, as Loren Mead sees it, is this:

> We are surrounded by the relics of the Christendom Paradigm, a paradigm that has largely ceased to work. But the relics hold us hostage to the past and make it difficult to create a new paradigm that can be as compelling for the next age as the Christendom Paradigm has been for the past age.[16]

The problem, however, is deeper than that. Christendom has shown an extremely tenacious ability to survive. Arguably it was mortally wounded when it took its first big philosophical hits from Kierkegaard, Nietzsche and Heidegger, but it remained an investment portfolio for the Christian church for the rest of the twentieth century. The difficulty was that it had exhausted its political capital by the end of the nineteenth century, when modernity no longer required its religious legitimation.[17] Most of us, of course, were never informed of this reality, so since then we have all been living off the interest until finally the whole Christendom project can no longer pay out any more dividends; the pension funds are now finally exhausted. To a progressively non-churchgoing population in Europe, Canada, Australasia and the coastal regions of North America Christendom has simply ceased to exist. Whatever the various remnants of church–state arrangements that still linger on, or the historical reality of beautiful church buildings and cathedrals that Christendom has bequeathed to us, Nietzsche was right: Christendom has become terminally implausible. For better or worse we now have to make our way in a post-Christendom world. The challenge for the Christian church in the twenty-first century is how to completely reimagine itself and at the same time to regain some genuine and serious political capital.[18]

The apparent anomaly of the present-day US

The anomaly we hinted at in our introduction now needs to be further investigated: What about the US, where Christendom arrangements still appear to be abundantly evident? It is, of course, a very different form of Christendom from the investment portfolio that took shape in Europe. The latter did not survive the attempt to replicate it in the vast open spaces of colonial America.[19] Nor could European Christendom arrangements hope to survive the Declaration of Independence. The first amendment enshrined in the American constitution remains deeply embedded in the psyche of the American people. We need now to investigate further the apparent contradiction of a deeply pluralist Christian society that developed its own version of Christendom.

To help us we turn first to a renowned sociologist, Peter Berger. As early as 1961 Berger recognized the apparent incongruity of the Christendom phenomenon that still held sway in modern America:

> There can be little doubt about the prominence of the religious phenomenon in America. Religion occupies a conspicuous place in American society, is accorded considerable social prestige, and appears to be a matter of active interest to large numbers of people.[20]

And his assessment of why this is so constitutes one of the most devastating indictments of the role of religion in American public life that we have ever come across:

> [T]he Christian establishment is important to America, including the state and all dominant institutions, precisely because *it contributes nothing distinctively its own* but serves as an excellent medium for conferring upon successive generations the "optimistic ideology" of the society.[21]

"The failure to see this," Berger concludes, "makes impossible any meaningful Christian thinking about the American situation."[22]

Significant theologians in both Canada and America have now caught up with Berger and his sociological analysis, adding theological fuel to the fire that they hope will consume the vestiges of Christendom.

With the help of theologians like Douglas John Hall, Stanley Hauerwas,[23] Walter Brueggemann,[24] George Hunsinger[25] we can identify most of the aspects of this "optimistic ideology" to which Berger refers. They are:

(1) A preference for a *theologia gloria* based on the modernity myths of power, prosperity, progress and success.

(2) An apparent blindness to the fact that at the heart of the Christian faith is a *theologia crucis* that embraces power-lessness, failure, godforsakenness, annulment and ambiguity rather than triumphalism.

(3) A preference for the prosperity gospel or a narcissistic me-and-Jesus piety that is either totally devoid of any social justice or political relevance or is hopelessly accommodated to consumerist culture.

(4) A simplistic bibliolatry, with a general distrust of theology and critical thinking.

(5) A failure to recognize that the megachurch phenomenon has virtually nothing to do with the New Testament or the historical experience of the Hebrew people and is, in fact, often a cultural adaptation to the celebrity culture of the US.

(6) A simplistic faith in the universal worth of liberal democracy which it is the duty of the US to export to the rest of the world.[26]

In summary: If, as is often claimed, the Enlightenment exhibited a prejudice against prejudice, then American theology and church life, as Bonhoeffer clearly noted, often exhibits a profound prejudice against self-criticism.[27] In this sense Jürgen Moltmann is correct when he asserts that the greatest testimony to the enduring success of modernity is the US. Modern America has been besotted by its own particular myths. Notions such as the Chosen People, Manifest Destiny, the Redeemer nation and the Great Experiment have held Americans in awe of their own seemingly endless capacity for renovation.[28] Most nations owe a debt to both the successes and the failures of the past. The US apparently owes no such debt and so tries continually to reinvent itself:

> As the self-government of the people, America is what Franklin Roosevelt called it: a bold and lasting experiment. What America is

to be, must therefore be continually redefined, and what America is, must continually be re-interpreted. In January 1993, President Bill Clinton stressed this aspect, and demanded "the vision and courage to reinvent America." It is true that in his inaugural address he stressed the inner political side of this renewal of America on behalf of the poor and the weak; but he also reaffirmed America's world-wide mission: America must continue to lead the world we did so much to make.[29]

By any accounts this is a remarkably truncated version of recent history, but this messianic complex still fuels America's dangerous interventionist strategies in other nations' affairs.[30] As we have noted already, the US was born out of a curious mixture of reformed Protestantism and modernity rationalism. Unfortunately it was the latter that won the day as successive generations of Americans traded their biblical covenantal heritage for the glories of the "American dream."[31] It is the successful marriage of modernity and the "American way of life," as George Bush senior opined, that has made modern America the remaining superpower in the world today. Of course, that is simply another way of referring to empire, which the biblical apocalyptic literature regards with deep suspicion.

Unfortunately, fundamentalist Islam tends to read the Koran in the same way (i.e. in terms of a negative assessment of empire) and so divides the world into believers and infidels, with the US seen as providing the military and economic hardware for the latter.

Both the imperialistic version of the modernity story and the Islamic condemnation of it are dangerous ideological illusions as each seeks to outwit the other and in so doing unfortunately transform the early twenty-first century into a very dangerous place in which to live. As long as the US continues to bankroll the modernity project, the apparently successful forward march of progress and emancipation now epitomized by globalization will be won at a considerable price. It is a price the free world cannot afford to pay, because it threatens the very economic, environmental, ecological and political security of the future: a destiny which does not belong to one nation only but is the duty of humanity in general to bequeath to successive generations.

Modernity and a distinct form of ideological Christendom have made a successful marriage in modern America. But, it is hoped, the divorce papers will soon be signed and then we will see if either is capable of flourishing on its own.

Metavista – welcome to the post-secular world

It is one of those ironies of contemporary cultural history that the collapse of Christendom was supposed also to announce the victory of something called secularization. The old secularization thesis went something like this: The industrial revolution in the nineteenth century ushered in a new era of economic prosperity and expansion which, accompanied by the victory of Darwinism over Christian theism, led inexorably to the secularization of society.

We will examine the secularization story in more detail in chapter 8, but for now we need to see that the old secularization thesis is showing some considerable signs of ill health; indeed, it is possible to point to something surprisingly new in our present cultural metavista (meta-space), a reality that is gathering pace all the time and demonstrates that religion is always much more adaptable to current cultural trends than many sociologists of religion realize.

We begin with another story – actually, part of a speech – which indicates that the notion of rampant secularity in society is (for some people anyway) merely a ghost of Enlightenment epistemology. The speech was delivered by the internationally acclaimed rock star, Bono, from U2, at the national prayer breakfast in the White House in September 2005:

> When churches started demonstrating on debt, governments listened – and acted. When churches starting organizing, petitioning, and even – that most unholy of acts today, God forbid, lobbying – on AIDS and global health, governments listened – and acted.
>
> I'm here today in all humility to say: you changed minds; you changed policy; you changed the world.
>
> Look, whatever thoughts you have about God, who He is or if He exists, most will agree that if there is a God, He has a special place for the poor. In fact, the poor are where God lives.
>
> Check Judaism. Check Islam. Check pretty much anyone.

I mean, God may well be with us in our mansions on the hill. I hope so.

He may well be with us as in all manner of controversial stuff. Maybe, maybe not. But the one thing we can all agree, all faiths and ideologies, is that God is with the vulnerable and poor.

God is in the slums, in the cardboard boxes where the poor play house.

God is in the silence of a mother who has infected her child with a virus that will end both their lives. God is in the cries heard under the rubble of war. God is in the debris of wasted opportunity and lives, and God is with us if we are with them. "If you remove the yoke from your midst, the pointing of the finger and speaking wickedness, and if you give yourself to the hungry and satisfy the desire of the afflicted, then your light will rise in darkness and your gloom will become like midday and the Lord will continually guide you and satisfy your desire in scorched places."

It's not a coincidence that in the scriptures, poverty is mentioned more than 2,100 times. It's not an accident. That's a lot of airtime, 2,100 mentions. You know, the only time Christ is judgmental is on the subject of the poor. "As you have done it unto the least of these my brethren, you have done it unto me" (Matt. 25:40). As I say, good news to the poor.[32]

When Christendom began there was no division between the secular and religious spheres, at least not as we understand them today.[33] There was simply political rule (the secular) and the rule of the church (the ecclesia). Both were public domains where justice and compassion had to be seen to be operating; both were subject to divine governance. Augustine could distinguish between them and call them two cities, but not for one minute did he think that because he was a bishop or a religious man he had no right to contribute to the debate about how they conducted their various affairs.

Similarly, in the Middle Ages or the premodern era the word *religio* simply meant "being virtuous." It was to do one's public duty before God, church and nation. There was no separate private sphere called religion that had to be clearly demarcated from law, politics, art or commerce. The secular referred to those who did not belong to a religious order, but everyone lived under the "sacred canopy" of the Christian faith, and those who sought to live a virtuous life did so publicly. It is a curious reality that it seems to be this world Bono is happier living in, because in some crucial aspects the premodern and the postmodern have now joined hands. Bono appears not to have read Kant, because he certainly does not subscribe to the rules of engagement that Kant drew up in relation to science, morality and religion, all of which were reinscribed within the limits of Absolute Reason. Bono's ethical judgments and religious sentiments all seem to belong to the same fabric and he is obviously not aware of the unstitching that needs to take place if we are to be truly scientific in Kant's terms. In fact, what was true in the Middle Ages is true for Bono today: the songs he writes, the public lobbying he organizes and the ethical judgments to which he is committed all appear to be located within the same religious narrative, or – dare we say – fiduciary framework. In Bono's case it is, to be sure, Judaism, Christianity and Islam, which all operate with some version of what the liberation theologians call the preferential option for the poor, where he prefers to take his stand.

If Bono hasn't read Kant, neither does he appear to have read the masters of suspicion with their equally reductionist accounts of the nature of religion. He does not seem to believe, like Freud, that religion is just like sucking our thumbs, an infantile nostalgia for a heavenly parent. Neither does he seem to agree with Marx that religion is the opiate of the people to inoculate them against the iron law of materialist economics.

Bono also does not seem to believe, like Nietzsche, that religion is simply antimaterialistic Platonism for the masses. Religion may indeed be only one perspective on things as Nietzsche suggested, but then Nietzsche and the other masters of suspicion were all torched by the same high-octane perspectivism that blew up in their faces. To the postmodern mind science, too, is just another perspective and one that owns no more legitimation than religion. Similarly, in the postmodern world the religious perspective does not require to be privatized or issued with a health warning as mere opinion or private value. The Enlightenment middle wall of partition between public and private has also collapsed. Welcome, indeed, to the post-secular world where religion, like any narrative, can hold its own in the public sphere. Welcome, indeed, to cultural diversity, where religion devoid of the Christendom straightjacket appears to be starting to make a comeback. Welcome, indeed, to a new cultural ingenuity where religion once again prophetically calls us to account for what we have done or not done unto the least of one of these.

In the next section we turn to a very different narrative. It is one that recounts the most desperate and distressing narrative of dispossession ever to blight the history of humanity; one to which Bono's speech refers; and indeed, his speech was deliberately aimed at reawakening our conscience to the fact that the emancipation narrative of modernity has not delivered what it promised in much of the Two-Thirds World. This story of dispossession, corruption, corporate greed and eventual desertion is a narrative that in many ways could be called the bastard child of modernity. It is a story that is becoming increasingly dangerous and apocalyptic in terms of our corporate survival in this globalized world – although that is not how it used to be told.

Metavista – welcome to the post-colonial world

"I have sometimes seen, in the morning sun, the smoke of a thousand villages where no missionary has ever been." These twenty words from the fiery Scots preacher Robert Moffatt transformed the life of a young cotton mill owner destined to become perhaps the most famous explorer and medical missionary of our time, David Livingstone (1813–73). Livingstone began his life of service, hardship and exploration in response to the words of the Great Commission (Matt. 28:19–20). His motto and motivation:

> "All authority is given unto me." *The same power is available*!
> "Go and *evangelize all nations.*" The same program is operative!
> "Lo, I am with you." *The same Presence is assured!*[34]

Different words, from a different theological tradition, which formed the last paragraph of a book that effectively ended the first quest for the historical Jesus – the words of author, celebrated German concert musician and theologian Albert Schweitzer (1875–1965), who spent the last 50 years of his life as a medical missionary in the continent of Africa and was later (in 1953) to win the Nobel Peace Prize for his efforts:

He comes to us as One unknown, without a name, as of old, by the lakeside, He came to those men who knew Him not. He speaks to us the same word: "Follow thou me!" and sets us to the tasks which He has to fulfill for our time. He commands. And to those who obey Him, whether they be wise or simple, He will reveal Himself in the toils, the conflicts, the sufferings which they shall pass through in His fellowship, and, as an ineffable mystery, they shall learn in their own experience Who He is.[35]

Albert Schweitzer was born two years after Livingstone was buried and honored as a national hero in Westminster Abbey. He began his endeavors because he was convinced that historical critical research could not disclose the real Jesus; rather, we must follow the Suffering Servant in his life of service and ministry to the displaced and marginalized of our world.

The heroic achievements of many of the early pioneers and missionaries could not however, disguise what was really going on:

The Protestant missions of the 18th and 19th centuries were never pure missions of the gospel … They were kingdom-of-Christ missions, and therefore spread, not only the Bible, but "Christian values" too, which meant European, American and modern culture. Christianization and civilization often went hand in hand. In the Victorian age these cultural missions were deliberately pushed forward in Africa and Asia.[36]

Livingstone witnessed with his own eyes the brutal reality of the slave trade in Africa and determined to use his considerable influence to end what William Wilberforce later referred to as "the rape of Africa." Schweitzer gave much of his time to treating what was then the medical scourge of Africa, leprosy. How would both men have reacted to the contemporary HIV/AIDS pandemic which is now scourging and raping Africa and threatening to rob that great continent of a prosperous and hopeful future?

Post-colonialism – what is it?

Colonialism has been with us ever since the great conquests by respective European nations in the sixteenth century. Post-colonialism, however, is a relatively new phenomenon and there is still widespread discussion among literary theorists, sociologists, economists and theologians about how best to define the post-colonial reality in Africa and elsewhere.[37] A working definition could be simply that it is characterized by substantial *economic, political, social, religious* and *humanitarian* challenges and changes following the end of the colonial era. We look briefly at each of these in turn.

The economic sphere, not surprisingly, is still characterized by a clash of cultures: predatory capitalism, which keeps many countries in Africa in a structural system of economic dependence, versus a still largely agrarian economy. Inevitably, it mirrors what is also happening in the West, namely an increasingly obvious economic gap between the rich and the poor and the extension of what can only be termed the poverty trap.

The political realities are evidenced in the struggle between liberal democracy on one hand and increasingly despotic and corrupt dictatorships or the upsurge of old tribal hostilities, and in some countries (like Sierra Leone, Somalia and the Sudan) the breakdown of any semblance of law and order and a return to religious strife, genocide and barbarism.

Africa and, to a certain extent, Southeast Asia manifest a dialectical social and cultural identity. There is collusion with the West, and widespread disillusionment with it at the same time. In both continents the effects of Westernization are every-where to be seen, particularly among the young, where the American ideals of prosperity, individual freedom and cultural hip trendiness are part of the fabric of everyday life. At the same time there is the re-emergence of indigenous African and Asian cultural identities, and both together give rise to the post-colonial phenomenon of hybridity in regard to racial and cultural identity.

The religious prospects for Africa appear to be taking shape around the axis of a vibrant, pluralist and explosively growing Christianity versus an increasingly militant Islam as well as the revival of indigenous African religion.[38] The same is taking place in Southeast Asia, but with the added pluralism of sizable Hindu, Buddhist and Sikh populations. One of the most interesting facets about the post-colonial religious situation is the way Christian theologians are rediscovering the relevance and importance of the Bible to their particular context of oppression:

> It [post-colonialism] seeks to situate colonialism at the center of the Bible and biblical interpretation. The Bible emerged as a literary product of various colonial contexts – Egyptian, Assyrian, Persian, Hellenistic and Roman. Postcolonial criticism tries to look at these narratives and investigate them for colonial assumptions, imperial impulses, power relations, hegemonic intentions, the treatment of subalterns, stigmatization of women and the marginalized, land appropriation, and the violation of minority cultures. In reading these texts, it endeavors to revive and reclaim silenced voices, sidelined issues, and lost causes.[39]

The humanitarian reality of the HIV/AIDS pandemic, accompanied by the upsurge in other preventable diseases, particularly in sub-Saharan Africa and increasingly now also in the poorer parts of Southeast Asia, can only be described as apocalyptic. It is scandalous how few governments and policymakers still do not realize that the HIV/AIDS pandemic is the greatest humanitarian disaster ever to befall the human race. It is this pandemic that increasingly threatens the economic, socio-political, cultural and religious identity and future of both continents.

In an internationally acclaimed speech at the London School of Economics in February 2005, titled "Responding to the HIV/AIDS Epidemic: Prospects for near and distant futures," the Executive Director of UNAIDS, Dr Peter Piot outlined the main reasons why the HIV/AIDS pandemic is an utterly exceptional global crisis and threat which should be treated as such. Because of the critical importance of this subject, we provide here a brief overview of that speech.

HIV/AIDS: prospects for the future

In the first place, unlike every other humanitarian disaster before or since there is at this time still no plateau in sight in regard to the spread of HIV/AIDS. Both the severity and longevity of its impact create special and unforeseen challenges to effective public action.

Thus, in Botswana, Swaziland and other parts of southern Africa the HIV prevalence rate among adults is around 40 percent and still rising. At the same time, the epidemic is globalizing increasingly rapidly, from West Africa to Eastern Europe, from China and India to the Caribbean and Central America.

And in country after country, the tipping point is being reached – that ominous point, which varies between countries, after which AIDS no longer remains concentrated in so-called "hot spots" but becomes a generalized explosion across the entire population. This has already happened in several countries in West Africa, including Nigeria with its population of nearly 140 million. Within the next decade, the Asia-Pacific region, with a population five times that of sub-Saharan Africa, could easily become the next epicenter of the epidemic, with every small increase in HIV prevalence translating into tens of millions of people infected.[40]

Secondly, the impact of HIV/AIDS is uniquely multi-dimensional and far-reaching. In Africa we are witnessing country after country literally "undeveloping" as the whole fabric of society disintegrates, drastically reversing economic growth, making countries politically unstable, devastated by widespread poverty and hugely increased mortality rates. Life expectancy in parts of Africa reduced from 65 in the early 1960s to 37 in 2006.

Thirdly, the slow response to HIV/AIDS on the part of national governments, the churches and various aid agencies is due to the fact that at the center of this pandemic are the sensitive issues of sex, gender inequalities, commercial sex, homosexuality and drug use. If this disease had not been transmitted through sex and drug use then the phenomena of stigmatization, isolation and shaming would not have been so prevalent. Consequently, it is just such negative social responses that contribute to the rapid spread of this pandemic. Sexual practice and morality are still deeply problematic areas of intellectual and social debate in the cultures of today.

Piot called for an equally exceptional response to the worsening HIV/AIDS pandemic – much increased activism across all sections of public life, including government, the media, social welfare programs, the churches, the business community and education, He asked for the doubling of international funding, which in 2004 stood at $6.1 billion – only about half of what was required for 2005–06. Quoting the International Commitment to Development

Index Piot drives this point home: "No wealthy country lives up to its potential to help poor countries. Generosity and leadership remain in short supply."

Finally, Piot called for exceptional implementation and on-the-ground action. "Money raised and political will garnered has to be translated into bringing proven, successful services to the people who need them, whether it be treatment, HIV prevention, or impact alleviation." In addition, particularly women and children need to be protected from sexual exploitation, rape and domestic abuse which in some countries in Africa and Asia are not regarded as genuine crimes punishable by law.

Not quite so simple

These, then, are the post-colonial realities that exist in many continents and countries in the Two-Thirds World, or majority world.

The legacy of colonialism, or the post-colonial era, is often seen as the direct consequence of the inequalities engendered by modernity. Liberation theologians in both Latin America and Africa have been quick to note that the progress and emancipatory rhetoric of modernity did not travel very well. In fact, development, Western aid, and technological and medical assistance always seemed to come with a price. So often all these factors translated into cynical and ruthless business and trade agreements designed to make Western countries and businesses richer and the Two-Thirds World poorer. The practice of widespread corruption in government and business that typifies many countries in Africa and Asia today is, according to some, a legacy of the same practices which characterized the colonial era.

This was, and still is for many cultural analysts, the standard rhetoric previously used to describe the post-colonial era, and we have all deployed it in different ways.[41]

However, blame and shame tactics have worn very thin and after 50 years of trying to understand the post-colonial realities we are beginning to see things differently, not surprisingly aided by the educated sociologists, economists and journalists within the Two-Thirds World who understand their cultural realities far better than we do in the West. International symposiums on the subject are coming up with very different approaches:

Neither colonialism nor dependency has much credibility today. For many, including some Africans, the statute of limitations on colonialism as an explanation for underdevelopment lapsed long ago ... Dependency is rarely mentioned nowadays, not even in American universities where it was, not many years ago, a conventional wisdom that brooked no dissent.[42]

What are the reasons for the rejection of the old imperialistic colonial dependency theories? Simply the fact that there are now too many exceptions to the rule. We have only to look at what has been taking place throughout the world; in the new Europe since the collapse of communism, the economic renaissance within China and the other Asian tigers, Mexico's initiative to join with the US and Canada in NAFTA, and the successes in Uganda and Senegal in the face of what other African governments seem to regard as an inevitable slide into high HIV/AIDS infection rates, to see that cultural attitudes and values play a previously unnoticed role in the ability of different countries to improve the life expectancy and standard of living of its citizens.

To a Western mind, however, the modernity and postmodernity projects are so significant and all-consuming that it is difficult to see either behind them or in front of them and catch a glimpse of other cultural realities coming into view. Yet premodernity, modernity, postmodernity and post-colonialism understood as interrelated and interdependent cultural phenomena all co-exist in our world today. The historical fact remains, however, that the supposed cultural benefits of globalization that the West is presently enjoying did previously arrive off the back of the economic and cultural horizons of most of its former colonies. This means that the global reality is now a more startlingly pluralist smorgasbord of cultural possibilities than we could ever previously have imagined. New voices and stories are emerging continually and new cultural horizons are coming into view.

Metavista – welcome to the post-individualistic world

We return again briefly to an aspect of the secularization thesis. Secular humanism was once thought to be the most obvious and long-lasting achievement of modernity. The victory of the "scientific and technological project" brought with it some very serious political mandates – none as historically wide of the mark as the myth of the so-called social contract, yet apparently politically convincing. Propounded by Thomas Hobbes, Jean-Jacques Rousseau and John Locke, the "social contract" amounted to a political theory constructed around the alienated will of the self-interested and self-motivated individual.[43] If, indeed, all of us are predisposed to act in our own self-interest, and if (as Hobbes suggested and Kant later explained) our natural wills are already hardwired in that direction, then political practice must be based on some form of negotiated contractual arrangements. Politics becomes possible only when we attend both to the inalienable rights of the individual (freedom, equality and the right to happiness) and at the same time maintain a democratic social contract that attempts to create the greatest happiness for the greatest number.

Secular humanism, however, was not based simply on the myth of the social contract in terms of political theory; it was also constructed around an equally spurious philosophy of individual subjectivity. From Descartes to Heidegger the individual ego or subject has stood at the center of the philosophical debate concerning human identity and has finally collapsed under the burden of far too much philosophical freight. Whether it be Descartes's individual self-conscious thinking or doubting ego, Kant's individual subject arrayed with the a priori categories of the mind, Fichte's and Hegel's transcendental philosophy of the self-postulating divine Subject made public in world history, Kierkegaard's anguished existential ego that must take the leap of faith, or Heidegger's individual *Dasein* burdened with temporality, finitude and inauthenticity, the move from philosophy to phenomenology that went via Edmund Husserl and Merleau-Ponty could simply not save the already overburdened human subject.[44]

With the advent of postmodernity this philosophy of subjectivity and the valorization of the individual human ego or subject has died the death of a thousand qualifications. Derrida sought to discredit phenomenology altogether by demonstrating that there is no neutral, internal self-consciousness that is not already mediated to us by the phenomena of language and signs. We never find ourselves in some perfect moment of self-conscious anonymity, because we are always conditioned by temporality and language; consequently our consciousness is always invaded by *alterity*.[45] The ideality of the self-conscious "I am" is already deconstructed by the fact that this "I am" has been named and therefore superseded by what Wittgenstein referred to as the linguistic limits of our world.[46]

With Foucault the subject-object dichotomy out of which idealism was birthed does not exist because the human subject is simply the product of a vast labyrinth of dispersed power systems. Baudrillard, on the other hand, enslaves the human subject to the media-driven discourses of the hyper-real whereby the subject surrenders to the high-tech world of objects that now assume autonomous powers independent of social relationships. We are back with the world of *The Matrix*. Lyotard dispenses with the metaphysics of subjectivity in favor of a Wittgensteinian world of language games and the regime of phrases.[47] Deleuze and Guattari, on the other hand, following Jacques Lacan, dissolve the human subject into a monistic essentialist desiring machine.[48]

Postmodernism's execution of the human subject has as serious consequences for us today as the idolatry of the individual subject in modernity. If the holocaust revealed in all its fury the theory of aggression that characterized modernity's obsession with the self, then the HIV/AIDS pandemic reveals the hopelessly inadequate nihilism of the postmodernist's deconstruction of the individual subject. Forty million individuals infected with a deadly virus that is transmitted through human sexuality reveals the desperate need to locate a theology and philosophy of human subjectivity that will help us rediscover ourselves as another rather than competitive, isolated, alienated, individual subjects.

Again, we turn to Paul Ricoeur for help. Ricoeur represents the tradition in continental philosophy referred to as the French incarnational tradition, which sought to overcome the difficulties of both idealism and empiricism in regard to our understanding of human identity. As Stiver correctly observes:

> Because of the centrality of anthropology in Ricoeur's philosophy, in some ways he represents the modern "turn to the subject." His turning to the subject, however, is at the same time a turning *away* from the subject. Ricoeur's subject is not an autonomous, individualistic soul

but one inseparable from the body, the world, language, and other people.[49]

Following in the footsteps of Gabriel Marcel and Maurice Merleau-Ponty, Ricoeur became an exponent of the embodied self or, as Marcel put it, "the lived body."[50] The human body is not an evolutionary accident that somehow incarcerates the human mind or spirit in a lump of matter. There simply is no disembodied mind. Similarly, the "lived body" is not some kind of material extension to all that really matters, namely the mind, soul or will. Nor is the human body a machine that simply registers stimuli from the external world. In fact, cognitive science would claim exactly the opposite, denying any semblance of the mind-body dualism that has infected the idealist tradition since Descartes:

> The mind is inherently embodied. Thought is mostly unconscious. Abstract concepts are largely metaphorical. These are three major findings of cognitive science. More than two millennia of a priori philosophical speculation about these aspects of reason are over. Because of these discoveries, philosophy can never be the same again.[51]

It would appear that Nietzsche was again on to something! We exist in the world as animated bodies. This, as Michael Polanyi asserted, is the tacit dimension of knowledge. We engage the world, we indwell the world, and our intimate day to day involvement with the world is in and through our embodied existence. The human body – indeed, the integrated bodily structure of consciousness – is never fully available to our self-conscious mind or ego. George Lakoff and Mark Johnson estimate that 95 percent of all thought is unconscious thought transmitted through bodily processes.[52]

We will go further than Ricoeur and claim that bodily existence is political existence. We are part of a vast network of inter-dependent bodies. What we do with our body in both social and sexual relations is like a stone thrown into a pond, the ripple affect (or in the case of HIV/AIDS, the domino effect) of which can be either constructive or catastrophic.[53]

We are also, of course, embedded in language and signifiers which, like our embodied self-identity, also mediate to us a peculiar sense of otherness. We do not create language, language creates us. Indeed, we receive ourselves as a gift of language. We did not choose our name, for instance; we move into self-conscious existence already named, and after a while our name identifies who we are to ourselves and to others. Our name becomes a signifier for the various bodily characteristics and personality traits others recognize, but it also signifies who we are to ourselves, and these are not identical – all of which designates both my individuality and my otherness.

This mysterious otherness is best expressed in terms of our so-called narrative identity, which is always conditioned by temporality. The self that moves through time has a past, a present and a future; in other words, there is both continuity and discontinuity when it comes to self-identity:

> People change. Physically, we are not literally made of the same constituents as we were years before. Moreover, we change in other ways – experiences, character and personality. Yet we continue to speak of the same person.[54]

Ricoeur locates the continuity of identity in our character which "designates the set of lasting dispositions by which a person is recognized."[55] Yet, as he also allows, our characters are often the result of choices we make, the relationships we lose and keep, the traditions that incorporate us into social expectations and loyalties, the cultures that demarcate certain social etiquette and behavior. It is our narrative, our personal story, that allows us to hold continuity and discontinuity together. Narrative mediates to us both freedom and change and constancy and commitment. Add to all of this the ethical self and the critical otherness of conscience; the interpersonal self and the genuine otherness of other people and their moral claims on our lives; and, in theological terms, the summoned self, defined by covenantal community loyalties and relationships and we have a much more nuanced notion of the self as another which breaks apart the limitations of identity in terms of isolated individuality.[56]

And yet both modernity and postmodernity are polluted by empty, shallow notions of individuality or the dispersal of the self as an active agent in social and semiotic systems. In the post-

postmodern world we will need to reimagine self-identity as that which owes debts and allegiances to myself as another. In taking full account of our otherness as a mediated narrative identity we deconstruct the aggressive, competitive, insecure, isolated individual that typifies so much of our consumer society.

Conclusion

This, then, is the metavista world we now inhabit. It is an extended hyperspace that awaits a new legitimization. It is not simply one cultural space among many; it is a global-impact culture. It trades off the various successes, distortions, illusions, ideologies and penetrating narratival perspectives of the past. It is like all hyperspaces and metaframeworks – it is a breeding colony of new ideas and possibilities. For a moment – and it may only be a brief moment – it has stabilized around some fundamental yet conflicting cultural stories. The cultural pluralism of this metavista world – a new age of imagination – awaits further reconfiguration around a reimagined encounter with the narrative world of the Bible. This metavista world awaits the invention of a new missio-ecclesiological narrative of faith, hope and love that will provide the church with some genuinely new socio-political capital.

In our next two sections we will address these and other pressing concerns.

Part Two

5

Cultural Engagement and the Refiguring of the Scriptures

"The 'Triumph of Orthodoxy' regarding Scripture is yet to come, if it will come at all. Lay people, pastors, theologians, even entire traditions are confused about what the Bible is, and what roles it plays in the life of their communities. They scratch their heads more than ever, wondering how they should be reading their Bibles. They find it difficult to name the Bible's character and work in their churches, let alone the Church at large and the wider world. They adapt only painfully to the conclusions of historical-critical biblical scholarship. Growing groups of Orthodox, Catholics, Protestants, and radicals look back to precritical biblical exegesis for ressourcement and hermeneutical training. Yet these same traditions find themselves unable to adopt or even endorse each other's reading practices."

(Telford Work)[1]

In 1997 the British and Foreign Bible Society conducted some research into the Bible reading practices of regular churchgoers of all denominations in the UK. The results were both astonishing and, for many church leaders, deeply disturbing. The research discovered that 18 percent of regular churchgoers (defined as people who went to church at least twice a month) had never read anything in the Bible for themselves in their entire churchgoing life! Quite by accident the research also turned up another startling statistic: a further 14 percent of regular churchgoers had never read anything in the Bible themselves in that particular year. Those two figures added together meant that for 32 percent of regular churchgoers in the UK, at that time, the Bible was largely a closed book.

The startling nature of these initial results clearly warranted some further, more focussed research. Consequently, a more extensive research project was undertaken to investigate how the

Bible was used in pastoral practice by priests and ministers of all denominations. Again the initial results were not very encouraging, showing a pattern of busy and overworked pastors and ministers who, regardless of theological training or persuasion, resorted to an ad hoc, make-it-up-as-you-go-along approach to using the Bible in their various and diverse pastoral vocations.[2]

Clearly there was a problem with the role and use of the Bible in the church, but those of us involved in the ongoing research were not sure exactly what the specific nature of the problem was or how to go about trying to do something to fix it. Thus began an extended partnership with the School of Religion and Theological Studies at the University of Cardiff in Wales which was launched with an international consultation in May 2000, when over 40 ministerial and pastoral practitioners gathered at the University of Cardiff to discuss these and related issues. The following year a part-time researcher was employed who began to research much more thoroughly the various practices, preferences, idiosyncrasies, failures and successes of ministers and pastors, from all denominations, who were willing to be involved in the project.

The following is a brief summary of the research results.

(1) The Bible was regarded largely as a "product" utilized in a variety of pragmatic ways that tended to reinforce rather than challenge existing theological convictions or stances. Historical-critical approaches to the Bible tended to be marginalized in favor of more hermeneutically neutral pastoral resources. The overall impression was that the Bible was used only superficially rather than critically or innovatively in both worship and Christian ministry.

(2) The Bible was still largely viewed as a book to be read and studied as such, rather than as a multimedia resource. Consequently there was only minimal use of web- and online-based material. "It was noted how theological education solely based on printed pages imposes a use of the Bible becoming increasingly obsolete in twenty-first century Britain."

(3) There was a decided lack of diversity in the use of the Bible for ministry, while at the same time a turning toward a

narrative, storytelling approach in pastoral ministry. "When it came to 'actual' Bible use very few went off-piste, but stayed within the fashionable 'runs' of practice. The rise in importance of storytelling, reflecting 'the narrative turn in theology' by conservative, radical and liberal theologians alike, and moving the emphasis of use from the historical and literary to the imaginative and practical, was evident everywhere."

(4)   There was practically no creative reflection or analysis given to the use of the Bible in different ministry and pastoral contexts, both in terms of time available and inclination to do so.

(5)   The "one-man band" approach to Bible teaching or training was to some degree being superseded by team and group approaches to Bible study and use (which, of course, can simply exacerbate the problem).

(6)   The initial results show that things are not all bad by any means, but also highlight some stark limitations in regard to the role of the Bible in pastoral practice. "In the end, it is clear that the Bible still plays a significant part in contemporary pastoral practice: informing the practitioner, identifying the group, enriching pastoral conversations, allowing dramatization and imagination, and providing direct counsel for life today. Yet the paucity of reflective comment starkly revealed a largely activist Christianity in the UK today in danger of losing the capacity to evaluate and improve its pastoral practice."[3]

The six-year project has now produced some innovative and practical resources to help ministers, pastors and laypeople alike to be more creative, imaginative and reflective in their use of the Bible in pastoral ministry.[4]

Clearly, however, this research project did not highlight an isolated problem. The fact is that even in this day of good, accurate Bible translations, multimedia resources, vast improvements in lexicons, Bible commentaries, and various aids for Bible study and meditation, plus an unprecedented number of publications seeking to make the study of the Bible a joyous and educative exercise,[5] the Bible still remains a closed book for the vast majority of people, both inside and outside the church.

So what really *is* the nature of the problem? And what can be done towards finding a solution to this crisis?

What is the problem with the Bible?

A conversation with the proverbial man or woman in the street, a discussion with faith-based or non-faith-based focus groups, or a quick surf of the web, will all produce the usual catalogue of problems the Bible apparently poses to anyone interested in religion or the Christian faith in contemporary culture. Here is a book, made up of 66 different books, in two unequal parts, dealing with quite diverse religious subject matter made up of an equally diverse collection of different genres of literature fashioned together in an apparently ad hoc manner over thousands of years by countless writers, editors and other contributors, most of whom we know virtually nothing about!

Add to this list the manifold differences in historical and cultural contexts between then and now, the lack of intact original manuscripts, numerous historical and theological inconsistencies and contradictions, the strange relationship that exists between historical narrative, fiction and myth, and finally, the often disturbing accounts of apparently God-induced genocide, patriarchy and violence, and it is no wonder that conspiracy theories about the Bible, its unholy origins and its discontents abound![6]

Bible Societies and other Bible-based parachurch organizations often underestimate the considerable public relations exercise they face when talking glibly about a biblical worldview, or the place of the Bible in public life, or, indeed, the Bible's contribution to public morality.[7]

Keeping in mind this considerable list of difficulties it is equally not surprising that a number of significant and dubious theological maneuvers have been devised in recent centuries to get us through this minefield of apparently deadly theological and historical explosive devices.

The most obvious one is the fundamentalist and literalist approach that claims the Bible is the infallible and inerrant word of

God apparently dictated, over time, by the Holy Spirit to a number of human secretaries who wrote down what they were instructed to write; consequently, the Bible is literally the historically and theologically accurate utterly reliable word of God that must be read and believed as such before full salvation can be enjoyed.

There are clearly a number of softer variations on this theme that all belong to the same family tree,[8] but suffice to say that the bibliolatry that flows from this apparent miracle of divine dictation leads to an obscurantism and a pathology of religious neurosis and judgmentalism that is clearly deleterious to the persons who hold such absurd beliefs and the practice of sane religion in general.

The second way to try and ward off these formidable difficulties is the conservative evangelical approach that does not claim literal verbal or propositional inerrancy for each text of the Bible, but asserts that the Bible contains certain absolute truths about God and his relationship with humanity, the creation and Jesus Christ (often understood as a proper name!).[9] The significance of God's relationship with Israel, the church, women, the poor and marginalized, those of other faiths, etc. is less clearly defined in this schema, thus immediately presenting a veritable host of problems with the whole viewpoint. It is rarely pointed out that this approach owes little to what the Bible asserts about itself and much more to the eighteenth-century rationalistic, universalizing tendencies of Enlightenment epistemology.[10] There is a direct line of descent from Gotthold Ephraim Lessing's (1729–81) ugly, broad ditch between the necessary truths of reason and the accidental truths of history to this conservative evangelical assertion about the absolute or necessary truths of salvation enunciated by the Bible.[11]

In both of these attempts to explain the nature and purpose of the Bible, the perils and probabilities of history are traded for a universalizing equivalent that in reality exists only in the field of advanced mathematics, namely so-called a priori truths that can be arrived at simply by a process of logical deduction. To claim that the Bible contains absolute truths vouchsafed by God solves nothing in regard to the problem of identifying exactly what these absolute truths are, what criteria we use to locate them and what language we would use to describe them (given that the limits of our language are the limits of our discernable world, as Wittgenstein commented).

Not surprisingly, to both of these conservative answers to the problem of the Bible's identity and role in the life of the believer and the church there is an equally unconvincing liberal alternative.

The first owes its existence to another trend within the Enlightenment knowledge industry referred to as nineteenth-century developmentalism, which traces its origins to Julius Wellhausen (1844–1918).[12] The developmental thesis claims that what the Bible really informs us about is the development of human religion from its early, primitive forms through ethical monotheism to its later, more ritualistic, priest-dominated or cultic equivalents. For nineteenth-century Protestant New Testament scholars the latter was often synonymous with something called early Catholicism and was usually regarded as a degenerate from of legalistic authoritarian religion![13] Liberalism forsakes any real identity between God and God's words or acts in favor of the history of the development of human religious responses to the divine, often in the process bracketing off any ontological or epistemological assertions about the existence or otherwise of such a divine reality in the first place.[14] A logical extension of the liberal viewpoint is to accept that the Bible is, after all, a broken vessel, a totally historically and culturally conditioned talisman of the religious search,[15] which actually exemplifies just how dangerous, misguided and demonic, as well as potentially liberating and salvific, such a quest can be.[16]

We have briefly traversed what for many is familiar territory and we have done so to contend that all of this is only part – and probably not the most serious part – of the problem. It is, after all, perfectly possible to accept that the Bible is a totally historically and culturally contextualized amorphous collection of diverse religious writings covering a period of thousands of years; that the theological relationship between the two testaments is, for some, difficult to discern and theologically contested; that there are manifest historical errors and inaccuracies and some apparent theological contradictions, as well as a baleful legacy of patriarchy, ideology, idolatry and a fairly tawdry treatment of women, and at the same time to claim that the Bible is also Scripture, in other words, the living word of God for a living church and a gospel of salvation, liberation and forgiveness for individuals, communities and nations. These two apparently contradictory facets of the Bible as Scripture can actually be theologically and practically melded together within some schema of divine inspiration, hermeneutical inevitability, or christological realism which in the end of the day forsakes any attempt to try and justify, exonerate or excuse any other Bible than the one we actually have.[17]

For those who have simply given up on the whole apologetics exercise and got on with good, historically informed and hermeneutically robust exegesis, there is much to commend and much to be thankful for – but that still does not fix the problem of the apparent equivocation over the significance, function, importance and centrality of the Bible to Christian existence in the world today. To get to the heart of this crucial issue we must look in other directions and at another formidable list of problems.

The role of the Bible in the Christendom Project

To put the issue baldly and somewhat simplistically: with the possible exception of the early Reformation period, the fact is that the Bible has never been central to the life and witness of the church during the whole Christendom project, which has obviously covered most of the time the church has been in existence. This was the disturbing reality that our initial research uncovered. Most certainly, from the second century onwards the Bible was utilized creatively, intuitively, authoritatively, prophetically, kerygmatically, ethically, practically and (to a much lesser extent) politically by the church and its leaders over the many centuries of its engagement with diverse and various cultural contexts and temporal realities. However – and here is the nub of the issue – Christendom inevitably marginalized the Bible as the chief source of the church's ecclesial and political identity, because it offered a politically expedient alternative. The marriage of the church with temporal power – be it emperor, king, nation, state or empire – compromised the church's primary relationship to the Scriptures as the fundamental source of its spiritual and ecclesial political existence in the world. Even the system of dual authority between church and empire that was worked out in the early stages of the Christendom settlement was modeled on the notion of imperial rule and remained so throughout the Orthodox, Catholic and Protestant extensions of the Christendom experiment.

Stuart Murray makes this point succinctly and accurately:

> Having accepted political support, and understanding this as divinely providential, theologians naturally adjusted their interpretation of the Bible to reflect and undergird the new context. They used it to legitimize a social order that benefited both church and state, not to challenge the system. The traditional "prophetic minority" critique was supplanted by a "moral majority" stance ... Texts like Romans 13, written to help marginal churches survive in a hostile environment, were now interpreted in ways that reflected Christendom requirements by inculcating loyal and uncritical citizenship.[18]

In other words, the raw apocalyptic energy of biblical messianic eschatology with its obvious critique of earthly kings, kingdoms and thrones in favor of the one compelling vision of a kingdom where God rules, justice and righteousness prevails, and genuine shalom exists, has rarely surfaced in the church's attempt to define its ecclesial and political existence through the story the Bible recounts.[19] In fact, for most of its existence – at least in the modern period – the church has found it convenient to believe that religion and politics are two quite separate spheres to be kept firmly apart, while all the time reading the Bible through this bifurcated lens.[20]

The hegemony of the historical-critical paradigm in the modern period

It is rarely noted that the origins of the historical-critical approach to the biblical manuscripts began with Baruch Spinoza and a thoroughly political critique of the role of the Bible in public life.[21] Spinoza, a victim of the anti-Semitism spawned by the ferocious wars of religion that tore Europe apart in the seventeenth century, viewed the Bible as the source of all such religious zeal and so deliberately sought to limit its dangerous influence on the popular imagination. Accordingly he prescribed that the Bible be approached as a historical and culturally conditioned document like any other book, that the truth of the Bible be seen in its illustration of innate moral truths accessible to human reason, and that the study of the Bible be limited to the scholars and teachers who had mastered the techniques of the new scientific approaches to historical critique.[22]

It is ironic that the consequent rise and eventual hegemony of the historical-critical paradigm from the eighteenth century onwards happened through acquiescent obedience to Spinoza's proposals and led to what James Smart referred to as "the strange silence of the Bible in the Church."[23] In the process the Bible was not only depoliticized, it also increasingly became the arcane territory of a scholarly elite whose esoteric disciplines opened up a rift between the academy and the life and witness of the church – which remains to this day.[24]

At the same time, as Karl Barth noted, there developed a form of scholarly reverence before the inevitable progress of history that often blinded many of the practitioners of this new science, not only to the positivism of their own views of history, but also to the Babylonian-type captivity of eighteenth- and nineteenth-century bourgeoisie liberal culture to its own ideologies.[25]

For the so-called baby boomers of contemporary ministry, now in their fifties, who grew up and learned their homiletic and pastoral craft according to the practices, procedures and ideologies of the historical-critical paradigm, the results were clearly seen in the research project undertaken by the BFBS. There are those still wedded to historical-critical methodologies who assert that the only way to counteract bad historical-critical study of the Scriptures is to advance the cause of good historical science that closes the gap between the academy and the church.[26] Clearly, there is much to commend in such laudable intentions and there are many fine scholars actively engaged in that enterprise. But the answer to this problem is more complex than such a view allows. The corresponding rise of hermeneutics during the very same period as the hegemony of the historical-critical paradigm alerted us to the multidimensional nature of the biblical narrative.[27] As Paul Ricoeur explains, there is in any text three worlds that require simultaneous investigation and are inherently related: the world behind the text, the world within the text and the world in front of the text.[28] Historical-critical research, utilizing all the tools at its disposal, has greatly increased our knowledge and awareness of the historical and cultural worlds behind the text, but it has been much more limited in its ability to illuminate the world within the text and the world in front of the text. To access those two worlds we have had to.rely on sociological, literary, hermeneutical and cultural studies which a purely historicist approach often leaves completely out of account.[29] Even more to the point, what if Ricoeur is also right in his assessment that the world behind the text is not nearly as generally available to us as many of the practitioners of historical science presume?[30] While acknowledging that we owe a debt to the past and cannot, therefore, simply indulge in fictionizing, Ricoeur reminds us that history remains a largely interpretive exercise, and, indeed, the science of scriptural investigation is not primarily a historical project at all; it is a literary narrative discipline that clearly acknowledges the polyphonic hermeneutics of textual identities.[31]

We will return to these important issues shortly. Suffice to say that while not everyone would agree with Walter Wink's prophetic comment that the historical-critical paradigm is now bankrupt, having been hoist with the various petards of its own objectivist, historicist and positivistic presuppositions,[32] there is nowadays a growing acceptance of the fact that the hegemony of the historical-critical paradigm has now come to an end and that during the course of its long ascendancy it virtually closed the Bible for many pastors, ministers, scholars and believers alike.[33]

The problem with knowing how to indwell the biblical narrative

In what is actually a very helpful and well-researched book, John Goldingay describes and assesses the various models of Scripture that have dominated the modern period of theological thought concerning the nature and significance of the Bible for the church. He discerns four primary models: Scripture as witnessing tradition, Scripture as authoritative canon, Scripture as inspired word and Scripture as experienced revelation.[34]

The difficulty that such a comprehensive classification presents, as Goldingay himself admits, is that in each case something else intrudes into the primary relationship between the believer and the story the Bible tells. There is something called tradition, canon, word and revelation to which Scripture must be answerable before we can properly grasp its nature and allow Scripture to properly grasp us.

This problem is compounded by the assertion that such terminology means that the message of the Bible, or the story the Bible tells, can be experienced and understood only indirectly. The Bible is accordingly best understood as the history of, or a witness to, the transmission of religious tradition, or as a function of its canonicity, or as an inspired account of divine speech, or as the experience of God's self-disclosure in history, or through a succession of history-like speech acts.

The question immediately arises: Is the same true for an understanding of the Bible as primarily a unified story or narrative with a beginning, a middle and an end? Are we claiming that the reason the Bible is a closed book for so many people is that the primary category it falls into is not tradition, canon, word or revelation, but narrative, and that unless you know the general rules of narratology you will not be able to understand how the Bible works?

The question above is really two questions, and the answer to the first part of the question is yes, while the answer to the second is no! We are claiming, with others, that the primary way the Bible was understood up until the modern period was as a unified narrative that narrates the identity of its primary agents and tells the story of God's interaction with the cosmos.[35] If we approach the Bible in this way we will eventually learn how to indwell this story and be fundamentally transformed by its perspicacity.

Such a claim requires immediate location and justification within the recent history of narrative theology.

The Bible as narrative – discerning the rules of engagement

Karl Barth

The claim that the Bible is fundamentally a unified narrative or story goes back in the modern period to Karl Barth and his designation of the early stories in Genesis as not fundamentally word or history but "saga,"[36] by which he meant the imaginative theological portrayal of how God indwells the world and conforms the world to his salvific intent. Saga is history-like, but not history as we understand it today. Like Barth we also believe that this is the primary starting point for all theology. We do not start with a historical investigation into the sources or traces of the biblical literature or by comparing it with other historical artifacts, neither do we start with the primacy of something else, be that canon, history, speech acts, revelation or whatever. Rather, we begin with a God who acts, and because God acts a world is created, and because there is a creation God tells the story about what he intends to do with that creation, and because there is a story we find ourselves part of it, and because we are part of it we can live in it or indwell it and, thankfully, also understand it.

Now if you say to me that I have just given you a list of so-called primary or foundational presuppositions and you would like to know how I justify them, I will have to say, as I do to all similar apologetic maneuvers, I am sorry I cannot. But I will also say, as did Barth, that you do have to start somewhere, and I have decided to start with the primacy of the story that preceded me, or to use Ricoeur's terminology, that prefigured me, because actually that is how reality works. We are already inscribed in language, textuality and storied-ness when we enter the world.[37] Just as the baby intuitively knows how to turn and find the mother's breast, so human beings intuitively, prethematically or instinctively, know how to be a story, intrude into the story of others, learn a story, recount a story and live a story; and if that is the case, it is because God tells his story before us. And that, I think, is what the Bible is fundamentally all about.

Again, you may say to me, "Well, that last bit of your argument does look like a justification, because storied-ness and textuality are what you say the world is made of."

My reply to that would be simple: "That is fine if that is how you want to view things, but I am not claiming that this is a foundational argument that proves this is the way things really are in the world. I am simply saying that this insight is part of a fiduciary framework that provides us with a comprehensive vision of the true, the good and the beautiful and so also gives us a tacit dimension to how we might be able to indwell this world in which we are presently situated."

Erich Auerbach

The next chapter in the story of narrative theology arrives via Erich Auerbach and his celebrated book *Mimesis*.[38] In his comparison of the biblical literature with that of the Homeric tales he stumbles upon something he believes is totally distinctive – in fact, unique – in the story the Bible tells. The biblical story, he asserts, makes an imperialistic claim upon us: this Story brooks no dissent and disallows any competitors. This Story simply takes over all other stories and incorporates their limited schemas into its own vision of universal history.[39] It is an omnivorous story that simply eats up all others. The stories of the Egyptians, the Philistines, the Assyrians, the Babylonians, the Persians, the Greeks and the Romans all appear in the story the Bible recounts, but are reinscribed within the primary intentions of God's Story and are accordingly stripped of their pretensions to be totalizing stories of their own.[40]

This point is made well by George Lindbeck in what is now regarded as a classic statement of post-liberal theology, *The Nature of Doctrine*:

> A scriptural world is thus able to absorb the universe. It supplies the interpretative framework within which believers seek to live their lives and understand reality. This happens quite apart from formal theories. Augustine did not describe his world in the categories we are employing, but the whole of his theological production can be understood as a progressive, even if not always successful, struggle to insert everything from Platonism and the Pelagian problem to the fall of Rome into the world of the Bible.[41]

Hans Frei

Hans Frei utilized these basic insights from both Barth and Auerbach to write one of the most important theological treatises of the modern era, *The Eclipse of the Biblical Narrative*, and at the same time found the Yale School of narrative theology.[42] Frei took over the insight that the Bible recounts not simply a story about reality, but *the* story about reality. Scripture is a complete linguistic world of its own, an all-consuming text: "Consequently, all other stories must be inscribed into the biblical story, rather than the biblical story into any of them. Insofar as we allow the biblical story to become our story, it overcomes our reality."[43]

Frei asserted that this is how the Bible was both read and understood from Augustine up until the seventeenth century, and this is also how Barth defied the hegemony of the historical-critical paradigm.

Already, if we accept these insights, it is clear why the Bible remains a closed book for so many contemporary Christians. In previous chapters we have been describing vast and complex cultural realities: modernity, postmodernity and now metavista, the post-postmodern world in terms of narrative theory. All such cultural stories easily become imperialistic, not necessarily because of their inherent credibility and persuasiveness, but simply because we become so personally invested in them – indeed, at times commoditized by them. This makes them all-consuming narratives demanding our prior allegiance and so displacing the biblical story from its primary place as literally the story that rules the world. The authority of the Bible, to use that often maligned designation, is simply that it recounts the story of God's dealings with the cosmos, and what other authority could the Bible possess than this? If this is the case, then this story could not help but absorb all other stories within its terms of reference – correcting them, confounding them, judging them and, like the story of Babel, at times dispersing and disempowering them.[44]

Modernity sought to tell a bigger and better story of progress, emancipation and enlightenment than Scripture itself. But it could do so only by first minimizing the significance of sin and evil, then depoliticizing and marginalizing the story the Bible recounts. Once that was achieved, the next step was also to divest Scripture of its unity and story shape, reducing it to a series of isolated micro-narratives and pericopes with no thematic tension and no eschatological resolution.

Postmodernity has sought to reconfigure that failed modernity story around the particularity of texts and so stay with a series of contested micro-narratives.

Post-postmodernity, we are claiming, is seeking to re-engage with the textual world of the Bible and reimagine the community that reads such texts – and so it is to this task that we must now turn.

Configuring the story the Bible recounts

To begin with, we take note of the fact that the fourfold system of medieval exegesis operated in terms of four interrelated aspects of the textual world of the Bible:

(1) the literal meaning, which did not mean the historical meaning, but rather the plain sense of the text
(2) the allegorical meaning
(3) the tropological meaning
(4) the anagogical (or eschatological) meaning.

The following rhyme explains what each means respectively:

The letter shows us what God and our fathers did
The allegory shows us where our faith is hid
The moral meaning gives us rules of daily life
The anagogy shows us where we end our strife.[45]

The second form of meaning, the allegorical, also became associated with typology, because many of the Church Fathers saw in the first testament allegories or types that prefigured their consequent fulfillment in the second testament.[46]

Now it is very interesting that while the typological and the allegorical meaning was what the Reformers most distrusted, Frei realized that it is precisely this convention, which he terms *figuration*, that allows the Bible to be perceived as a unified narrative.

Put simply, figural or typological reading means reading the history of the "other" into the text; or, as Loughlin puts it:

Figuration was at once a literary and a historical procedure, an interpretation of stories and their meanings by weaving them together into a common narrative referring to a single history and its pattern of meaning.[47]

Dispensing with Auerbach's notion of an imperialistic and voracious story (which, of course, is highly vulnerable to the postmodern incredulity toward metanarratives), Frei notes that it is precisely by way of typology, or figuration, that many of the biblical writers linked the two testaments into one unified story, especially in the Pauline corpus (Jesus as the new Adam, the heir of Abraham and the Wisdom of God), Hebrews (Melkizedek and Jesus the High Priest), the synoptics (Jesus as the Son of Man and Suffering Servant of God) and the gospel of John (Jesus as the Logos or Creative Word).

What actually takes place is that the old is configured into the pattern of the new. So Scripture, viewed from the perspective of the whole human race is indeed a unified story with a beginning (Adam and Eve, created in the image of God, and so representing all of humanity), a middle (Jesus the Christ, the redeemer of humanity), and an end (the new resurrected humanity); or to put it differently, a creation, a recreation and a new creation.

It is also the case that from Ireneaus through Athanasius to Augustine the middle of the story was determinative of the meaning of the whole. For the former the whole story went through a recapitulation that changed its dramatic content and intention through the incarnation of the Logos. For the latter the coming of the Christ serves to reveal and embody the central meaning of the whole story as the history of the divine *caritas* (grace), in other words, the love of God and neighbor in and for the sake of the history of divine grace. From the second century up until the modern period this is typically how the church read the story that Scripture recounts:

> This underlying unity in the message of the Bible, definitely revealed to the Christian in the gospel, was generally understood by patristic and medieval interpreters to produce, not a flat uniformity of doctrine, but a new richness and variety, a kind of unquenchable fountain whose scattered drops all reflect the one Mystery of Christ.[48]

This way of reading Scripture reveals how Scripture can be one, unified story told through a multitude of narratives, even though the overall story and the narratives that recount this story are not the same. There is a difference in time and place between both and the narratives can repeat or reposition aspects of the story, or leave them out of the telling altogether (witness, for instance, the differences between the books of Chronicles and Kings, and, indeed, between the four gospels). With the Christ event, however, the story receives its unity, because this crucial chapter in the story illuminates the meaning of the whole. Scripture tells the story of God's engagement with the cosmos first through creation, then through Israel, then through the sending of the Messiah, and then, finally, through the Spirit-filled church. In that sense, therefore, the creation and the history of Israel prefigure the coming of the Messiah, but with the Christ event the story so far is configured in terms of a unified whole, and with the birth of the church the whole story is reconfigured around the faith community, whose story it is to tell and recount. But more of that later – sufficient to say at this stage that the latter reconfiguration also explains why the early church looked to the rule of faith, the creeds and tradition as the interpretive matrix through which it could tell the one central story. All exercised what George Lindbeck has called a Christological maximalism, in other words, all held to the central significance of the Jesus story, especially his death and resurrection, as the narrative center around which the whole drama of Scripture, as well as the revelation of its central agent, revolved.

This also means, of course, that Christians and Jews read a different story. The former claim that the apocalypse (i.e. the uncovering of the meaning) of the whole story occurs with the advent of the Christ; the latter claim that the two testaments relate two different stories of two different faith traditions. The Christian claim that Jesus the Messiah expresses the hidden meaning of the whole story does not, however, imply supersessionism. As Paul makes clear in Romans 9–11, both the Jewish and the Christian stories have yet to be ecclesiologically united and eschatologically fulfilled.

Auerbach was also the main contributor to Frei's next major observation. Frei referred to the biblical texts as realistic narratives. By this he meant that within the biblical texts the identity of an agent was revealed through the combination of contingency, character, intention and circumstance. Again, the situation is described well by Lindbeck, an observation which he also refers to as *intratextual narrative theology*:

> This type of literary approach can be extended to cover, not simply the story of Jesus, but all of scripture. What is the literary genre of the Bible as a whole in its canonical unity? What holds

together the diverse materials it contains: poetic, prophetic, legal, liturgical, sapiential, mythical, legendary and historical? These are all embraced, it would seem, in an overarching story that has the specific literary features of realistic narratives as exemplified in diverse ways, for example, by certain kinds of parables, novels and historical accounts. It is as if the Bible were a "vast, loosely structured, non-fictional novel" (to use a phrase David Kelsey applies to Karl Barth's view of scripture).[49]

This is one of the most important aspects of the biblical story and it is worth going back to what Auerbach saw as the basis of this observation. Again, he contrasted the biblical narratives with those of the Homeric tales and concludes that what makes the biblical stories unique is that they are always "fraught with background." The heroes of the Homeric adventures remain fundamentally the same. They may age, change direction, lose their companions, but the essence of who they are is never put at risk, nor could that essence ever be tragically annulled. "Odysseus in his return is exactly the same as he was when he left Ithaca two decades earlier." Not so Abraham, Isaac or Jacob, for example. However,

> Abraham's actions are explained not only by what is happening to him at the moment, nor yet only by his character (as Achilles' actions by his courage and his pride, and Odysseus' by his versatility and foresightedness), but by his previous history; he remembers, he is constantly conscious of, what God has promised him and what God has already accomplished for him – his soul is torn between desperate rebellion and hopeful expectation; his silent obedience is multilayered, has background. Such a problematic psychological situation as this is impossible for any of the Homeric heroes, whose destiny is clearly defined and who wake every morning as if it were the first day of their lives: their emotions, though strong, are simple and find expression instantly.[50]

What makes the biblical story so compelling and forthright, and, indeed, unique, is that each character can come to grief because circumstances, intentions and background can all collide. It is not just their actions, intentions or character that decides their fate, but the contingency and constancy of the still unraveling story. If God were not faithful to the covenant, if he did not stand by the contingency of his previous promises and actions, then Abraham and Sarah (and, indeed, Hagar), Isaac and Rebekah, Jacob and Rachel, Moses, Joshua and David would have no future.[51] It is not that they would be written out of the story or superseded by a collection of new heroes and heroines, it is that their identities would become too distilled and fragile either to bear the continuing narrative or to hold the tension of the plot. The *emplotment* that the central characters in the biblical story experience is fraught with background or thick with the implications of the previous story. As such they are defined by the intratextual nature of the biblical story.

This is why Frei concluded that Jesus *is* his story, because he is part of a drama that preceded him and his own part in the drama is one of exceeding risk. This is why Satan has the foresight and the wit to tempt Jesus from his prescribed vocation by endeavoring to test and so possibly to undermine his sense of self-identity. Many are the exegetes who have failed to notice the subtlety of the querulous assertion addressed to Jesus by the devil in, Luke 4:3: "*If* you are the Son of God then makes these stones bread." To damage irretrievably Jesus' sense of who he is, is also to succeed in effectively getting him to betray the reason for which he came.[52]

Biblical characters are not stereotypical or literary types such as tragic heroes; they are active agents and therefore unique irreplaceable persons who, like all people, exhibit an "intention-action" pattern. What they do is what they are, embroiled as they also are in the plot that is unfolding behind, within and in front of them. "Thus the identity of Jesus is given by his intention to enact the good of men on their behalf in obedience to God."[53]

Again, as Auerbach suggested (and Frei concurred), both history and fiction demonstrate this realistic tension between character, intention, circumstance and plot. That is why the gospels, according to Auerbach, are most like nineteenth-century novels rather than like any parallel in ancient literature.

This latter point is also taken up by Ricoeur, for whom there is no fundamental narrative difference between history and fiction, for each text creates a world of its own, opening up before us a world in which we can live, revealing to us a host of imaginative possibilities that can reconfigure our own lived horizons.[54]

Reconfiguring the story

We come now to the central issue of how we, the contemporary disciples of Jesus, or the contemporary readers of the biblical text, actually learn how to indwell the story and so find ourselves within the world that the text opens up before us.

This is not a question that is totally inimical to those who are engaged in the historical-critical investigation of the different worlds of the text. So, for instance, N.T. Wright has made much of the assertion that the biblical story is a five-act drama: the first act is Creation, the second the Fall, the third Israel, the fourth Jesus the Messiah, and the fifth the church[55] – we, the contemporary participants in this drama, find ourselves in the fifth act, supposedly ready, willing and able to improvise and play our part in the ongoing story.[56] There will, of course, also be a sixth and final act to the drama – the eschaton, which will also completely reconfigure the whole drama.[57] Similarly, within this schema the church plays a crucial role in the resolution of the drama as it lives out its corporate vocation to be the second Israel witnessing to the risen Christ and thus living within the tension of the already and the not yet.

The problem, however, with this depiction of the overall plot, drama or story is that it remains fundamentally a historical project and not a literary narrative description of a multidimensional story. This may seem a surprising claim to make because Wright speaks frequently of "narratival worldviews" that are composed of underlying stories, symbols and subversive praxis.[58] But the difficulty with all such historical projects is that while the historian or the reader may imaginatively enter into these narratival worldviews, and investigate and describe them, they remain projects of the past and the story and its various sub-plots cannot be performed, lived or enacted again. Rather, the church lives in the traces, the still reverberating resonances, the dramatic configurations, of the story of Creation, the Fall, Israel and Jesus, but we can no longer personally or collectively indwell those worlds, because they are assigned to the vicissitudes of past history. This is the fundamental difference between history and narrative. Narrative allows the contemporary reader to indwell the whole story, because each episode of the story is recapitulated, expropriated and reconfigured in the event of the reading and in the collision of the narrative with the context of the reader.

This is similar to what Hans Gadamer intended by his description of hermeneutics as the fusion of horizons.[59] When two worlds fuse they create a new interpretive and imaginative possibility; when two texts collide, each forfeits some of its meaning, truth and significance to create a new world, a new lived possibility. The energy and substance of the previous textual world is passed on to the world of the reader or recipient. Consequently, the world of the text is loosed from the confines and restrictions of history as it engages our text, our world, our culture, our identity, and a new story is formed.

What is utterly distinctive about narratives is that they are always *someone's* story. They may have universal resonances or significance, but they are not the story of everyman or everywoman. Narratives are fundamentally particular stories about a person, a nation, a culture, an empire, and the biblical story is the particular story of the God who dwells with his people, Immanuel, God with us. This story develops and reaches out to others not by way of universal significance but by way of covenant and election. This is *God's particular* story, not *our universal* story. It is often hard for contemporary Christians to realize or appreciate this in this day of crass and rampant individualism, but we are not necessary to the plot – God began this story without us and he could end this story without us as well. We are invited into the story not because the drama depends on us but because God chose to celebrate the story of his triune life with us and amongst us.

This means that however and wherever the church re-enacts this story or the reader learns how to indwell this story, a fundamental reconfiguration takes place that creates a new world, a new history, a new possibility of fresh adventures, a new imagined opportunity, most certainly not just one damn thing after the other, and most certainly not just the duties and responsibilities that history allows us to discharge. Stories create history and undo history, they reconfigure and rupture history, and, consequently, they are not merely the product or the refuse of history.[60] Stories are primary, while history follows the plot, sequencing the story into time; consequently, both the historian and the reader have to locate the story in order to indwell it and then imaginatively retell it.

Amos Wilder makes this point forcibly:

> If we ask a prestigious body of modern critics about the relation of story-world to real world, they will reply that it is a false question. For one thing the story goes its own way and takes us with it; the storyteller is inventing, not copying. He weaves his own web of happening and the meaning of every part and detail is determined by the whole sequence. We lose our place in the story if we stop to ask what this feature means or refers to outside it. More importantly, these students of language will ask us what we mean by "real world." There is no "world" for us until we have named and languaged and storied whatever is. What we take to be the nature of things has been shaped by calling it so. This therefore is also a storied-world. Here again we cannot move behind the story to what may be more "real." Our language-worlds are the only worlds we know![61]

As we have indicated already, historians owe a debt to the past; they are not given a license to fictionalize, but once the plot is exposed and grasped they are implicated in it and their own imaginative *emplotment* entails that the original story is now reconfigured. The story most certainly arrives fraught with background, but it collides with the vagaries and vicissitudes of the foreground and in the process a new world is formed.

The consumption of history by other historians, the entering into the world of the novel by the reader, and the indwelling of the biblical narrative by the believer all go via the same route: the world of the text, the structure of narratives and the density of the various plots, and it is these realities that we must further investigate in our next chapter.

6

Constructing a Biblical Theology for Cultural Engagement

"Each day, it seems, thousands of Americans are going about their daily rounds – dropping off the kids at school, driving to the office, flying to a business meeting, shopping at the mall, trying to stay on their diets – and coming to the realization that something is missing. They are deciding that their work, their possessions, their diversions, their sheer busyness are not enough. They want a sense of purpose, a narrative arc to their lives, something that will relieve a chronic loneliness or lift them above the exhausting, relentless toll of daily life."

(Barach Obama)[1]

The extraordinary movie accomplishment *Angels in America* (2000) not only swept the board with 11 Emmys, but also managed creatively and ingeniously to tell four stories at the same time, linking them together by a dramatic plot situated in the homosexual community of the 1980s; a group of individuals endeavoring to grapple with the life-threatening phenomenon of HIV/AIDS. Based on the Pulitzer Prize-winning play of the same name by Tony Kushner, this remarkable piece of narrative storytelling grips our attention and elicits our admiration by the remarkable depth of the various subplots that meld together to produce a multilayered narrative that leaves the viewer wondering at the end of the movie what exactly was it really all about![2] As one observant critic put it:

> This [production] isn't about gays, it isn't about AIDS, it isn't about Jews and it isn't about Mormons. Its theme is the necessity for people to change, the scariness of change, while most of us would prefer to just let things stay as they are.[3]

Set in the Reagan years and portraying some real-life characters while at the same time conjuring up ancestors from the past and looking toward some divine vindication in the future, the movie exhibits a number of distinctive features that illustrate some of the basic characteristics of what, as we saw in chapter 3, Ricoeur refers to as *emplotment* – the way narratives impact us, invite or entice us into their frame of reference and how a new world is formed out of this experience.

The construal of the text

First and foremost narratives that confront us in textual form open up a multidimensional world where we, the viewers, readers or participants are invited to become involved in the task of meaning-making. Even at the level of discerning the author's intentions in writing a particular novel, movie or drama, in the sequencing of the plot and the grasping of the significance of the various episodes in the drama there is a necessary construal of meaning that only the viewer or reader can make.[4] We might do so, to begin with, merely out of curiosity or interest, but interest invites us to decide how, why and whether we will imaginatively participate in the unfolding drama.[5] Each drama, movie, play, poem, novel, or narrative meets us as another world of meaning and beckons, entices or seduces us to participate in that world and so to render that world differently, indeed to reconfigure the plot according to our own imaginative reality. In all of this the role of the constructive imagination, embedded as it is in various cultural, philosophical and theological narratives, is crucial.[6]

George Steiner grasps and expresses this reality with poise and erudition:

> All serious art, music and literature is a *critical* act. It is so, firstly, in the sense of Matthew Arnold's phrase: "a criticism of life." Be it realistic, fantastic, Utopian or satiric, the construct of the artist is a counter-statement to the world. Aesthetic means embody concentrated selective interactions between the constraints of the observed and the boundless possibilities of the imagined. Such formed intensity of sight and of speculative ordering is, always, a critique. It says that things might be (have been, shall be) otherwise.[7]

In his seminal work *The Uses of Scripture in Recent Theology,* David Kelsey makes this very point. He seeks to describe and configure what actually happens when theologians construct a metaphor that defines the relationship between God and the Bible and the Bible and the church. Kevin Vanhoozer, reflecting on Kelsey's work, notes that theologians often line up their doctrine of God with that of Scripture because they construe these relationships in similar terms or metaphors.[8] What actually takes place is an "imaginative construction" ("construal") of this relationship that necessarily determines how we think God is present in, and works through, the Bible and the church.[9] Kelsey provides three examples which Vanhoozer nicely summarizes:

> God's presence in and through Scripture may be construed in an ideational mode (as in B.B. Warfield, where God's presence is like the presence of truth), in the mode of concrete actuality (as in Karl Barth, where God's presence is like the presence of another person) or in the mode of ideal possibility (as in Rudolf Bultmann, where God's presence is like the presence of an existential possibility).[10]

In other words, with Warfield, God is present to us in and through the Bible as objective truth, and it is the task of the church to codify and explain that truth in doctrinal content. With Barth, however, God is present in the Bible as an active personal agent whose identity is revealed in the narrative of Scripture and reconfigured in word and sacrament,[11] while for Bultmann, God is present as the promise of authentic existence which must be grasped and appropriated (and therefore also reconfigured) by the individual and the church.[12]

In his own theology Vanhoozer construes this fundamental relationship between God and Scripture in terms of communicative action. God is the primary communicative agent who in and through Scripture creates the covenant of discourse and the discourse of the covenant.[13] In other words, God gets things done through the convention of speech acts that draw us into the relationality of language, aimed as it is at creating covenantal communities. At this juncture in his argument Vanhoozer draws heavily on the speech act theory of J.L. Austin and J. Searle, later considerably refined by W. Alston and N. Wolterstorff.[14] Accordingly, it is at this stage in his construal of the relationship between God and the text of Scripture that we lose the overall category or metaphor of narrative that we have been endeavoring to retain. Ultimately, for Vanhoozer, narrative is replaced with a philosophical theory of language.[15]

To construe the text in terms of the relationship of the author to the narrative work, the relationship of the characters to one another, the relationship of the various episodes of the drama to one another, and the intentionality of meaning, is exactly the way readers or viewers enter into the world of the text after that world has collided with their own and solicited their participation in the reconfigured new world that emerges from that fusion or collision.[16]

We can illustrate this reality with reference to the creation narratives. When God situated Adam in the Garden of Eden he also solicited his help and co-operation in tending the flora and fauna in the garden. In other words, God provided the raw material, which Adam crafted and worked into something else. Similarly, God brings the animals to Adam to be named and abides by that act of designation (Gen. 2:8–20). In all of this we see that the addition of a human being to this environment who resembles and represents his Creator (Gen. 1:26–27) immediately alters the script. The narrative changes because another active agent is now involved in the process of writing and editing.

We may legitimately ask: Were Adam and Eve part of God's original authorial intention? We assume that this is the case, because they are created in God's image and invited to participate in the ensuing drama. Consequently, we construe the relationship in that manner and then immediately realize that these particular agents have now become co-writers of the creation script!

In construing the relationship between God and Scripture in this way we are not replacing the dynamics of narrative configuration with reader response theory.[17] This is not simply a question of how the reader responds to what he or she reads or hears. Rather it is the question of how the reader, participant, viewer or hearer inevitably becomes implicated in the script, and it is really ideological power play to claim that this is not similarly true of how the historian reconfigures the meaning of the original stories or how the exegete locates the meaning of the text in something called authorial intention. Historians and exegetes carry no immunity from the reality of emplotment.

The world we inhabit is a labyrinth of unfinished narratives, stories and plots. As we intentionally or accidentally bump into them and enter these often strange, perplexing and disquieting worlds, so we become implicated in their intertwining, overlapping, sometimes imploding and at other times rapidly expanding plots and subplots. As George Steiner contends, we may have to make a wager on transcendence, that there is in fact a hidden code, teleology, or design to these narratives that it is our task to decipher. But to do so necessitates that we construe the text, the story or the plot in a particular fashion. To refuse to do so as individuals and communities is to refuse to indwell the text and to become hearers only of the word and not doers (Jas. 1:24–25). In other words, what has taken place is a failure of constructive imagination.

The structure of the narratives

We have already hinted at a particular construal of the emploted narratives that will become the convention we will adopt. A five-act play is, after all, a literary convention and Wright admits that in construing the narrative in this fashion he is giving more space and significance to the story of the Fall than many biblical writers themselves do.[18]

On the other hand, Gerard Loughlin, in his construal of the narrative, opts for only three overlapping stories:

> It is the story of God and the Hebrews, of God and the Christ of God, of God and the Church. In the Bible, the story of Jesus of Nazareth recapitulates or retells the story of Israel's encounter with and formation by the "I am" to Moses, the "It is the Lord who speaks" to the prophets. The story of Jesus – the narrative of his journey from the wilderness to the house of his "Father" – recapitulates, retells, the journey of God's chosen children from slavery to new life: the coming forth of God's servant Israel. The story of Christ is the retelling of God bringing forth God's people, from death to new life through parted waters ... [T]he story of the Church is the third story, and it may only just have begun.[19]

Each mimesis is, of course, not just a remembering but a retelling, and each retelling is not just a repetition but a recapitulation, and each recapitulation is, of course, a re-creation of the original story. It consequently becomes an expanded and reconfigured story as the previous story is taken up, broken open and reapplied in the retelling that ensues from the first, the second and the third. But why just three stories? For Loughlin it is because it is the story of the triune God whose very being constitutes both the truth and the meaning of each story and the whole narrative:

> There are three stories, and together they constitute the threefold story of God. They are the stories of God with God's people, the stories of Father, Son and Spirit. They are the stories of the economic or revealed Trinity. They are the reason for any talk of Trinity at all. It is the experience of God with God's people, as Father, Son and Spirit, that impels the trinitarian naming, and that naming is the only and sufficient reason for the threefold telling of God.[20]

Here, once again, the construal of the relationship of God to the Bible and the Bible to the church is developed by way of the same metaphor – the triune narration of the one God.

However, we are going to pose the question of truth and meaning as an intratextual issue. In other words, we are going to contend that the truth and meaning of the overall narrative does not depend on its conformity to a particular historical state of affairs (Wright) or to a particular doctrinal formulation (Loughlin), but to the reformulation (*perichorsis* or mutual indwelling) of each story in the other and the recapitulation of the same plot density in each. In that sense we opt for *four* stories: Creation, Israel, Jesus the Christ and the Church – all of which, it is imperative to realize, are *unfinished* stories that are accordingly, by direct design, retold and redrafted through the others and consequently invite our participation at every stage of the journey.

Four stories – four subplots

The quote from Barach Obama at the beginning of this chapter reiterates a familiar theme in American culture. So much is on offer in today's consumerist societies that life easily fragments into isolated and competing agendas.[21] We rush from one episode to another, one environment to another, one relationship to another, one story to another; not surprisingly, therefore, we easily lose any sense of a united and purposeful plot to all that we seek to do and become. Indeed, one of the most problematic aspects of living in a society that has been as insidiously consumerized as modern America is that civil society implodes into a Disney-like hyperreality where many of its citizens are unwittingly the victims of a Matrix-like form of social control.

Obama's phrase *narrative arc* is an interesting one: it is reminiscent of Ricoeur's hermeneutical arc whereby we move from a naïve understanding of the text, a first naïveté, to a critical naïveté or a second naïveté.[22] Dan Stiver superimposes Ricoeur's narrative theory upon this hermeneutical arc, so that we can include the move from prefiguration to configuration to reconfiguration in terms of our construal and appropriation of the text.[23] What is fundamental about a narrative arc, however, is that the end takes us back to the beginning, and so we must start the work of narrative interpretation all over again. Similarly, we are never finished with either the stories or the subplots, because they all intersect. It is equivalent to playing an instrument during the performance of an unfinished symphony comprising four distinct movements that are nevertheless held together by four inspirational and haunting overtures which are not only played simultaneously but are continually reiterated within the grand scheme of the whole symphony. It is time, therefore, to read the musical score and find our own place within it.

The creation story

A recurring failure of many exegetical and theological accounts of the creation story is that they presume to take account only of the two distinct creation stories located in Genesis 1 – 3. In reality, however, the creation narrative consists of the first eleven chapters of Genesis, and if we read it in this way we cannot fall foul of the inevitable Protestant temptation to ascribe far too much significance to what happens in Genesis 3. In fact, Claus Westermann claims that when we read the story of creation in this fashion then we see that the theological point of the early Genesis stories from the expulsion from Eden to the Tower of Babel is "to show that man created by God is defective man."[24] Similarly, exegetes have argued that based on such a reading one will not find the idea of a fall from a state of perfection in Genesis, nor will one find there the Augustinian notion of inherited sin or guilt. Rather, both these interpretations of the Fall episode so beloved by Reformed theologians stems from an over-literal interpretation of what is neither cosmology nor biology but a story.[25]

The first 11 chapters of Genesis, which tell the story of the prehistory of the cosmos and humankind, take us through four interlocking themes. We construe these themes in the following fashion and will shortly explain why: Creation and Covenant, Election and Exile, Imaging and Idolatry, and Nations and Empire. Now let us endeavor to tell the story by utilizing each of these four configurations or subplots as they occur naturally in the drama.

Creation is God's first saving and redemptive act (Gen. 1 and 2). God makes room within his own triune life for a sheer gratuitous act of love that brings into being a splendidly diverse, complex, ordered, interdependent cosmos that forms the context for the sustainability, evolution, preservation and fecundity of a colorful carnival of life. Psalms 8, 19, 33 and 145 speak of a creation that shares in the celebration of God's glory and power.

Within this largely ecological context of creation God conducts an experiment. He introduces into this complex ecology of life other actors with whom he will share everything he has made – gendered human beings, esteemed and appointed as partners, created in his *image* and likeness, consequently *elected* to represent and resemble their creator in being equally creative, fruitful and relational (Gen. 1:26–27).

This vocation of *imaging* goes horribly astray when the partners, not satisfied with being merely created in the image and likeness of God, want, instead, to be the same as God. To be the same as God is to know how to separate good and evil, something human beings cannot successfully accomplish, so the first act of *idolatry* precipitates a terrible rift in every set of relationships the humans are designed to enjoy – with their creator, with the creation and with themselves – which, inevitably, results in an *exile* in terms of place (paradise) and vocation (the joyful and fulfilling preservation of creation, Genesis 3).

The inability successfully to separate good and evil introduces into the creation not first and foremost the problem of evil, but the problem of violence, as we see when Cain's jealousy swiftly results in fratricide (Gen. 4). From here on God has a problem on his hands, which is essentially how to curb humanity's propensity for gratuitous violence. Alongside a creation blessing to be fruitful and multiply, God now has to introduce a providential *covenant* of sorts with Cain to try and contain the pernicious slide into violence. Furthermore, up until God's *covenant* with Noah after the flood, God continually worries about the humanity experiment, and, indeed, almost terminates the partnership.

The Adam and Eve, Cain and Abel and Noah stories illustrate that human beings are not essential to the plot but are, rather, invited into the plot by *election*, whereby they represent their creator in preserving the creation, creating communities and curbing violence (Gen. 5 – 9:17). Unlike the Babylonian creation myth (the *enuma elish*), violence is not inscribed within the created order in the Genesis account but is the result of a fall from our common vocation to *image* our creator and so to be the means of blessing to and preservation of the whole created order.

The creation narrative continues in Genesis 10 with another way to curb humankind's leaning toward systemic violence, namely the establishment of *nations*. Though all descendants of the sons of Noah, they nevertheless reconfigure God's plan for diversity in terms of race and ethnicity. The strange story of Noah's drunkenness and his uncovered nakedness hints at unresolved difficulties and disputes between the *nations* that, indeed, soon become a recurring aspect of the overall story (Gen. 9:20–28).

Finally, in Genesis 11, the reality of a common culture, language and land introduces the menacing specter of *empire* with the *idolatrous* story of the Tower of Babel. This threat God quickly dispels with his basic *creation* tactic, which is more diversity, but this time in terms of language and location, which in turn forms the basis for more national diversity.

We have dispersed the various themes throughout the narrative as befits a narrative that has a kind of *diaspora* or *exile* at its core, but clearly, even at this stage, there is a pattern of coupling going on.

As Karl Barth suggests, we can see already that the *creation* forms the external basis of the *covenant* and the *covenant* the internal basis of *creation*.[26] Similarly, the representative, rather than the ontological, status of the first human beings means that in and through them God *elects* the whole human race as his partners in *creation*. What is fascinating about that *election*, however, is that since the confusion of good and evil, when *imaging* turned into *idolatry*, it is best advanced and expressed in situations of *exile* that form a partial solution to the problem of spiraling violence. Furthermore, that problem is again contained when *empire* is refused and *nations* welcomed into the still unfolding drama of *creation*.

Now let's turn to the second story to see how things develop there, and how the same four pairs of interlocking themes can be identified.

The Israel story

It is a recurring deficiency of many Protestant evangelical readings of the biblical narrative that it can be told without the inclusion of Israel at all! An over-individualistic concentration on the Fall as a second story instead of an episode within the first story results in a stunted engagement with the biblical text which almost inevitably leads to an interpretation that individual salvation was the whole purpose of God's creative act.[27] Consequently, we quickly jump from the Fall episode to the coming of the Messiah whose death and resurrection fixes the personal sin question – and hey presto! we're back on track! The anti-Semitic, Marcionite and Enlightenment individualistic consequences of this reading are totally overlooked. To the contrary it is really only when we get into the Israel story that all our interlocking overtures sound forth with a new vitality and vibrancy, mainly because this story consumes so much of the overall narrative.[28]

The renewal of the Adamic promise of blessing to Abram at the start of Genesis 12 alerts us to the fact that a new *creation* is now coming into being. It originates in another *exile* as Abram leaves the home of his ancestors and ventures forth in obedience to the divine summons. It appears as if the *creation* of Israel through Abraham, Isaac, Jacob and Joseph is another God-created strategy to curb the spread of sin, evil and violence in the created order. Similarly, it is an extension of God's original blessing of human fruitfulness, protection and multiplying to others through this *elected* (chosen) nation and it is configured anew in God's *covenant* with Abraham in Genesis 15:17.

Covenant-making now becomes a recurring theme for the Creator God. It may well be that these *covenant* agreements and ceremonies reflect Near Eastern royal grants and suzerain-vassal treaties, but the fact remains that they all consolidate Israel's relationship with their God and express different aspects of what this covenant relationship means – a *covenant* which, the Psalmist explains, God will never forget (Ps. 105:8–10).

The covenant-making God enters into relationships of mutual obligation and in each case agrees to maintain and fulfill the agreement as the initiating partner. The two *covenants* with Abraham (Gen. 15:17, 17) involve an unconditional promise to fulfill the grant of the land and to make of Abraham and his descendants flourishing *nations*. When Israel's hopes are dashed through slavery and *exile* in Egypt, it is the exodus tradition that becomes the main way of reaffirming her *election* and of overcoming the menacing specter of *empire*. After the exodus from Egypt, led by Moses, the Sinaitic *covenant* is based on the giving and receiving of the Torah (Ex. 19–24; Deut. 4:44–47 – 5:32; 29 and Josh. 24), which, as Psalm 1, 19, 119 and 147:19–20 make clear, is Israel's covenant charter, the means by which she fulfils her obligation and vocation to *image* God's relationship with humanity and the *creation* to the *nations*.

Time and time again the Psalmist and the prophets return to these two interrelated themes. When Israel celebrates her unique vocation as God's *elected* people she does so by remembering the means by which she fulfills her vocation to the other *nations*, which is to be the community that celebrates and lives by the Torah (Deut. 4 – 7). When the *nations* turn against Israel and ravish both her citizens and the land, she laments and calls for the creator God to fulfill his *covenant* promise of protection (Ps. 74, 79, 137). In Deuteronomy 27 – 30 these relationships are reinforced, so to abide by the duties of the Torah is to guarantee that the land will itself be blessed and fruitful. One of the most remarkable sections of the whole story narrated in Numbers 22 – 24 is the story of the pagan diviner and prophet Balaam, a story that reiterates God's sovereign blessing upon his *covenant* people even in the midst of her sinfulness and unfaithfulness. Second Isaiah returns throughout chapters 40 – 55 to the creator God who will fulfill his covenant promises and end the agony of the *exile* in Babylon.

The Torah and Land are the two signatory gifts of the *covenant*, but when God makes another *covenant* with the righteous priest Phinehas (Num. 25:10–13), that promise implies the provision of a lasting priesthood to manage and honor the sacrificial system and the key place of the Temple in Israel's national life (Lev., 1 Kgs. 6 – 8; Ps. 24; Isa. 6).

Similarly, the Davidic covenant involves an unconditional promise to establish the Davidic lineage and so bring Israel into line with other *nations* who look to the sovereignty of the monarch to *image* their relationship with their gods (2 Sam. 7:5–16).

By means of four divinely instituted covenant gifts – the Torah, the Land, the Monarchy and the Temple (where God dwells) – Israel in her cultural, socio-political and religious community life is to be like the sun, a shining light of life giving sustenance to all the *nations* of the earth, who will eventually align themselves with her *election* status and repent from their *idolatrous* ways returning again to the one creator God (Isa. 49:6).

What happens, however, when Israel, the means of blessing to the nations, slips effortlessly into her own form of *idolatry* (cf. the Elijah and Elisha narratives in 2 Kgs. 1 – 9)? What happens when the first and second commandments are disobeyed, when Israel brokers dangerous economic and political arrangements with *empires* and *nations* as a replacement security for total allegiance to the creator God (Judg., Isa. 28 – 30, Hosea)? What happens when Israel ignores her covenantal and community duties to the poor, the widow and the foreigner and the rich get richer off the backs of their own citizens (Amos)? What happens when pride and arrogant exclusivism turn Israel's *imaging* vocation into *idolatrous* pretension (Jonah and Amos)? What happens when Israel cries, "All is well, eat, drink and be merry for tomorrow we die," when all are asleep and like a thief in the night the "Assyrian comes down like a wolf on the fold" (Jeremiah)? What happens when all of Israel is engulfed by *exile*, and Land, Monarchy, Temple and even the practice of the Torah are no more (Jer., Ezek. and second Isa.)?

What happens when Israel has to learn to sing the Lord's song in a foreign land (Ps. 137)? What happens when Israel has to turn again to the *nations* as part of God's design to halt the slide into violence and so seek the welfare of the city (Jer. 29:7) What happens when Israel feels the coercive, brutal force of *empire* and loses her own national identity? What happens when Israel feels the pain of the dark night of the soul and cries out in bitterness for God to take revenge on *empires* (Ps. 88, 109)?

It is at this point that we must pause for a moment from the narrative and take full cognizance of the central significance in Israel's story and history of the reality of the Exile. Much Old Testament scholarship now views the Exile as the central defining crisis in Israel's national life:

> The Torah (Pentateuch) was likely completed in response to the exile, and the subsequent formation of the prophetic corpus and the "writings" as bodies of religious literature (canon) is to be understood as a product of second Temple Judaism. This suggests that by their intention, these materials are not to be understood in their final form diachronically – that is, in terms of their historical development – but more as an intentional and coherent response to a particular circumstance of crisis.[29]

What this crisis produced was an unprecedented reuse of previous materials, along the lines we have been suggesting, that reinvigorated the prophetic tradition in an explosion of counter-reality rhetoric. Just when the suffocating coercion of *empire* holds all in its thrall, when Israel is displaced, disoriented, disordered and denied, then Hosea proclaims a new victorious entry into the Land, Isaiah a new Davidic monarchy and a new Zion, second Isaiah a new exodus and a new *creation*, and Jeremiah a new *covenant*, where Torah allegiance will become a matter of inner conviction and motivation rather than of external performance and adherence (Jer. 31:31–34).[30]

It is at this time, too, that the wisdom literature grieves for an irretrievable loss (Lam. and Ps. 74), and Job and the writer of Ecclesiastes enter into a tribunal-like dispute with the creator God. So just when the narrative stutters and strains for new beginnings and momentarily loses direction, when the traditions of Israel are dispersed and dislocated and go underground,[31] then Wisdom makes her play to articulate a practical counter-cultural ethic (Prov.) that will allow Israel not just to stay the course but to engage in a defiant articulation of hope for another deliverer.[32]

And it is just at this time that Daniel, the Song of Solomon and other second Temple apocalyptic literature resume the penetrating critique of *empire* and that old eschatological and messianic traditions are revisited. The reuse of old material reverberates around the central overtures of *creation* and *covenant, election* and *exile, imaging* and *idolatry,* and *nations* and *empire.*

(We will dispense with the convention of using italics for emphasis in the remaining two stories.)

The Jesus story

The intertestamental period witnesses to the fact that several different attempts at the restoration of the Israelite storyline have taken place (Nehemiah and Ezra), and, consequently, the overall narrative has fractured into a number of competing possibilities. As N.T. Wright and others contend, the narrative in second Temple Judaism was contested by four significant power groups: the Essenes, the Zealots, the Pharisees and the Sadducees. Each had its own spin on the restoration possibilities.

Exile is also still real enough, even though the Jews are back in the Promised Land because the land is now in the control of another menacing and cruel empire, that of the Romans. Israel, however, still lives by her memories and the new possibilities of her sacred story which, according to Wright, is undergirded by four basic questions:

(1) Who are we? We are Israel, the chosen people (*election*) of the Creator God.

(2) Where are we? We are in the Holy Land, focussed on the temple; but, paradoxically, we are still in *exile.*

(3) What is wrong? We have the wrong rulers; pagans on the one hand, compromised Jews on the other, or halfway between, Herod and his family. We are all involved in a less-than-ideal (*an idolatrous*) situation.

(4) What is the solution? Our god must act again to give us the true sort of rule, that is, his own kingship exercised through properly appointed officials (a true priesthood; possibly a king [*to image the creator god*]); and in the meantime Israel must be faithful to her *covenant* charter.[33]

Not surprisingly, each of the competing groups within second Temple Judaism provided different answers to this set of fundamental identity questions.

The Pharisees represent the sectarian solution, which is to purify the inner sanctuary of personal life, if not the outer sanctuary of the land, by strict adherence to the purity codes and the Torah, to honor the covenant charter, and to maintain the religious and political polemic against the Sadducees and high priests, the self-appointed religious elite.

The Essenes, on the other hand, embrace the monastic solution – flee to the desert (with Qumran symbolizing exile), be the vanguard of a restored and renewed Israel through practicing covenant purity and piety, and wait for the coming king and/or priest to liberate the nation. The military solution had been tried already through the Maccabean revolts which had re-established Jewish national identity for a brief moment in history, although it was not to last. The ensuing Hasmoneans first became compromised and Hellenized Greeks and then Roman puppet procurators.

The advent of the Roman Empire left the Zealots still waiting for a political messiah to emerge and overthrow the pagan rulers through insurrection and rebellion.

The conservative solution as practiced assiduously by the Sadducees and chief priests was to maintain the power and control of the Temple and indulge in political compromise with the Romans.[34]

Then into this cauldron of competing interpretations of Israel's central narrative steps an unknown rabbi from Nazareth who probably, to begin with, was a disciple of another formidable prophet, John the Baptist (Luke 3 and parallels). His reconfiguration of the story, however, not only constructs for him a considerable reputation among the poor, marginalized and overtaxed peasants, but draws suspicion and open condemnation from just about all the other opposing power groups. He arrives preaching a new message of repentance because the coming kingdom of God is now near (Mark 1:15).

No one seems to require an explanation of this strange phrase ("the kingdom of God") because it incorporated and configured afresh the old message of creation and covenant. A new kingdom could only mean a restored creation when the nations will either give up their idolatrous ways or be dashed to pieces by a new holy war. The king will once again take up residence in the Temple and the covenant charter will express his loving and gracious reign among the whole creation, and exile will at long last be no more for God's elected nation. On the other hand, the nations will hear the good news of salvation as empires crumble to dust.

In a similar fashion to what has happened in Old Testament studies, Wright contends that the message of the kingdom could have meant only one thing to oppressed and discontented second Temple Jews, namely a promise that at long last the exile is coming to an end (Luke 4:14–30). With this implicit promise in mind Jesus codes his own interpretation of the kingdom in a series of surprising parables that contain hidden messages for those who have ears to hear (Mark 4; Matt. 13). That is why the people eagerly gathered to hear how and when the prophet Jesus would deliver on this kingdom promise, because the motif of the coming kingdom in Jesus' preaching could not be restricted to words alone. It was given an entirely new spin through healings, exorcisms and other mighty acts through which Jesus demonstrated that the end of exile, the promise of creation blessing and fruitfulness, was already breaking in; accordingly, blessed were all those who celebrated with him the reality of the poor having good news preached to them, the lame being healed, the captives being set free and sinners forgiven (Matt. 11:2–19; Luke 7:18–35).

Not surprisingly, through all of this dramatic saving kingdom activity we hear rumors and murmurings about the return of Elijah, Moses and the prophets, all portents of the appearance of another messiah figure (Mark 8:27–29 and parallels). Such an imaging vocation that will expose and denounce the idolatry of the religious and political leaders of second Temple Judaism is surprisingly reconfigured in the image of the suffering servant of second Isaiah (Luke 9:22–27 and parallels) and the Son of Man of Daniel 7.

Perhaps because both these figurations from the previous narrative could be understood in either a corporate or an individual sense Jesus shares this same imaging vocation with a community of disciples and followers who represent the twelve tribes of Israel (Luke 6:12–16 and parallels) These ordinary people are called, equipped and expected to live out the kingdom life and so reject the idolatrous military, sectarian and compromise solutions to Israel's story (Luke 10 and parallels). The birth and baptism narratives contend that this elected savior possesses a representative status as the son of the living God who will stand in David's line and through whom the nations will be blessed (Luke 2).

All of this leads to the inevitable confrontation with the compromised religious leaders and the representatives of empire when Jesus sets his face toward Jerusalem (Luke 9:51–55). He brokers that confrontation through cleansing the Temple, making it ready for the return of God to his rightful dwelling place (Luke 19:45–48 and parallels). Now the narrative of the new creation and covenant rehearsed by this new Messiah imaging the end of exile comes to a dramatic crescendo and climax as Jesus takes upon himself, in vicarious suffering, the sin, evil and violence of the nations who again and again contend to become empires. For all of the other representatives of the Israel story – the Pharisees, Zealots, Sadducees and Essenes; the ordinary people, friends and foe alike, who in the end betrayed him – the story ends at this point. Jesus, the perceived pretender to the throne of David, dies the cruel death of crucifixion that the representatives of empire have devised for all would-be trouble–makers (Luke 23:36–56 and parallels) While the women weep, Jesus surrenders all he has left – his own life – and once again a lantern, a messianic light to the nations, is extinguished.

The church's story

The church, of course, would have no story if it were not for a remarkable sequence of events that not only reconfigured the Jesus story but also started a new story. Resurrection, ascension and Pentecost were the totally surprising *novum*. A startling new creation that orchestrated the possibility and the reality of a second Israel, a new covenant people of God whose election fulfilled the ancient prophecy to Joel (Joel 2:28–32) and, of course, to Jeremiah and Ezekiel (Jer. 31:33–34; Ezek. 36:26–27; 39:29) about a new messianic age when the Gentiles would now be included within the original Adamic and Abrahamic blessing.

The totally central and fundamental place in all this of Jesus' resurrection simply cannot be underestimated:

> Only by his resurrection from the dead did the Crucified attain to the dignity of the *Kyrios* (Phil. 2:9–11). Only thus was he appointed the Son of God in power (Rom. 1:4). Only in the light of the resurrection is he the pre-existent Son. Only as the risen Lord is he always the living Lord of the community.[35]

Now the story becomes one of witness, acclamation and surrender to Jesus the *Kyrios* (Lord), the anointed one (Messiah), the pre-existent Logos/Wisdom and divine Son, the enthroned Son of Man and the new Adam, the head of his Body the church – Jesus, who *is* the *image* of the living God (not merely created in his likeness – Col. 1:15–16; 3:10; Rom. 8:29; 2 Cor. 3:18). It is this Jesus who now receives from the Father the gift of the Spirit and pours it out on the *ecclesia* in a dramatic reversal of the idolatry of the Babel story, so that all the nations can hear the liberating message of salvation and reconciliation and return to Zion (Acts 2).

The Acts of the Apostles begins with a promise of a new exile and diaspora (Acts 1:8), and the rest of the story is written as a fulfillment of that prophecy so that the good news of the Jesus story can be reincarnated in the life and witness of the second covenant people of God that will now include both Jew and Gentile (Acts 15). It is this message of liberation and eschatological hope that thunders out first in Jerusalem, then in Judea and Samaria, and to the ends of the earth.

The church's first great theologian, the apostle Paul, is wrenched out of the Pharisee version of the story and equipped to lead and direct the newly elected people of God to stand by and uphold their new covenant charter, which is allegiance to Jesus, the Christ of God (through whom the demands of the Torah are fulfilled), and co-option into the faith community that bears his name (Acts 9:1–31; Gal. 1:11 – 2:21). It is this same apostle who believes that the creator God will stand by all his covenant promises so that both the first and second Israel, whose different stories after AD 70 go their separate ways, can remain a means of shalom, blessing and fruitfulness to all the nations (Rom. 9 – 11). Paul utilizes the familiar overtures of Creation and Covenant to recast the Jesus story around this axis (Col. 1:15–20; Rom. 1 – 11 and 1 Cor. 15). The election/exile schema prefaces almost all of his epistles, as it also does 1 and 2 Peter. Imaging and idolatry provide the background for the new Adam typologies of Romans 5:12–20 and 1 Corinthians 15:45–49 as well as the central idea behind the Pauline theme of God's justifying righteousness. Finally, recent scholarship has noted that the duality of the nations and the empire forms the socio-economic and political background to Colossians, Philippians, Romans and 1 Thessalonians.[36]

It is similarly within the familiar grand scheme of nations and empire that the writer of the Apocalypse shares his vision of a new heaven and a new earth, when the great perpetrator of evil and violence will finally be put to the sword and the whole family of the imaging people of God will see the end of idolatrous empires and gather to worship the Lamb upon the throne.

Then, of course, this remarkable story of the sojourn of Father, Son and Holy Spirit with the whole created cosmos will come to an end, and no doubt a new story will commence. Before that great and victorious day the church, the anointed and elected people of God, will need to indwell the four episodes of this grand narrative and utilize the four densely configured plots of Creation and Covenant, Election and Exile, Imaging and Idolatry, and Nations and Empire to forge a genuinely new political and ecclesial existence that will simultaneously reconfigure and reimagine the mission of this community for the world at large.

It is to a consideration of this enormous task that we must now proceed.

Metavista: The Political Capital of the Bible in Cultural Engagement

"When I survey the great vault of corpses and mutilated bodies that begins with Hiroshima and Nagasaki, that stretches to the Indochinese corridor, where our government dropped the explosive equivalent of one Nagasaki bomb every week for seven years, and that extends now to the torture chambers and deathsquad barracks of Central America and beyond; and when I contemplate the even greater vault of corpses that awaits us in the future and that will surely signify the end of Western civilization and perhaps of life itself on earth, should something serious not soon be done to reverse the nuclear arms race; and when I remember Deak's strictures about a casual, indifferent, and callous people, then I am forced to the painful conclusion that today to be an American is to be an executioner or, what is much the same thing, an accomplice to the executioners."

(George Hunsinger)[1]

It is a remarkable tribute to the continued influence and faithful engagement with the political theology of Karl Barth that such a penetrating political analysis of modern America, written in 1985 by George Hunsinger, can still be heard amidst the strident clamor of rightwing religious and political nationalism and anti-Islamic rhetoric.[2] It is the kind of theological and political acumen that the last three Republican administrations, despite openly and fervently professing belief in the Christian faith, have been quite unable to apply to their own political proclivities. Instead, those who have espoused, and still do espouse, such political sentiments as Hunsinger endorses, have been reduced to becoming frustrated auditors to expensive war machines that have taken on dubious imperialist adventures in other sovereign areas, resulting in countless military and civilian casualties and the increased destabilization of already fragile political constellations. The enthusiastic support of modern America by the British prime ministers Margaret Thatcher and Tony Blair in this regard is at least in part due to their respective inability to distinguish between the ideology of contemporary liberalism and shrewd international politics.[3]

Indeed – to be even more controversial – it could be legitimately advanced that any candid long-term political assessment of the role of America in the modern world would have to ask the question: Did the era of international terrorism actually start when Truman authorized the dropping of the atom bomb on Nagasaki and Hiroshima?[4] The question arises because, as Hunsinger makes clear, up until the mass bombing of cities and innocent citizens by Hitler and Churchill in the later stages of the Second World War, the callous extermination of innocent populations had been regarded not as a political expediency but as a crime against humanity for which the perpetrators should be brought to justice. As Hunsinger explains:

> "What was universally condemned by church members and decent people generally in 1937, and considered fit only for dictators in 1939, was between 1940 and 1944 accepted as a 'military necessity' and a normal part of the procedure of war, both by the general public and the large majority of church people, both Protestant and Roman Catholic." Having enlisted in the aims of the war, Christians lost all will to resist, all sense that there even was something to resist, when the conduct of the war became wantonly immoral.[5]

It is a sad testimony to the state of modern liberal democracy that we no longer expect such candid and forthright self-analysis from our political representatives, because this was not always the case in American politics. Arguably we have only to go back to Gerald Ford and his drive to rid the White House of the scandal and double-dealing that had beset the political administration during the Nixon years, or Abraham Lincoln and his Second Inaugural Address concerning the state of the union at war with itself over the issue of slavery, to see another form of sanguine and much more biblically attuned political judgment.

The political role of the US in the modern world

Hunsinger stands in the tradition of another American, one whom Karl Barth both admired and suggested more American

Christians should read, William Stringfellow, whose book *An Ethic for Christians and Other Aliens in a Strange Land* was written during the controversies of the Vietnam War. Stringfellow gave up an illustrious legal career to work in East Harlem. He was a firm advocate of helping people read modern America from a biblical perspective rather than, as the religious right currently does, allowing American cultural ideology to read the Bible for us.

A good example of someone following the latter course is Richard John Neuhaus, erstwhile leftist progressive turned conservative Catholic. Neuhaus both endorses and encourages the "chosen nation" myth that conflates modern democracy with Americanization and apparently legitimizes America's emancipatory role in the international affairs of the modern world.[6] All conscientious objectors to such nationalist propaganda are simply branded disloyal Americans who have capitulated to the processes of liberal secular government!

Stringfellow, on the other hand, in the midst of the controversy that engulfed the American bombing campaign in Vietnam, goes to St John of Patmos to find a hermeneutical key to his present political conundrum. He sees in the Apocalypse a contrast between the two cities Babylon and Jerusalem. America, he claims, is presently identified with the former because it has embraced a culture of death, which is how John symbolically understood the demonic principality of Babylon.

Stringfellow, an early exponent of the theology of the principalities and powers, anticipated a lot of Walter Wink's critique of modern America as a nation obsessed with a culture of death and the myth of redemptive violence,[7] and as Christopher Rowland explains, he concluded that

> Babylon is a description of every city, an allegory of the condition of death, the principality in bondage to death, and ultimately the focus of apocalyptic judgment. Jerusalem is about the emancipation of human life in society from the rule of death. It is a parable, he says, of the church of prophecy – an anticipation of the end of time.[8]

How is it that Hunsinger and Stringfellow are able to come to such forthright and penetrating political analyses concerning the role of their own nation in international politics? In Stringfellow's case it is because he is alive to the biblical apocalyptic literature with its constant vigilance and hermeneutic of suspicion toward the potentially demonic manifestations of empire. In the context of the modern world that vigilance simply has to be directed toward the only remaining superpower whose influence on the world stage for good or ill is everywhere to be seen. In Hunsinger's case it is because he takes as his model for political engagement the Barmen Declaration of 1934, written largely by Karl Barth and directed toward enabling the Confessing Church in Germany to disentangle itself from the ideology of Hitler's National Socialism. The Barmen declaration exemplifies a shrewd Christological realism, confessing as follows:

> Jesus Christ, as he is attested for us in Holy Scripture, is the one Word of God which we have to hear and which we have to trust and obey in life and death.
>
> We reject the false doctrine, as though the Church could and would have to acknowledge as a source of its proclamation, apart from and besides this one Word of God, still other events and powers, figures and truths, as God's revelation.[9]

To use the Barmen declaration in our present context implies the following: while rejecting any analogous revelatory moment to Jesus Christ – be that the international role of modern America, free-market capitalism, Islamic theocracy or Aristotelian virtues – we, like Barth, can still welcome the appearance of other words of liberation and good sense manifested in any political system that advances the cause of world peace and international justice.[10] In other words, we do not have to indulge in the refusal, castigation, and continual lambasting of the so-called naked public square, or liberal democracy, mixed as it is with a peculiar nostalgia for previous political systems, which has been the wont of other representatives of current political theology both in America and Britain.

Engaging the protagonists – theology and modern democratic liberalism

Jeffrey Stout has made this very point as he engages with what he refers to as the slide toward a theology of resentment. His target is John Millbank and the radical orthodoxy coterie who, as Stout rightly asserts, appear to accept what now actually lies in ruins, namely the account by modern liberalism of how the secularization of modern society actually came about. More of this in our next chapter; suffice to say at this juncture that the theory proposed that all attempts to found a genuine Christian account of political authority in the modern era were dissolved by the anti-religious liberalism inherent in modernity itself is now what it should always have been: a theory without any supporting evidence. Having revived a totally discredited theory, Millbank and his associates indulge in a highly otiose and tendentious reading of Augustine in order simply to refuse any account of the secular at all.

Concerning all such attempts to engage in the politics of nostalgia and revive the back-to-Christendom rhetoric, Stout asks three fundamental questions:

> Is it not possible to discern the workings of the Holy Spirit, and thus some reflections of God's redemptive activity, in modern democratic aspirations?
>
> Is there nothing in the political life of modern democracies, or in the lives of those who are struggling for just and decent arrangements within them, that a loving God would bless?
>
> If the plentitude of God's triune inner life shines forth in all of creation, cannot theology discern some such light in democratic political community?[11]

If Millbank and his associates can answer yes to any of these questions, then their theology is a lot less radical and novel than they think and they have little theological justification for their wholesale refusal of the secular realm in political judgments. If, however, they answer no to such a set of questions, then, as Stout rightly contends:

> [Millbank] has little to offer besides nostalgia, utopian fantasy, and withdrawal into a strongly bounded enclave. In that event, he would owe his readers reasons for avoiding the conclusion that his theology has restricted divine sovereignty and inhibited charity toward the non-Christian other.[12]

Stout has similar strong words of criticism for Stanley Hauerwas, who he claims is another advocate of the politics of withdrawal.[13]

His detailed exegesis of Hauerwas's intellectual development is highly illuminating and on the whole fair. He gives praise where it is due, but regrets the substantial influence of Alasdair MacIntyre's account of the tradition of modern liberalism on Hauerwas's work. The beginnings of Hauerwas's distrust of modern liberalism began with the detailing of what he referred to in 1971 as "quandary ethics" – the tendency in post-Enlightenment ethics to abstract genuine human persons and decision-making from ethical theory and rely, instead, on universal maxims or rules to discriminate between good and evil actions or deeds.[14]

As others have noted, such universal maxims are rules of thumb based on thin stories, ultimately the Enlightenment quest for universal values or the abstraction of problem-solving divorced from real human activity, both of which lack the thick description of legitimating religious narratives or ethical traditions.[15]

Already in Hauerwas's work we can see two fundamental concerns combining. The first, following the example of his mentor, John Howard Yoder, was to burst into the smothering undergrowth of modern political and ethical theory and carve out some legitimate room for the political role of the church;[16] the second was his turning toward the importance of narratives in justifying both theological and political discourse. In all of this he was substantially aided and abetted by MacIntyre's influential critique of modern liberalism as a privatized, fragmented and ultimately polarized ethical and political tradition that relies on what the Enlightenment failed both to attain and to justify, namely universal truths about human character, virtue and judgment upon which we can all agree. MacIntyre's influence led Hauerwas to intensify his argument that ultimately the church is itself a community of virtue and character that relies not on universal moral truths but on the redemptive efficacy of the biblical story and its fulfillment in Jesus Christ.[17] This is the political space the church occupies and its task is to preach the gospel of the crucified Christ which provides an ethic for vicarious suffering (something which Oliver O'Donovan has also claimed modern liberalism cannot provide)[18] and at the same time live out in a community of character the ethics implied and detailed in the church's narrative of redemption.[19]

The crucial influence of MacIntyre on Lesslie Newbigin (whom Hauerwas greatly admired) should also be noted at this juncture.[20] It strengthened Newbigin's conviction that the modern secular liberal state (what Peter Berger called the journey of the homeless mind)[21] was, in fact, deeply antipathetical to the gospel story and amounted to a counter-narrative that must be confronted by a new mission to Western culture. Stout notes that at this juncture Hauerwas, like Newbigin, conflates liberal democracy and modernity as the epoch of vicious individualism and ideologically controlled violence. (The latter descriptor also embraces Hunsinger's critique.) This, claims Stout, inevitably leads to Hauerwas' becoming another advocate of the politics of withdrawal from the secular public square and the victim of a double dualistic bind:

> One cannot stand in a church conceived in Yoder's terms, while describing the world surrounding it in the way MacIntryre describes liberal society, without implicitly adopting a stance that is rigidly dualistic in the same respects that rightly worried Hauerwas in 1974.[22]

In a recent book Hauerwas has protested his innocence (somewhat unconvincingly) on the charge of embracing the politics of withdrawal.[23] A lot depends, of course, on how one reads Hauerwas's most recent work and also how one reacts to his jaundiced view of the language of justice. In my view, Hauerwas does not advocate a withdrawal manifesto; instead, he has rightly understood one of the pressing issues for any current political theology, namely: What is the political role of the church in contemporary political arrangements and how should the church react to and deal with what is, by and large, its present cultural captivity? Hauerwas's tendency is to be somewhat confrontational and bullish in both his defense of the church as a community of character and his impatience with the secular rhetoric of liberal democracy, both of which not only irritate Stout but lead him to conclude that Hauerwas is being politically irresponsible.[24]

On the other hand, Stout's account of the genesis of modern secular liberalism is a lot less sinister than that of MacIntyre, Newbigin or Hauerwas. Ultimately he sees the secularization of modern democratic theory as a pragmatic process of purging from political discourse any language that is bound to lead to disagreement, hostility or sectarian division. The problem does not lie with the secularists, but with those of religious conviction who cannot find any common biblical or theological ground on which to base their political theology and who thereby not only disagree with one another but tend to hamper rather than prosper the inevitably pragmatic business of democratic government. Stout does not want theologians to refrain from making political judgments or to abandon their Christian convictions and language. In fact, he takes religious people and theologians very seriously and encourages both to be actively involved in democratic political processes for the good of all. He invites ordinary believers and theologians, in the interest of their becoming better equipped to do so, to abandon their conflation of modernity with the tradition of liberal democracy, which he believes is a deeply flawed story, and to set about finding better theological and political reasons for strengthening the rhetoric and practice of democracy in an age of international terrorism.[25]

If one agrees with Stout, then the argument is this: Christendom arrangements and constitutional monarchy are by and large no more, and brutal dictatorships or lawless anarchy no one seems to want; on the other hand, liberal democracy accompanied by a certain amount of liberal secular rhetoric is what we currently have, at least in the so-called free world, so let's work with the system and see what we can all do to contribute to the vision and practice of human flourishing and international justice.

The truth here probably does not lie in an either/or mandate in favor of Hauerwas or Stout but, as is so often the case, somewhere in between. Clearly there have been some forces and strong voices within modernity that have taken an aggressive secularizing stance toward Christianity, seeking to marginalize or silence the Christian voice altogether (as, indeed, we will explain in more detail in our next chapter).

But it would not be accurate, and would probably be unwise, to conflate such a secularizing tendency with modernity per se. Stout is correct when he adjudges that political language is not by implication wedded to a secularized view of the world and politics; indeed, much of it is still located in the Judaeo-Christian narrative, and liberal democracy is not the same as the narrative of secularization. The latter, a flawed and inflated story if ever there was one, and one largely promulgated by atheist sociologists, we hope to explode and demolish in our next chapter. Stout is also right when he refers to the divided and schismatic voices of a now outmoded Christendom that were, and still are, unable to get their political act together in a way that truly respects and works with alternative points of view.

Biblical theology and political arrangements – what are the issues?

This forthright discussion of what is by and large a healthy debate in modern political theology has prepared us to ask the fundamental questions of any political theology that seeks to be a contributor to the debate about modern political arrangements. They are the following:

- What is the fundamental nature of the political act (note: not political theory)?

- Exactly what role does the church play in the political arena as a political community constituted by the ethical, political and religious vision of the kingdom of God?

- What resources lie to hand in the biblical narrative to fuel an imaginative and compelling project of political theology?

If we want to try and locate a current political theologian and ethicist who has attempted to provide a detailed and thorough answer to all three questions we need look no further than Oliver O'Donovan.[26] As many have noticed, O'Donovan is a tough read, but his shrewd and erudite historical and biblical judgment allows him to move beyond what has been one of the major limitations of Catholic natural law theology and the political theology of the liberation theologians: a tendency toward a highly eclectic and piecemeal appropriation of the biblical narrative.[27] If, as O'Donovan asserts, political theology has to do with exposing politics to the activity of God, that can come about only by a full and theologically reflective indwelling of the whole narrative of Scripture.[28]

O'Donovan sees the essence of biblical political theology as encapsulated in Jesus' message about the coming kingdom of God for two reasons. First of all, as we have already argued, the kingdom motif is dependent upon the creation and covenant schema for both its theological justification and its location. Secondly, it allows us to define the essence of the political act in the notion of kingly rule. It is here that we find a decisive analogy between divinely authorized rule or authority and an equivalent in the human realm of politics.[29] This also permits us to avoid a common failing with modern politics, at least within the Western tradition, which is the concentration upon the political institution and agency rather than the political act. Consequently, "the political act is the divinely authorized act."[30]

In developing such a political theology we also attend to the revealed history of Israel as it is offered to us in the canonical Scriptures, not some constructed history of Israel that supposedly sits behind the text.[31]

O'Donovan draws out four interrelated themes from the notion of kingly rule: salvation, judgment, possession and praise. In narrative terms this means that both creation and covenant, manifested in the kingly rule of God, lead to a nation of people who enjoy God's salvation and submit to his judgment because they are his possession who honor him in praise and worship.[32] From this theological analysis of Israel's unique relation to the electing God, O'Donovan draws a crucial (and some would claim highly contentious) conclusion:

> Out of the self-possession of this people in their relation to God springs the possibility of other people's possessing themselves in God. In this hermeneutic assumption lay the actual continuity between Israel's experience and the Western tradition.[33]

In other words, the narrative of Scripture does not belong to Israel alone. The second Israel (the church) opens the promise and blessing of God to the Gentiles as well, and the whole Western tradition stands in this relationship to the Judaeo-Christian faith. This was, and still is, our founding religious narrative and despite the ravages of aggressive secularism we in the First World still stand within its borders. Only on this basis are we permitted to reuse the biblical material in constructing a contemporary political theology.

From this biblical framework, and in dialogue with the whole tradition of political theology, O'Donovan annunciates six fundamental axioms which form the basis of his political theology:

1. Political authority arises where power, the execution of right and the perpetuation of tradition are assured together in one coordinated agency.

2. That any regime should actually come to hold authority, and should continue to hold it, is a work of divine providence in history, not a mere accomplishment of the human task of political service.

3. In acknowledging political authority, society proves its political identity.

4. The authority of a human regime mediates divine authority in a unitary structure, but is subject to the authority of law within the community, which bears independent witness to the divine command.

5. The appropriate unifying element in international order is law rather than government.

6. The conscience of the individual members of a community is a repository of the moral understanding which shaped it, and may serve to perpetuate it in a crisis of collapsing morale or institution.[34]

As we move into the New Testament, it is clear that through the incarnation, ministry, death and resurrection of Jesus the first covenant is fulfilled and recapitulated in the second. Jesus' resurrection and enthronement (ascension), whereby he is given all authority in heaven and earth, entails that the rule of God is now mediated through the Son in the power and person of the Spirit:

> To speak of God's rule from this point on must mean more than to assert divine sovereignty, or even divine intervention, in general terms. It means recounting this narrative and drawing the conclusions implied in it ... We cannot discuss the question of

"secular" government, the question from which Western political theology has too often been content to start, unless we approach it historically, from a Christology that has been displayed in narrative form as Gospel.[35]

It is at this point that O'Donovan takes note of the Pauline theme enunciated in Colossians 2:15 of the "subjection of the nations." O'Donovan asserts that this applies to all forms of political rule, namely that they have been disarmed and subjected to the rule of Christ, even though that rule is not yet fully revealed in the world as it is. In that sense he argues that secular authorities are now required, indeed authorized, to provide the social space for the church's mission to proclaim and live out the gospel to the nations:

The passing age of the principalities and powers has overlapped with the coming age of God's kingdom ... Secular institutions have a role confined to this passing age (*saeculum*) ... Applied to political authorities, the term "secular" should tell us that they are not agents of Christ, but are marked for displacement when the rule of God in Christ is finally disclosed. They are Christ's conquered enemies, yet they have an indirect testimony to give, bearing the marks of the sovereignty imposed upon them, negating their pretensions and evoking their acknowledgement. Like the surface of a planet pocked with craters by the bombardment it receives from space, the governments of the passing age show the impact of Christ's dawning glory. This witness of the secular is the central core of Christendom.[36]

Clearly, then, the secular (*saeculum*) in this schema does not mean what it tends to mean in modern political theory, namely an entirely neutral, extensive and self-legitimating arena of non-religious political debate. On the contrary, it refers to a chastened, highly reduced, yet conditionally divinely authorized forum of political judgment and political arrangement aimed at controlling evil and violence which, in turn, should acknowledge the church's right and responsibility to be the gospel-reconciling community.

By any standards O'Donovan presents us with an impressive, deeply thoughtful and extensive account of political theology that at every stage of its development is thoroughly earthed in the whole biblical narrative.

Before attempting some critical reflections and postulating some misgivings, we will do what we have been advocating from start to finish in this book, namely, attempt an exercise in cultural engagement. In that way we will also be complying with Stout's request actually to enter into the debate about present political arrangements without first requiring that everything is adjusted to meet our theological preferences.

Political theology in cultural engagement

Any definition of the political is itself a political act.[37] Politics as an academic discipline and as a practical form of government is a contested and disputed area, and any construal of how we wish better to understand the political act biblically and theologically is, as we have suggested already, precisely that: a construal based on our imaginative entering into and configuration of the biblical story. To refuse such personal responsibility in cultural dialogue and claim that we are simply reading off the plain theological or historical sense of what the biblical narrative tells us is, to my mind at least, to claim some privileged position of hermeneutical objectivity that is itself a highly political power play prone to ideological self-deception. Any notion of the practice of modern politics is distributed along a spectrum encompassed by the following four definitions:

(1) Politics as government: politics is associated primarily with the art and practice of government and the activities of the state.

(2) Politics as public life: politics is primarily and fundamentally concerned with the conduct and management of community affairs.

(3) Politics as conflict resolution: politics has to do with the expression, delineation and resolution of conflicts through compromise, conciliation, negotiation and other related strategies.

(4) Politics as power: politics is the power-brokering process through which the production, distribution and use of

scarce resources is, as far as is humanly possible, equitably determined in all areas of social existence.[38]

The first definition of the political act is the prevalent, mainstream notion of the nature of political discourse in both the UK and the US. It places very restrictive boundaries around what politics actually is, namely the activity of governments, state agencies and various powerful social elites. In that sense it is a thoroughly modernist, top-down, if not hierarchical, notion of political arrangements that relies on a process of democratic choice and consent. The last definition, on the other hand (as we have noted already in chapter 2), tends to comply with the postmodern, more diffuse and decentralized theory of political processes which can (and, some say, at times should) lead to bypassing the democratic process altogether and engaging in the politics of dissent and direct action. The first definition is a secularized descendant of the equally hierarchical, hegemonic and centralized form of government that typified Christendom arrangements which, some would claim, is evidenced in the UK by political anomalies such as the House of Lords. Here both church and state still hold hands in the process of political deliberation. The postmodernists suggest that if we encourage a discourse and practice of politics based on the last three definitions of what politics actually is, then such anachronistic political arrangements will eventually disappear and modern democratic arrangements will evolve into even more decentralized, bottom-up, organically distributed power arrangements that will involve far more citizens in the political process.[39]

If their analysis is correct (and many would question whether it is), then this would be an improvement on the present state of affairs, since voting figures in both the UK and the US clearly show that there is currently terrible apathy about present democratic processes and widespread disillusionment with how governments use their authority and power and, indeed, with the whole political process altogether. In that sense, it could be asserted that the old top-down, highly restricted form of hierarchical political government clearly is not working and neither does it count for much, at times, in the realm of international law.

What does the above analysis suggest in regard to O'Donovan's redefinition of the theological nature of the political act? For many it might suggest that his is another hierarchical, top-down construal of political arrangements using the analogy of divine kingly rule (although analogies are never univocal) that clearly favors the Christendom settlement and something rather ambiguously referred to as early Christian liberalism.[40] It might also suggest that O'Donovan demonstrates a proclivity toward constitutional monarchy[41] and that he, like Millbank and Hauerwas, also laments, and at times castigates, the so-called secular modern state which, it is claimed, has lost any coherent notion of authoritative rule or divinely instigated leadership.[42]

All of the aforementioned people could justifiably retort that I appear to be a typical postmodern who simply refuses any biblical notions of authority, hierarchy and rule that can by analogy be applied to current political arrangements. To which I would respond, tongue in cheek, "I'm sorry – I've always been a communitarian and a democrat and I am not about to change!" But in more serious vein, I would contend that this is not the way I construe the biblical narrative, which seems to me to arrive finally at a political space where both government and the church are no more (witness the absence of the Temple in the apocalyptic vision of Rev. 21), and where the worship of the Lamb also includes the glory and honor of the nations because they have been conformed to the gospel of the risen Jesus encapsulated in the mission of the church and anticipated in Philippians 2:9–11.

Let us return for a moment to Yoder. He asks just what the rule of Christ entails in the interim period between his enthronement to the Father's right hand in heaven and the eschaton. If *the rule of Christ* is not just an empty figure of speech, then it is clearly preparing for something and by implication actively engaged in doing something on earth as well.[43] The end in sight is outlined for us by Paul in 1 Corinthians 15:24–25 and it will entail handing everything over to the Kingdom of the Father after Christ has completed the subjugation of the principalities and authorities and indeed destroyed death itself. It is consequently the task of the church as the earthly body of Christ to live out the rule of the Son in what Yoder refers to as "an aftertaste of God's loving triumph on the cross and foretaste of His ultimate loving triumph in His Kingdom."[44] Accordingly the church is a political society identified by "baptism, discipline, morality and martyrdom."[45] The church must embody and preach a message of forgiveness, faithfulness, restraint and justice to the authorities as it witnesses to the Lamb who was slain, whose love will eventually dissipate and destroy that which rules through institutionalized power and control.[46] Indeed, as Mahatma Gandhi asserted, is this not what the meaning of history bears out? And is this not the hope to which democratic political rule bears witness?

In this sense we do agree with O'Donovan that something absolutely new has taken place in the death, resurrection and ascension of Jesus which must apply to political arrangements as well, namely that their authorization must comply with his rule and with the mission of the church to go to every race and nation with the message of the justifying righteousness of Jesus who is now both Lord and Christ, which is also what is entailed in fulfilling the Great Commission in Matthew 28:16–20.

At the same time, like Yoder, we could not agree with O'Donovan's second axiom, namely that any regime that should actually come to hold authority, and should continue to hold it, is a work of divine providence in history, not a mere accomplishment of the human task of political service. This statement is clearly qualified by the other five statements to which we referred earlier; nevertheless, to hold to such a view unreservedly is, in my view, to accede to – indeed, to be complicit in – any demonic, oppressive, barbarous regime that relies on the abuse of power and the instigation of institutional violence and terror, which is not a justifiable, or even desirable, expression of divine providence. Such a viewpoint implied in O'Donovan's second axiom could find no place, for example, for Bonhoeffer's politics of direct action and eventual martyrdom in regard to Hitler's National Socialism, nor could it accommodate the following statement about the same regime by Karl Barth:

> It could be that we are dealing with a government of liars and perjurers, murderers and arsonists, a government that wanted to put itself in God's place, bind consciences, oppress the church and make itself into the church of the Antichrist. It would then be clear that we can choose only to be disobedient to God in obedience to this government or obedient to God in disobedience to this government.[47]

Furthermore, Barth chose to advocate active violent resistance to the Nazi regime most certainly as a last resort, but nevertheless because theologically we are "here on the border of the church, within the realm of the not yet redeemed world."[48] In other words, this was a moment in history when to bear witness to the rule of Christ was to embrace martyrdom.

The movie *The Mission* makes the very same point in regard to the Jesuit missions to the South American Guarani Indians in the eighteenth century. The mission led by one Father Gabriel, helped by his acolyte and converted slave trader, Father Roderigo, is eventually ceded by the Spanish to Portuguese government forces who, aided and abetted by the very same slave traders, destroy the mission outposts. Father Gabriel, faced with this betrayal by his own religious superiors, chooses the way of pacifist self-sacrifice, while Father Roderigo trains the Indians in armed resistance. Both are killed, but the question – dramatically and deliberately framed through the action and musical overture of the film – poignantly rests over the sad denouement of the film: Were both these men being obedient to the witness of the crucified Christ in refusing submission to and actively resisting unjustly propagated evil and violence?

Conclusion – political theology and the biblical narrative

At this point, to draw out some conclusions, we return to the theological overtures we constructed from the whole biblical narrative in chapter 6.

First of all, if political arrangements are part of God's good creation order – fallen of course, but nevertheless now subjugated to the interim rule of Christ – and if such arrangements are affirmed by the Wisdom literature as an expression of God's covenant fidelity to Israel and later, of course, also to the church, then through the very same interim rule of Christ they should analogously reflect the eschatological reality of shalom, harmony, international peace and justice encapsulated in Jesus' message and in his personification of the righteous kingdom of God.[49]

Secondly, such divinely authorized political arrangements are directed toward curbing and controlling humankind's endemic proclivity toward violence and our consonant inability to apply justly the wisdom of Solomon and separate good and evil. This particular fallen human dilemma Alexander Solzhenitsyn neatly summarizes:

> If only there were evil people somewhere insidiously committing evil deeds, and it were necessary only to separate them from the rest of us and destroy them. But the line dividing good and evil cuts through the heart of every human being. And who is willing to destroy a piece of his own heart?[50]

Thirdly, in a post-Christendom situation such as we now find ourselves in, the church exists and conducts her mission to the nations in exile, the wilderness experience that constituted most of Israel's covenant history. Here, at times amidst the fleshpots of Babylon, at others under the oppressive strictures and tyranny of empires, where the mission of the church is curtailed or controlled, the church must, nevertheless, fulfill her task to image the kingdom of God, proclaim judgment, and actively resist the idolatry of the oppressors.

Fourthly, the mission of the church to proclaim and incarnate the reconciling good news of the crucified Savior to the nations as the elected people of God is the church's primary raison d'être and divinely sanctioned activity. Israel and the church share a mission to proclaim peace and shalom to the nations, and this disallows both the rigid Zionism that now largely determines the politics of the nation of Israel and the politics of fear and resentment presently espoused by the administration in the US. For the principalities and powers, now subject to Christ's authority, to hear and obey this gospel, political space should be allowed for this great eschatological task to be undertaken and ultimately accomplished. The mission of the church is, after all, the Spirit's task, against which no human authority can ultimately stand or prevail.

Finally, democratic government in both its secularized and its Christian form is a Western political arrangement dependent on the legitimating authority of the Judaeo-Christian tradition. It cannot, therefore, be imposed on other states and nations that adhere to another legitimating religious tradition, for instance Islam, where there is no separation between church and state and where theocratic arrangements are often preferred.

To fulfill all five requirements, two important and essential things are necessary. One is to take apart, from top to bottom, an erroneous story and popular myth that has seriously curtailed the mission of the contemporary church and has led to what can only be described as a debilitating loss of nerve and conviction. The other is to chart as accurately as possible the ebb and flow of contemporary mission history so that we may gain new insight into the necessary task of reimagining the church in the midst of our metavista, our post-postmodern cultural context.

These important twin tasks will occupy our attention in the next two chapters.

Part Three

8

Deconstructing the
Secular Imagination

"What happened in the late twentieth century has been unique and epoch-forming. Since around 1963, Britain has been in the brave new world of secular secularisation – that is, the permanent decline of religion."

(Callum Brown)[1]

As we come to consider how the church can recover its confidence and so live its narrative, we are bound to ask the question: Is it at all possible for the church to do such a thing, except as a cult, or a sect? Even if we do find individual churches that both belong to the mainstream and are thriving, are they not merely insignificant exceptions that cannot stand against the general rule that Christianity cannot survive against cultural and intellectual forces vastly greater than the Christian church itself? If a story can't be re-enacted in different historical and cultural circumstances has it any worth at all?

Amongst many explanations of the decline of religion in the West, it is above all the secularization story that suggests that the narrative of religion has come to an end.

We deliberately use the term *secularization story* rather than *secularization thesis* or *secularization theory*. Cox expresses very well the reason for this conscious choice of phraseology:

> Instead of conceptualising secularisation as merely descriptive, or as a scientific hypothesis to be verified as if conducting a laboratory experiment, it makes more sense to think of secularisation as a story. The practice of history involves comparative storytelling. There are many different kinds of stories, overlapping stories, stories of different levels of generality and even visibility. Historians who make the conventional distinction between narrative history on the one

hand and analytical history on the other run the risk of ignoring the narrative nature of analysis, and the explanatory nature of narrative. An analysis is often a story of how an historian has solved a problem. A narrative, far from being a simple arrangement of facts, usually serves some explanatory rhetorical purpose.[2]

In rightly discerning that the secularization thesis is not just a thesis but a story, and one which has a rhetorical purpose, Jeffrey Cox does not go on to analyze the nature of the rhetoric served by that story.[3] There is good reason to suppose that in the hands of some narrators the rhetoric is a tool with which to assault religion in general and Christianity in particular. In that sense it is a natural development from the broader attack on Christianity pursued with such force by the radical advocates of what Midgeley calls scientism,[4] which begins as far back as the middle of the nineteenth century but is today enthusiastically continued by Richard Dawkins and others. Their specific intent is to push Christianity to the margins of society such that the voice of the church is silenced.

It is important for our concerns to understand the place and function of the secularization story, but before we can approach that task there are some preliminary difficulties that need to be addressed.

Some difficulties with the secularization story

There are a few issues regarding the so-called secularization story which we need to deal with briefly.

What does the phrase "the secularization story" mean?

In the 1960s and 1970s some sociologists, including Peter Berger and Bryan Wilson, developed the principle that secularization inevitably follows modernization. The popular perception of this theory of secularization would seem to be that it describes the process by which modern societies (currently the West, but ultimately the whole world) leave religion behind as an unnecessary superstition that belongs to a more primitive age. In this populist version, secularization and secular humanism are often linked. Secular thought is identified as rational and scientific. It is on the side of reason, tolerance and freedom. Religion, on the other hand, is always inevitably connected to the opposite of these modern virtues. It is dangerous and harmful and children should be protected from it.

In most accounts of the secularization story the notion is advanced that the statistics relating to religious affiliation and attendance reveal an unremitting pattern of decline that entirely coincides with the modern period. Moreover, that numerical decline is mirrored by a decline in the influence of the church and Christianity. Thus the Christian story loses its credibility in the face of modernity. In reality, however, the numbers are much more complex. If there is a uniform story at all in terms of the major historic churches in Europe it would be the decline of church attendance and membership in the twentieth century since the end of the First World War in northern Europe and since the late 1960s in southern Europe.

Hugh McLeod tells us that Bryan Wilson defines *secularization* as "the process by which religion loses social significance" and Steve Bruce links secularization to the "irreversible trend towards individualism in modern societies." It soon becomes clear that a particular rhetoric is being served in both Wilson's and Bruce's descriptors, and McLeod goes on in his analysis of Bruce's categories or stages of secularization to indicate something of the ingredients of that rhetoric.

How robust is the secularization story?

The second difficulty relates to the question as to how robust the secularization story actually is, or even whether it has survived at all. As we imply above, Bruce is being required to defend the thesis. Why should this be necessary?

Jeffrey Cox describes the attack very well:

> Upon occasion I encounter the assertion that no one believes in secularization any more. Jay Demerath, an American sociologist of religion, recently put it even more emphatically: "For a long time there was a notion that society would just become secularized over time, that this was part of modernization and westernization, and that religion would disappear due to the legacy of the Enlightenment. I don't know any sociologists of religion worth their salt who really believed that."[5]

Cox refers to others with severe doubts about the secularization story and notes the comment of Simon Green that "It is the anti-secularization model which has made most of the running in recent British religious historiography."[6] But despite these references to the doubters, Cox makes it absolutely clear that the secularization story does remain very robust and that it does so because it offers a powerful mechanism to understand the place of religion in the modern world. This is a way of acknowledging the existence of religion while simultaneously stripping it of its significance. Cox goes even further and claims that ultimately "the secularization story is the only master narrative of religion in modern history."[7]

But if the secularization story is so powerful and so useful, why does it have its detractors, and how can some insist that no one believes it anymore?

We might best understand the reason for its weakness by first examining its strength. The secularization story does describe something. After all, there is a puzzle that demands an explanation. The question is simply this: Why has the church, so vastly influential for so many years, been experiencing widespread, constant and seemingly inexorable decline all across the Western world for so many years? Underneath that relatively simple question about statistics lies a rather deeper question: Why, after so many years when the story of Christianity operated as a founding narrative or worldview of culture and society at every level, has the impact of that story, and so, too, the influence of the church, gradually weakened to the point where, far from being authoritative, the voice of the church has become marginalized, vilified, scorned and ignored?

In constructing the claim that there is something about the modern world that makes it difficult for religion to continue in any kind of public or institutionalized form, the secularization story is both seeking an explanation of what has been and is also predicting the future. Initially it was suggesting that what was true for Europe yesterday and today would eventually be true for the whole world as the remainder of the world gradually modernized just as Europe had done. Indeed, there was almost an implication that it was Europe's duty, call and mission to assist such a process. Secular Europe would continue its task of enlightening the world as to the true shape of all things, just as Christian Europe had attempted to export the Christian story a generation earlier.

What, then, became unconvincing in such an explanation? The evangelizing and totalizing tone of the narrative gives the clue. There is a degree of arrogance and even imperialism attached to the suggestion that where Europe goes, the rest of the world is bound to follow.

However, the problems with the theory did not begin with the world outside Europe, but with Europe itself – parts of Europe did not yield up the influence of the Christian narrative and the Christian church so easily. But an easy explanation was at hand. The parts that had not followed the pattern were almost uniformly Catholic and not as impacted by industrialization and modernization as northern Europe. The prediction that these parts of Europe would eventually follow the same pattern as the rest of Europe has proved to be correct and has therefore strengthened the secularization story. Whether it should have done so and whether the dramatic social changes that have impacted Catholic Europe can adequately be explained by the secularization story alone is another matter.

Then another problem emerged, also within the Western world. America did not conform to the story as it should have done. This seemed to be a major embarrassment. It was difficult to argue that America was somehow either predominately Catholic or undeveloped in the way that the Republic of Ireland in the 1950s and 1960s clearly was. How could this leader of the modern world not conform to the broader secularization story?

At first, the situation of the US was seen as an exception to the general rule that had to be explained, and many alternative accounts were offered. For example, the very plausible idea that Christianity in America is in fact civic religion and hence a disguised form of secularity has been suggested amongst many other ideas. Gradually, though, the notion that America is the exception to be explained has receded in the face of growing evidence that the rest of the world is becoming both more developed and, if anything, more interested in religion and not less so.

These developments have shifted the debate to the point where instead of Europe being the norm and America being the exception, Europe itself is now seen to be the strange exception to be explained.

Grace Davie attacks this issue head on:

> It is simply not the case that the patterns of religious activity discovered in Western Europe are those of the modern world more generally. Indeed, if anything, the reverse is true. In terms of the parameters of faith of the modern world, the European case is beginning to look increasingly like an exception – a statement that many Europeans find hard to accept in that it flies in the face not only of their own experience, but of deeply embedded assumptions. Europeans are prone to believe that what they do today everyone else will do tomorrow. Or in terms of the subject matter of this series of lectures, Europeans are convinced that the relatively strong empirical connections between modernization and secularization that can be observed in Europe's historical evolution will necessarily be repeated elsewhere. Hence their conviction that as the world modernizes, it will necessarily secularize.
>
> Quite simply, it hasn't. And one look at the empirical evidence taken from almost every other global region suggests that it won't in the foreseeable future.[8]

Davie attempts her own explanation of why Europe seems to be an exception to the religious norms of humanity. She locates her core explanation in two areas. First she notes that the historical narrative is rooted in the particular and unique interaction of church and state as expressed in Christendom both in pre- and post-Reformation history. No other part of the world has experienced the unique church–state relationship found in Europe through the medieval period. The struggle of society and of many Christians to be free of such arrangements represents the first stage of secularization in its European expression. Second, Davie goes on to note the evidence that emerges from the European Values Survey, which shows that those values display high levels of affinity with Christian perspectives, to such an extent that Davie describes Europeans not so much as secular but as "differently religious." She acknowledges that the church as an institution has lost its authority and its position as a cornerstone in society, but says that does not mean that Europeans no longer see themselves as in some way Christian. She expresses this tension as follows:

> In short, many Europeans have ceased to connect with their religious institutions in any active sense, but they have not abandoned, so far, either their deep-seated religious aspirations or (in many cases) a latent sense of belonging.[9]

It is in this context that Davie has coined the phrase *believing not belonging*, which causes her to take issue with the notion that even Europeans are truly secularized in the sense that they have forever abandoned a framework of religious aspirations, even if the sacred canopy of Christendom has been significantly dismantled. Hence, as we have indicated already, her contention that Europeans are not less religious but "differently religious."

How might we assess the notion that Europeans are not so much *less* religious than populations in other parts of the world but rather, and quite simply, *differently* so?

For particular historical reasons (notably the historical connections between church and state), significant numbers of Europeans are content to let both churches and churchgoers enact a memory on their behalf (the essential meaning of *vicarious*), more than half aware that they might need to draw on that capital at crucial times in their individual or collective lives. The almost universal take-up of religious ceremonies at the time of a death is the most obvious expression of this tendency; so, too, the prominence of the historic churches in particular times of national crisis or (more positively) of national celebration.[10]

Secularization as a reaction to the power of religious institutions and not to the heart of religion itself

The emergence of Europe as the oddity to be explained leads us to the third difficulty within the secularization story. For understandable reasons, most of the scholarship that has questioned the classic version of the thesis is American. Religion looks a great deal more resilient in the US than it does in Europe or, interestingly, amongst their near neighbors in Canada. They do not deny that a form of secularization exists in the US (a fact that Jeffrey Cox is quick to pounce upon);[11] rather, their *description of what it looks like* is very different from European descriptors. And that difference offers a further clue about the phenomenon that the secularization story is actually describing.

At root, Europe has experienced a range of responses or reactions to Christendom, especially the Christendom of the immediate post-Reformation period. Those reactions have been very different in the various parts of Europe. The nature of the secularization story – including its flexibility and its narrative structure – lends itself to a process of adaptation such that it can always appear to be describing the phenomenon accurately while in reality probably itself being a part of the reaction it is describing.

The secularization story is itself deeply rooted in a very secular way of looking at the world, and the depth of that connection may well induce a lack of clear-sightedness in understanding religion in terms of the significance of its persistence. In short, a secular view of the world sees the continuance of religion as an aberration or a weakness to be deplored. At best, thriving churches need to be thought of as strange exceptions, or as sects or cults, in an attempt to ensure that religion remains in its place – privatized and outside of the public square.

Secularization as signaling a shift in popular aspirations

But there remains at least one more version of the secularization story that has emerged recently and needs to be discussed. As we noted in the Introduction of this book, Callum Brown, in his provocatively titled book *The Death of Christian Britain*, has given a unique and interesting twist to the secularization story. Brown challenges the secularization thesis by using detailed statistical data that calls into question the idea that religion in Britain has been in decline since the advent of modernity. He correctly documents that membership and attendance of British churches was much more resilient and lasted for much longer into the twentieth century than is often admitted. Brown suggests that the change in the place of the church in British life did not really take place until the 1960s. He mentions specifically 1963, the same year that the poet Philip Larkin famously suggested that sex was invented.[12]

Brown posits a different conundrum from that usually addressed by the secularization theorists. Instead of asking why Christianity in Britain has been in a state of steady decline both in numbers and influence for such a long period of time, he asks why Christianity maintained its influence before suddenly and dramatically collapsing over a very short period of time. He writes:

This book is about the death of Christian Britain – the demise of the nation's core religious and moral identity. As historical changes go, this has been no lingering and drawn-out affair. It took several centuries (in what historians used to call the Dark Ages) to convert Britain to Christianity, but it has taken less than 40 years for the country to forsake it ... quite suddenly in 1963, something very profound ruptured the character of the nation and its people, sending organised Christianity on a downward spiral to the margins of social significance.[13]

How does Brown answer the question he poses?

As we noted in an earlier chapter, his primary thesis is concerned with the rise of the women's movement. He claims:

[W]omen, rather than cities or social class, emerge as the principal source of explanation for the patterns of religiosity that were observable in the nineteenth and twentieth centuries ... [W]omen were the bulwark to popular support for organised Christianity between 1800 and 1963, and second it was they who broke their relationship to Christian piety in the 1960s and thereby caused secularisation.[14]

A number of writers have taken issue with Brown over the importance he places on a single factor. Grace Davie argues that Brown's analysis of the special relationship between women and Christianity does not help to explain the collapse of similar and parallel institutions (themselves the products of modernity) such as trade unions, political parties and a variety of other social institutions.[15]

But there are two other dimensions to Brown's argument which present potentially much more difficult issues than the question of the women's movement in relation to Christianity. The first has to do with the ending of the discursive power of the Christian story. Again, as we have already noted, the capacity of a faith narrative to resonate deeply with the aspirations of a population or people is the single most important guarantor of the place and significance of that faith. The decline of this dimension of Christian influence, perhaps more than any other measure of influence, is deeply disturbing for those who still identify with the Christian narrative. Brown makes the case (for him strongly related to the role of women) that for the first time since the beginning of the Dark Ages, a major religious tradition has completely failed to renew itself in the transmission of the story to succeeding generations. For Brown this signals the unprecedented end of faith – hence the title of his book.

Is Brown correct in his estimation that Christianity is doomed to die in Britain, and by extension in the rest of the Western world? Of course he may be correct, but there are a few reasons to suspect that he may not be.

In describing the death of Christian Britain, Brown is engaging in two quite different exercises. First he is documenting the decline of churches as religious institutions. There is certainly no quarrel about his statistics – far from it. The statistical case that he makes against the idea that the churches have been in decline since the late eighteenth century is both accurate and welcome. But that does not necessarily mean that he has understood the way in which religious movements (as compared with religious institutions) renew themselves. It is certainly true that religious institutions rely heavily on the transmission of the faith within families, but religious movements draw much more widely for their growth than that single approach. Movements in their initial phase thrive on discontinuity and only later on thrive on continuity. They have the capacity to break into new social networks and to attract adults that have not had previous contact with that faith tradition.

The story of the eighteenth-century church in Britain was one of both decline and growth. Overall, church attendance was low and in continual decline throughout the whole of the eighteenth century.[16] Religious revival and growing new movements operated simultaneously against the background of a wider decline and loss of social significance for Christianity. It was not until the nineteenth century that these new movements reached the tipping points where their numerical growth and social significance began to be understood. Of course we now see the eighteenth-century revivals through the lens of their later social significance, but at the time the broader story was one of decline and death.

The churches of the eighteenth century were not renewed by the transmission of the faith through families (continuity) but by the radical discontinuity of conversion. Much of this new impetus of renewal and growth was condemned by the structures of power and authority within the church and instead emerged from the margins to challenge existing religious narratives. That pattern of renewal from the margins changed the landscape of church life in a number of important ways.

The numerical balance between nonconformity and the Anglican Church shifted towards the new churches and away from the Anglican Church to an extent that would have been unthinkable and even unimaginable in the first half of the eighteenth century. Some of the historical and even socially influential nonconformist churches that were part of the mainstream in the eighteenth century were not renewed and hardly appear on the ecclesial radar today. The Anglican Church was changed by the challenge of the new churches, taking into its system features of the more dynamic nonconformist churches to such an extent that it is possible to argue that the Anglican Church, in its evangelical expression, almost became another variety of nonconformity. At the very least, the Anglican Church in the nineteenth century became a voluntary church as compared with a confessional church.

It is possible to argue that in the present century, however much the historic churches have suffered a haemorrhaging of attendance and membership, renewal will come, but from the margins and not from the center. If that is so we should be looking much more at what is happening to the newer Pentecostal and charismatic churches, to the arrival of newer immigrant churches, and to unpredictable movements amongst youth that depend not on the transmission of the faith in family life but on the activity of vibrant congregations with the capacity to make converts.

But Brown's second exercise is far more challenging than the purely statistical evidence that he cites. He takes time to investigate the base of discursivity that the Christian story enjoys. In order to do this he takes time to "listen to people rather than counting them as numbers, as they speak about themselves and their lives."[17] In doing so he believes that he has identified what he calls a "moral turn" that has enabled (in this case) British people to reimagine themselves "in ways no longer Christian."[18] It is this part of Brown's project that is both moving and convincing. The reimagining that he describes is not restricted to the power of the women's movement, although clearly that is one of the narratives that exercises influence.

What should we make of Brown's contention that the population of Britain since the 1960s operates with an entirely different imagination and narrative? To put it another way: Do we agree with Brown's contention that secularization actually began in the 1960s, or with Grace Davie's contention that the people of Britain and Europe – the people of the exceptional case – are not secularized as much as differently religious?

Escaping Christendom

Clearly there are a number of strands in this complex equation. The backdrop is a fairly widespread desire to escape a socially coercive and politically manipulative Christendom. This is not, in the first place, an anti-Christian theme. The various nonconformist churches (and later in Britain the Roman Catholic Church) were only too anxious to escape from the influence of an Anglican Church that had immense privileges in terms of political and public appointments and educational advancement.

The desire to escape the dominance of state churches took different forms in the various parts of Europe. In France it was often deeply anticlerical, whereas in Denmark or Spain the church was viewed much more benignly by large portions of the population even when they did not attend. (Indeed, not feeling any compulsion to attend may be even be part of that benign feeling.)

But the desire to escape a more formal Christendom structure in society did not necessarily lead to the loss of social significance for Christianity. Indeed, one can see how the social significance of Christianity actually increased during the nineteenth century, as attendance at Sunday school and attendance and membership of churches rose dramatically. Political influence and involvement in key social structures such as charities and schools was certainly higher at the close of the nineteenth century than it had been at the beginning. As we have already concluded, the objection to Christendom as a structure changed the shape of Christian allegiance. It is still open to question whether it has ended all Christian commitment.

Escaping the influence of Christendom did have a strong anti-Christian edge for some. From the middle of the nineteenth century we can detect the rise of a militant anti-Christian secularist tendency which has wanted to curb or end the influence of the church and Christianity in European life. This has been a radical movement that has always been a minority but a vocal and powerful one. The radical atheist tradition had a number of circles of influence and almost a genealogy of connected individuals. One such grouping was associated with a collection of individuals centered at an address in London, 142 The Strand, which was a printing house. The group included a young woman who was later to publish under the name George Eliot. T.E. Huxley, among others, frequented this group and they were in turn connected with the most radical of atheistic groups in the twentieth century, the Bloomsbury Set.

One researcher has made the curious discovery that many of the members of the Bloomsbury Set were the grandchildren of the members of that earlier evangelical grouping, the Clapham Sect, which had done so much to establish the social significance of Christianity in the early part of the nineteenth century. Their best-known achievement, the campaign to abolish the slave trade, had been accompanied by a much wider campaign to inform the social imagination of a new century. Now, a century later, their commitments were being challenged and dramatically undermined by their own grandchildren and others. An intellectual aristocracy formed, composed largely of Cambridge alumni:

> Thus Lytton Strachey, Leonard Woolf, Maynard Keynes, and Saxon Sydney-Turner found themselves, in the Saturday evening meetings of the society, engaged in discussion with G.E. Moore, Bertrand Russell, Roger Fry, E.M. Forster, Desmond MacCarthy, and others who were to become lifelong friends.[19]

This was a formidable coterie, and one whose ideas were going to set the temperature for the debate in the universities ready for that huge intake of students anxious to create another new age in the 1960s. Formal Christendom had gone and now the Christendom of social significance was under deep attack.

But why did a Christianity which had endured for so long, seem suddenly to collapse under the weight of this new assault?

In part Christianity in the late nineteenth century had taken refuge on some very weak ground. Throughout the nineteenth century the Bible had been under attack, and rather than defend the core narrative of Christianity, which (as we saw in earlier chapters) the theology of the nineteenth century was singularly ill equipped to do, there was a tendency to settle for a spiritualized utilitarian position. In essence, those who were leaders in the church and leaders in the land were not inclined to fight over whether Christianity was actually true and on what basis the Bible should be understood and taught. Rather, all accepted that Christianity provided a useful social glue.

The evidence for the social impact of Christianity was all around. Sunday schools provided a sound moral education for the next generation, and the Christian church contributed enormously to the greater good through its community, charitable and educational activities. The utilitarian settlement (nowhere debated and certainly never written down) essentially offered to the church a privileged position in society in terms of social influence, in exchange for an understanding that Christianity did not really belong in the public square. Christianity was to be a chaplain to society, not a prophet. In surrendering the ability to talk about public theology, truth, the basis for ethics, and the critical business of how we might live together in a troubled world, Christianity set itself up to be marginalized and eventually ignored.

Competing narratives

Christians had never imagined that churches would continue to offer their services to the community but that no one would choose to come. Why did they choose not to come? Because however socially useful the activities of the church might be, they were all based on a narrative that had lost not only its intellectual credibility but more especially its power to attract. It was out of tune with the emerging aspirations and social vision of a new generation of westerners. Grace Davie expresses this development in the following way

> Alternative ideologies emerged, moreover, to take the place of church teaching – ways of thinking associated both directly and indirectly with the European enlightenment. No longer were the certainties of Christian theology taken for granted.[20]

It is, of course, possible to protest that since Christendom is not the same as Christianity, the collapse of Christendom should not mean the end of Christianity. The missiologist Werner Ustorf argues this case and in so doing hopes to help Christianity to be renewed with reference to the ways in which it is expressed in other parts of the world[21] – vibrant churches but no Christendom. Others, such as Linda Woodhead, tend to opt for a weaker and rather vague future for Christianity as "spirituality."[22]

Grace Davie may be right in saying that Europeans are not truly secular, but only "differently religious," but her beginnings of a solution, which lie in describing a move "from obligation to consumption,"[23] are frankly weak and fail to acknowledge that a move in this direction would simply allow Christianity to be colonized by the consumer narrative.

In his book *The Cube and the Cathedral*, George Weigal points out the deliberate symbolism of the postmodern construction in Paris called The Cube.[24] It represents a celebration and indeed a declaration of the intent of secular power. It was deliberately designed with a vast space beneath its overarching structure – a space exactly and intentionally large enough so that the Notre Dame Cathedral could, if moved, be encompassed by the cube.

In thinking about the future of Christianity in the West, we are engaged in a contest of narratives. The future for Christianity does not lie in being accommodated to The Cube, or indeed to any other story. It is time for these other stories to be unmasked in their totalizing intention, for their trajectories to be declared and examined, and for Christianity to contest the space that others seek to conquer. Christians can have the courage to do so – not out of arrogance, but simply because there is a crisis of culture in the West. Christianity does not need to reinvent Christendom to answer the deep cry that comes from the human heart, but we do need to examine the shape of the church.

It is to the question of how we should do this that we must now turn.

Imagining the Missional Community

*"Therefore, leaders who want to cultivate missional communities in transition
must set aside goal-setting and strategic planning as their primary model.
Leadership in this context is not about forecasting, but about the formation
of networks of discourse among people. It's about the capacity to engage the
realities of people's lives and contexts in dialogue with Scripture."*

(Alan Roxburgh)[1]

In the previous chapter we alluded to Callum Brown's conviction
that something decisive happened to religion in the West in general
and in Britain in particular during the 1960s. He described a general
decline in religious affiliation of such momentous proportions that
it is unlikely to be reversed. Most other observers point to a more
complex scenario and one that contains many contradictions.

The most obvious contradiction is the extent to which Europeans
retain a strong Christian identity but increasingly absent
themselves from attendance at any public worship service and
decline to engage in any active membership of any denomination.
The national census in Britain records that just under 72 percent
of Britons describe themselves as "Christian" and yet only eight
percent attend public worship on a regular basis.[2] The contrast
between these self-descriptors and actual attendance is even more
acute in Scandinavia.

The changing shape of church

The overall statistics hide the extent to which there are underlying
changes in patterns of commitment and attendance. To illustrate
this shift from the British scene, we may note four changes within
church life that are potentially significant.

First, within the historic denominations there is an overall growth in the evangelical and charismatic elements within each denomination. In the case of the Anglicans and Baptists the growth of the evangelical wings is sufficiently significant to impact the overall policy and direction of the denominations. These two denominations appear to have arrested their decline and arguably it is the growth of the evangelical wing that is overwhelmingly responsible for this shift. In the case of the Methodist Church and the United Reformed Church the evangelical wing is not sufficiently strong to have changed the shape of those denominations.

Second, the so-called "new churches," which are entirely evangelical/charismatic in their orientation, have grown to the point where they have become a significant presence on the church scene.

Third, the growth of churches composed largely of Christians from African, Asian or South American backgrounds has become a noticeable feature of inner-city life across the Western world. In Britain some of the largest and fastest growing churches in the land are "black led" churches.[3] The largest church in Britain, with a weekly attendance of some 10,000 people, reports that more than 100 language groups are represented amongst its attendees.

Fourth, the question as to who occupies the mainstream is beginning to be redefined. For example, in 1972 the Assemblies of God had a membership only approximately 10 percent the size of that of the United Reformed Church. In short, the URC was a mainstream denomination, while the Assemblies of God was on the margins of church life, almost regarded as a sect from a sociological perspective. Within the next few years, however, it is likely that the Assemblies of God will exceed the fast declining membership of the URC. A new mainstream is emerging.

It is very easy for evangelicals/charismatics from Anglican, Baptist, New Church and Pentecostal churches to work together. They share a growing set of aspirations, theological horizons, vocabulary and spiritual experiences that enables them to see one another as part of a larger, though variegated movement. Moreover, the worldwide connections of this movement to the growing churches of Asian, Africa and South America have become increasingly important in developing ecclesial policy and direction.

While these changes within the ecclesial firmament could seem encouraging, a more cynical perspective might be to conclude that the arrival of significant numbers of Christians from the Two-Thirds World simply serves to mask the overall decline of the church. In this sense this influx is a potential distraction, just as the arrival of significant numbers of Polish Catholics has temporarily distracted the Catholic Church in Britain from addressing its serious long-term problems. Commentators who hold this view point out that the attitudes of the children of immigrant communities are much closer to those of the host communities. Moreover, age-related studies of religious beliefs and commitments reveal a huge march away from the church on the part of the young.

In short, any encouragement that one might be tempted to draw from the growth of evangelical Christianity is minor compared with the broader pattern of alienation from the churches. To return to our earlier comment, this does not mean that Britons, or indeed any other westerners, are on the way to embracing a purely secular vision – but neither are they anxious to belong to churches of any description.

So the question that inevitably presents itself is this: What kind of religious framework is formed which has no connection at all with a formal religious narratival framework?

Evidence from research conducted on the spirituality of the unchurched[4] suggests that people still have significant religious experiences in their lives, but increasingly lack the language with which to describe those experiences and so become deskilled in their capacity to explore the religious and spiritual significance of their lives.

Grace Davie paints a picture of a Europe that is aware that "the 'keystone' of the arch of European values is crumbling, but they are not altogether complacent about his situation."[5] She proposes a society which is much influenced by secular perspectives but nevertheless spiritually open. She locates this shift toward spirituality in the context of a broader shift from modernity to postmodernity.

Davie associates the period of modernity with industrialization and with metanarratives drawn either from Christianity or from the secular notion of progress. She believes that the postmodern context has produced a new openness to a religious search which she describes as a "Fragmentation/decentring of the religious narrative but also of the secular or anti-religious narrative." She describes the new situation as one where there is "a space for the sacred but often in forms different from those which have gone before."[6]

In locating shifts in attitude towards religion in a broader cultural context Davie is reminding us that it is not just the church as an institution that is struggling to find its place in the new rushing waters of postmodernity. Institutions of all kinds, from political parties and trade unions through to the Boy Scouts movement and the Mother's Union, all face a decline in formal membership and a challenge to reimagine their purpose and vision.

Stephen Toulmin's incisive essay *Cosmopolis: The Hidden Agenda of Modernity* suggests that the secularization story that we discussed in the previous chapter is, in fact, merely a product of the all-pervasive metanarrative of modernity. In three or four pages he outlines the major features of the grand story of modernity. He begins with these words:

> Those of us who grew up in England in the 1930s and '40s had little doubt what Modernity was, and we were clear about its merits. It was our good luck to be born into the modern world, rather than some earlier, benighted time. We were better fed, more comfortable, and healthier than our ancestors. Even more, we were free to think and say what we liked, and follow our ideas in any direction that youthful curiosity pointed us. For us, Modernity was unquestionably, a Good Thing; and we only hoped that, for the sake of the rest of humanity, the whole world would soon become as "modern" as us.[7]

But he concludes:

> From the start, that whole story was one-sided and over-optimistic, and veered into self-congratulation ... The worst defects in the standard account, however, are not matters of philosophy, but of straight historical fact. The historical assumptions on which it rested are no longer credible.[8]

Harsh words, and even harder sentiments, backed up as they are with a blow by blow account of the historical inaccuracies and assumptions on which the standard view of the benefits of modernity are based. The story of modernity is not only deeply flawed but has long since ceased to be a useful account of the world in which we live.

Mission in the West

But even though Toulmin and others have demolished the story of modernity, its demise as an explanatory framework does not take us back to where we were before its arrival. The accuracy of the secularization story lies in the recognition that Newbigin[9] and others have illustrated so well, namely that the story of modernity, in the rrhetoric of some secularists, can be deeply antagonistic towards the Christian story. It is not the ending of faith but the arrival of another faith.[10]

While the coming of postmodernity – what Toulmin calls the "point of transition from the second to the third phase of Modernity" – opens the agenda for the church and the Christian metanarrative, it does not easily return us to it. Instead we are in a unique mission field without direct parallel.

So how has the church reacted to the mission field in which we now find ourselves?

The problem is hardly new. Even in the late nineteenth century there was an awareness in England that all was not well. That concern centered on the persistent absence of large sections of the working classes from church life. In the case of the nonconformists, even though their growth continued, it had fallen behind the growth of the wider population.[11]

Few thought hard about these issues, because the individual denominations still saw their numbers increasing.

When the churches did think about such matters, they understood their responses to them broadly under two headings. First, there was a concern to meet the needs of the poor, or to engage in incarnational mission. (This theme was particularly strong in the Anglo-Catholic wing of the Church of England, which planted many congregations in the poorer areas of the growing English cities in the latter half of the nineteenth century.) Second, there was a concern to attract and evangelize the working classes.

All kinds of approaches were attempted, from the radical work of the Salvation Army through to the establishment of the various City Missions and the Methodist Central Halls. Few were thinking more deeply about the broader issues of the relationship between church and culture. These were localized problems that could be addressed – or so it was believed – with better programs, dedicated action and higher levels of commitment.

But that was all to change with the shattering advent of the First World War.

The late Christendom response

Toulmin's view that we have already experienced two distinct phases of modernity is an important one. He suggests that phase one ended somewhere around 1914. Up until this time, modernity was supremely confident about the future. In a curiously parallel way, Christianity was also deeply optimistic about its own emerging future, not least because the seemingly secure sending base of mission in Europe was beginning to experience significant success in exporting Christianity around the globe. Another reason was that the churches in the US seemed everywhere to be meeting with success.

The modern missionary movement celebrated its successes of the nineteenth century at the Edinburgh Missionary Conference of 1910. The watchword of the Student Christian Movement, which was "to finish the work of the Great Commission in our generation," represented the flavor of the event. However, the cataclysmic tragedy of the First World War forced Christian leaders and thinkers to realize that all was not well with Christendom. The issue was not church attendance – which was at an all time high in most of the Western world. Nor was there a worry about the influence of the church with children and young people – again, Sunday schools and youth groups were in a very healthy state. Many church leaders were, therefore, greatly pleased with the social and political prestige that they enjoyed.

Theological responses

At a deeper level, however, some perceptive leaders recognized that in terms of a more profound influence on the worlds of culture and ideas, and therefore on the shape of the future, the church was becoming increasingly marginalized.

But the theological reaction hardly helped the church to recover its mission. That is because at the time the ascendancy lay with an emerging liberal theology which felt able to accommodate itself to the brave new world of the twentieth century. Robert Wuthnow points out the pitfalls of aligning the church so closely to the emerging world of science, technology and progress.[12]

The evangelicals, so dominant in the nineteenth century, so influential in the creation of the ecumenical movement, were largely bypassed and ignored. The liberal establishment embraced the ecumenical movement, not so much in its original vision of a church strengthened for mission, but more in a vision of a church united to deal with the challenges of the modern world – the thought was: if not a renewed Christendom, then at least a streamlined and more efficient one.

Liberal scholarship increasingly embraced the secular world and in doing so became shipwrecked. The ecumenical movement, now expressed largely through the World Council of Churches, could hardly avoid being aboard the same shipwreck. Lesslie Newbigin describes the coming collision as he recounts a key World Student Christian Federation Conference held at Strasbourg in 1960:

> The new vision was of the world, not the Church, as the place where God is to be found. Consequently "the mission and renewal of the Church in our day depends on acceptance and affirmation of the secular world in place of traditional Christian tendencies to reject it." The most articulate exponent of the dominant mood was Hans Hoekenkijk whose address called us "to begin radically to desacralize the Church" and to recognize that "Christianity is a secular movement – this is basic for an understanding of it."
>
> On a theological level I had to recognize the big element of truth in what was being said, but I was acutely aware at the same time of what was being ignored or denied … On a personal level I found the event very painful. It was painful to experience the contempt with which missions were held.[13]

If that was the beginning of the decade of the 1960s, a decade in which secular theology would increasingly gain ground, the end of the decade was even more shattering for Newbigin.

The event that closed the secular sixties for Newbigin was the "shattering experience" of the fourth assembly of the World

Council of Churches at Uppsala, where the ecclesiastical *soixante-huitards* took over the show – epitomized by a vaudeville artiste's singing of the satirical "there'll be pie in the sky when you die" to rapturous applause. "The scars left on the body of the Church by that traumatic decade," wrote Newbigin 15 years later, "will take a long time to heal."[14]

The Evangelical Renewal

Marginalized for many years, evangelicals had been quietly gathering strength. They had established a whole range of new institutions, notably Bible colleges and theological seminaries, as well as renewing older bodies such as the Evangelical Alliance. A growing interest in biblical scholarship helped in the development of educational institutions of note. Evangelicals had been heavily involved on the campuses and in a related set of activities amongst various professional bodies, especially through the work of the Inter-Varsity Fellowship.

Just as significantly, the products of the evangelical colleges had steadily grown many local congregations and their reputation as competent and dedicated pastors and leaders enabled them to be welcomed into congregations that previously would have seen themselves as rather more liberal in their theological orientation and view of society. The long years of marginalization had not resulted in a renewed vision of society. Indeed, it would be accurate to describe the predominant view as rather pietistic in tone. Separation from the world rather than the transformation of the world reflected an extractionist theology.

In keeping with this theme, many evangelicals looked with fondness to past revivals as representing a model for hope. The Welsh revival and the Methodist revivals of the eighteenth century were seen as the ideal to wish for. Prayer for revival in terms of the future, and prayer for conversions for the moment, were more the hallmark of evangelicals until the early 1970s. The crusades of Billy Graham, which had produced many of the converts who found their way to the growing Bible colleges, were seen as the way in which the church could be strengthened.

The evangelical cause was greatly strengthened from the mid-1960s by two related developments. First, evangelicals cautiously embraced the older classical Pentecostals, who had previously been regarded by evangelicals as peculiar sects, or even been listed as cults in some evangelical publications. Their vigor and strength enabled the evangelical cause to be taken much more seriously. Second, the growth of the charismatic movement – "a second wind of the Spirit," as some called it – also added many to the evangelical cause, which increasingly looked less like a "party" and more like mainstream orthodox Christianity.

The stature of Billy Graham was important in marking a new direction for evangelicals following the Lausanne Conference of 1974. This "coming of age" for evangelicals allowed them to take both the world and mission seriously. No longer was mission to be seen exclusively as evangelism, but from now on the social content of the gospel could be embraced.

However, significant as all this was for the growing worldwide confidence of the evangelical cause, the task of growing the church in the West, and particularly in Europe, did not look any easier. Most evangelicals despaired of the degree to which society seemed to be marching away from Christianity, and even though evangelical causes were much stronger than they had been, the greater numbers did not result in the broader culture taking Christianity seriously. Across Europe the churches were in drastic – some felt terminal – decline overall, however much the evangelicals might seem to be prospering.

With a growing sense that Western secular culture was becoming increasingly secular and hostile to Christianity as it approached the closing decades of the twentieth century, evangelicals looked for solutions to the hemorrhaging of church membership and attendance in most parts of the Western world. It had become apparent by the 1980s that the revivalist hopes of the charismatic movement were misplaced. However much some individual charismatic and Pentecostal congregations had grown, the hoped for scenario in which a renewed church would see hundreds of thousands clamoring to become Christians in the context of signs and wonders came to be seen as a false hope.

Evangelical leaders began to look for solutions to the problem of decline. There was a widespread recognition that however fondly they still regarded Billy Graham as a leader of integrity, the day of crusades (and indeed the language of crusades) was over in the

West. New solutions would need to be found. The 1980s and 1990s saw a succession of solutions presented – many of them emanating from North America.

Programmatic responses

The revivalist themes of the charismatic and Pentecostal movements still persisted and manifested themselves in spiritual tourism around the centers of the Airport Vineyard Church in Toronto and an Assembly of God congregation in Pensacola, Florida. But many of the same leaders who flirted with these unusual spiritual manifestations were also busy buying into programs of one kind or another. The Church Growth Movement, whether formally or informally, was the parent of many of these programmatic approaches. Purpose Driven Church (Rick Warren and Saddleback Community Church), Seeker Targeted Church (Bill Hybels and Willow Creek), Cell Church and G2 all offered programmed solutions to the problem of church decline. Wimber and the Vineyard movement offered an interesting combination of charismatic experience and Church Growth pragmatism.

Some of the underlying insights of these various programs were helpful. For example, the attempt to mobilize members around their giftedness, the conviction that Christians need to build significant relationships with unbelievers, and the awareness that churches need to be places of welcome and sensitivity are all valuable principles. But the basic approach of all these programs is deeply flawed.

There are at least three fundamental difficulties with them.

First, many of these programs are actually attempts to explain and systematize situations of growth that are, in fact, unique or highly distinctive. The growth of Willow Creek has more to do with the creative leadership of Bill Hybels and the team he created than it does with the 7-step strategy that they subsequently formulated by thinking about what they were doing. Communicating the 7-step strategy does not, in fact, lead to the replication of other Willow Creek situations, especially outside of the US. While Vineyard as a kind of ecclesial branding has had more success in the replication stakes, conversations with Vineyard church planters reveal that their success does not lie in replicating a particular model, but comes much more from their ability to attract and recruit creative leaders.

Second, at a very deep level, most of these approaches to the growth of the church actually represent the very best of an old model. However hard they try to disguise it, each in its own way relies on attracting new members to an essentially passive, audience-oriented model of church. It is what Alan Hirsch calls the classic evangelistic-attractional model.[15] Obviously there is a percentage of the population that is attracted to such a model of church, but in improving the model one is primarily increasing the likelihood of that "market segment" attending one church rather than another. Of course there are always enough stories of conversion to convince leaders that they really are reaching beyond transfer growth, and while there may even be some notable exceptions to the general rule that transfer growth is the main factor in the growth of these churches, it is hard to argue that the overall situation of the church is being significantly transformed through the import of church growth programs.

Third, most of these models have the church, and not mission, as the main object of their activity. The idea is not to change the world but to grow the church. Of course it is possible to argue, as some do, that a larger church will have a beneficial impact on the broader society, but in reality it is much more probable that the church will have been sidelined as just another consumer choice, a private matter for consenting adults, but not something that can possibly represent public truth. Mission must have the world as its focus. The church is certainly involved in mission, and in that sense its health is important, but it must never become the object of mission.

The Gospel and our culture

Lesslie Newbigin's sense of shock following the events of Upsalla in 1968 were compounded following his retirement in 1974 when he returned to Europe to take up a teaching post at the Selly Oak Colleges in Birmingham. His subsequent reflection on the situation of the church in the West led to the publication of his remarkable book *The Other Side of 1984*, in which he raised for the first time a key dilemma facing the church in the West.[16] Newbigin's core contention was that the crisis was not the absence of faith, but rather the full frontal attack of another faith – the secular Enlightenment project.

Other publications followed and around them grew a movement which became known as the Gospel and Our Culture project. It was embraced enthusiastically by, among others, the General Secretary of the then British Council of Churches, and the early advocates were mostly from the historic churches – individuals who would have seen themselves as inheritors of a broadly liberal theological view but were unable to embrace the secular theological turn that many theologians and pragmatic church leaders had taken in the 1960s.

Before long, evangelicals were also embracing Newbigin's analysis and a new kind of alliance between liberals and evangelicals began to coalesce around a program that Newbigin started to develop. The intention was to conduct a broad-ranging analysis of culture and its underlying belief system.

Although the Gospel and Our Culture project in the UK substantially ran out of direction in the early 1990s, two other projects that had received considerable momentum as a consequence of Newbigin's work did continue in the US. A research program headed by Wilbert Schenk resulted in a substantial body of writing under the heading The Missiology of Western Culture Project. The Gospel and Culture Network in North America simultaneously engaged in a research and writing project under the broad heading of Missional Church. The newly invented word *missional* was intended as a descriptor of churches in the West that saw their own context as one of mission, as compared with churches in the West that had a concern for overseas mission or traditional foreign missions. A missional concern included the notion of mission to Western culture as well as the immediate community contexts in which churches in the West found themselves.

Some of the same scholars, thinkers and writers were involved in both The Missiology of Western Culture Project and The Gospel and Culture Network.

Unfortunately, what happened in practice – however unintentionally – was that a concern for the missional church once again shifted the focus away from culture and towards ecclesiology. As we will see below, deep tensions began to develop between those who wanted to see the church as redefining its whole relationship with what was by now a deeply postmodern context and those who saw the challenge as shifting the church from maintenance to mission – a more sophisticated recalibration of the church, but not its fundamental reimagining.

The Emerging Church debate

The debate about the future of the church in the West in the context of mission has, to some extent, come to be polarized around what has become known as the Emerging Church. In part, this polarization is generational, but that alone would be too simple as an explanation. Not only can one find representatives of an older age group among the "emergents," but some younger practitioners are among those who are looking to transition the existing church towards mission, having moved significantly beyond the older Church Growth school but at the same time not being willing to abandon existing forms of the church.

It would also be too simple to say that the "emergents" are thoroughly postmodern and that those committed to the transition of the existing church have at least one foot in modernity, but there is some truth in that categorization. What is true is that nearly all of those on both sides of the debate have been heavily influenced by Newbigin and are well aware that the task facing the church in the West is huge. New programs will not be enough to enable the church in mission.

The missiologist Alan Roxburgh describes the two polarized groups as the Liminals and the Emergents. He describes them in the following passage:

> For me, the picture became startlingly clear during a recent conference. In one room, a group of eight hundred to nine hundred young leaders sat dressed in T-shirts and blue jeans, blogging away on their Macs and participating in journey groups. Meanwhile, next door, a group of fourteen hundred to fifteen hundred Liminals wearing Polo shirts, Dockers, and loafers feverishly jotted down notes from the latest, greatest speaker on how to make their churches more effective. It wasn't just a generational difference either – each group had leaders of various ages. And while they

were all attending the same conference, there was still virtually no sense of connection between the tribes.[17]

Not surprisingly, Roxburgh believes that these two groups or tribes need each other if we are to arrive at a newly imagined missional church:

> We need to recognize that each tribe has gifts the other needs. Each requires the other to understand the nature of the changes we are all experiencing. The Liminals can receive from the Emergents their gifts of imagination, critical evaluation and feedback, and holy restlessness. The Emergents can receive from the Liminals the gifts of history, tradition, habits, capacities and foundational theologies handed down to them through years of schooling and discipleship.[18]

Roxburgh's analysis suggests that the two groups are responding very differently to the deep and abiding problem of discontinuous change in Western culture, a change that is impacting every aspect of life, especially that of institutions, and significantly that of the church as an institution.

In discussing the five phases of change that he believes our culture is presently passing through he makes this comment:

> The shift in frameworks we need is how to imagine Christian life, congregational formation, and leadership in this world of discontinuous change. It is no longer a matter of how we get from our known world into a new world – that conversation is over! We are already living in a world drifting between the two. The questions now are: first, how do we as leaders learn to understand and function is this new world of discontinuity? And second, how do we cultivate our church structures to invite God's people to live and thrive in the midst of this uncertainty since we have no idea where it will end?[19]

Notice that there is no discussion of programs or of models of the church. Much of the debate between liminals and emergents (even on the radical end of the emergent spectrum, which sees no place for organized or institutional church at all) is still about models of church life, even if the model is a reactive choosing of no apparent model at all.

The Church of England has largely sidestepped the debate about models by calling for a "mixed economy". Some could see this cynically as a hedging of bets, given that no one knows what a future church might look like. A more sympathetic reading would be to say that there is great wisdom in moving away from a debate about ecclesiology in general, and models in particular, and towards a debate on mission. That does not mean that we can avoid all questions about the church, but paradoxically, if we want to reimagine the church it is best to begin with a new awareness of the task of mission. Scripture is a key resource for that task.

So, to conclude this chapter, a few propositions.

First, Christendom might have once been the problem and it certainly helped to produce a secular reaction to the institution of the church.

Second, Christendom has now gone and it not likely to return.

Third, Christendom undoubtedly acts as a shadow in terms of our imagination concerning the church both defensively and reactively (as liminals and emergents).

Fourth, the church is constituted by mission and we need to think about that mission in terms of both the life of the people of God as we live with one another and the life of the people of God as we live in relationship to the world. These are both important dimensions of living the story that we desire to tell, and they will occupy our next two chapters.

Reimagining a Counter-cultural Life

"Of course, there are a lot of people around who think they have what are called 'alternative' values: neither the values of the market, nor the values which the market has destroyed. One of the characteristics of the world since 1945 has been the generalization of eccentricity – what is sometimes called pluralism but is really the desubstantialization of all values except those of the market. The moral world, like the material world, is supremely represented as a shopping mall: it is now open to us to stroll between the shelves and pick out, or opt for, as the phrase has it, whatever takes our fancy – Buddhism, scientology, environmentalism, feminism, gay liberation, animal rights, Jehovah's Witnesses: in the emporium of pluralism you can have what you want and it is politically incorrect – that is, a restrictive, anti-market practice – to suggest that some commodities should not be put on sale. But the good is not something that we choose to acknowledge – it is something that we have to acknowledge. A true, a substantial value, is not something we have opted for, it is something that has imposed itself on us – as an obligation."

(Nicholas Boyle)[1]

As we attempt to escape the imagined lengthening shadow of Christendom and think about the church in the context of mission we quickly discover how difficult such an exercise actually is. The futurology business is generally a hazardous exercise, but that does not mean that we cannot imaginatively engage with the future based on present experiences of mission. To a significant extent that task will always mean a call to the Christian community to act in a counter-cultural manner, and this will be challenging.

In attempting to tackle that task there are four resources that we can bring to our aid.

The first is that of Scripture itself. We can study the Bible and attempt to empathize with the mission of Jesus and the process of entrusting that mission to his immediate followers. We can consider what it must have been like for the 12 to be sent out and for the 70 to be similarly commissioned. We may enter imaginatively into the discussions conducted by the Council of Jerusalem when they considered the critical missiological question: Must a follower of Jesus first become a Jew? There are many other key texts that can inform our missional journey at the level of imagination as it extends to engagement in mission.

Our second resource is that of church history. The church has responded to a variety of cultures in different times and in doing so has looked astonishingly different in its various localities. Even in terms of the story of Europe and the constant call to convert that continent, to reconvert that same territory after the Dark Ages, and then continually to renew the church through mission, the shape of the church has not been one of gradual change and development, but more one of convulsive upheaval. (Had they been able to meet, what would St Aidan of Northumbria have made of Calvin of Geneva?) The very fact that the church has been able to exist in such different guises, shaped and reshaped as a response to mission, can provide some creative fuel for our imagination, at least in terms of possibilities. In times of crisis the church has had to learn to live in such a way that counter-cultural values are vividly expressed. It has sometimes been noted that the monastic mission that spearheaded the re-evangelization of Europe in the Dark Ages not only *preached* the gospel but *demonstrated* it through a radical lifestyle. For example, in a period dominated by a warrior culture in which the strong took what they wanted, the monastic emphasis on a self-supporting lifestyle helped to re-establish the dignity of work, without which a society cannot be healthy. In a society where work has value, the poor and the powerless have a place of security and contribution.

Our third resource is that of the cultural context in which we find ourselves. We must have the confidence to believe that the Holy Spirit is both judging the cultures created by humanity and shaping and renewing them. We are called to a partnership in mission and therefore, since the initiative in mission always resides with God, we are both looking for his activity and seeking to reimagine our own life as a Christian community in dialogue with that which has already gone before us.

We will say much more about these first three resources and their creative theological interaction in the final chapter.

Our fourth resource, which we comment on in more detail in this section, is that of the contemporary church which is growing explosively around the world. Here we must be careful, though, because this is not primarily about numbers but primarily about the enormous diversity in terms of the shape of the church.

Lamin Sanneh argues that a world Christianity has emerged as "a variety of indigenous responses through more or less effective local idioms, but in any case without necessarily the European Enlightenment frame."[2] It is this amazingly diverse expression of Christianity emerging in places as culturally diverse as China, Chad and Chile that allows us to imagine the immense freedom that we have to conceive of what it means to be followers of Jesus, sharing together as a band of sisters and brothers.

Living counter-culturally as the community of the church – not just as Christians

The little phrase *sharing together* which is used in the previous paragraph is somewhat mischievous in its insertion – intentionally so. The reason is simply this: there are those who want to reconceive Christianity without the church at all. They believe it is possible to live as individual Christians without any reference to any organizational structure, even of the simplest kind.[3]

There are some obvious difficulties in such a position, though, not the least of which is that Jesus did seem to have some kind of church in mind when he commissioned his disciples, even if he may have been thinking of a "Jesus synagogue." We must remember that Jesus never abandoned either the synagogue or the Temple or the family liturgies such as the Passover; nor it seems, did the earliest church. Moreover, one can argue that however divorced individuals are from the church and however effective in their personal Christian witness, they are themselves the beneficiaries of an earlier communal life. More importantly, there is a case that suggests that a radical destructuring of communal life to the point where there is only the individual and never the community in any shape or form is to be over-influenced by an individualistic Western culture and under-influenced by the gospel.

Of course there is a place for missional communities that have very little structure and are fluid in their operation, perhaps in order to engage with many of the "tribes" of younger people, for example. But our conviction is that the very act, or process, of the creation of community is part of what it means to live counter-culturally as a Christian in the West. However much we might be out of love with the church as it is presently constituted, it is simply not an option to be forever living apart from Christian community. Some expression of communal life flows naturally from the encounter with a Triune God.

Called to be a missional community – the call to the West

The debate about the shape of a church thoroughly committed to mission in its immediate context began in earnest in the West during the 1990s. In many parts of the Western world the coming of the millennium caused Christians to look at the final decade of a whole millennium with a degree of evangelistic urgency – but now a new concern for mission, as compared with a more longstanding interest in the narrower topic of evangelism, began to appear.

In large measure a broader interest in mission had been occasioned by the kind of debate that Lesslie Newbigin had provoked through his use of terms like *mission* to *Western culture*. To some extent, also, large-scale immigration to the West from lands where the church is exploding with growth has occasioned a combination of puzzlement, fascination and joy. Sanneh notes:

> We have been given intimations of what is afoot in the world by the growing presence in the towns and cities of the West of members of new religious movements. In places as varied as Moscow, Paris, Amsterdam, Glasgow, London, New York, Atlanta, Washington, D.C., Chicago, and Los Angeles, new charismatic healing churches have sprouted as the far-flung offshoots of the worldwide Christian resurgence.[4]

The presence of such significant communities of Christians, with their strong emphasis on mission, will become increasingly important. They are part of the future of the church in the West, even if Western Christian churches are not entirely sure how to work with such a contribution.

The early debate about a missional church in the West tended to focus on what missional churches would do – what they would look like and what their programs would consist of.[5] That debate tended to be rather technical and almost managerial in nature, echoing earlier Church Growth teaching. But the debate soon began to move away from a consideration of the technology of mission towards an awareness that we are dealing here with art, not science.[6]

Two key drivers that helped to create a different kind of exploration were, first, a growing realization that no matter what program a church had, the leadership issue had to be faced; and second, the perception that no matter what a local church did, the cultural context in which a local congregation found itself was at least as critical in terms of mission as were internal factors.[7] In short, the problems are deep and long-term – there are no quick fixes available. Both the leadership and the contextual issues point to the need for deep cultural change within the life of the Christian community – what Alan Roxburgh refers to as "adaptive change."[8]

The key issues

What, then, are the key issues that will enable the church to grapple with fundamental cultural change?

At the purely technical level there are a variety of strategies, mechanisms and even programs that we can usefully employ to provoke change and engage in change management. But what needs to happen first (or at the very least in parallel with technical change) is the reimagining of the nature of the Christian community and of its task.

That reimagining needs to take place in two very different ways. First, a missional church has to engage with some core themes that flow naturally from the foundational narrative of the church. Second, a missional church has to recover its spiritual confidence as it seeks to create a community that lives in dynamic relationship with that narrative. So let us now return to the rules of engagement we discerned in chapter 3 in terms of how the church can become a subversive missional community in the context of the metavista world now emerging.

A missional narrative

Retelling the story in creative dialogue with contemporary culture

We have commented on a number of occasions in this book on Callum Brown's assertion that something happened in the 1960s to decisively shift the ground in terms of the credibility of the Christian narrative. We might not accept his explanation as to the causes of that shift, but it is undeniable that something cataclysmic did take place in the early to mid-1960s all across the Western world. The cultural aspirations that seized the imagination of the "beat generation" appeared to render the Christian story not just unbelievable but also unacceptable.

To a very large extent that shift was not so much the rejection of the Christian hope as expressed by its founder as much as it was an unequivocal reaction against the highly individualistic notion of a Christianity that had been reduced either to a morality tale by theological liberal, secularizing tendencies or to a story of personal redemption by the evangelicals of the mid-twentieth century. Such reductionist accounts of the Christian narrative were simply no longer convincing for a generation looking for a founding narrative that could act as the basis for experimentation with a brave new world.

The first fruits of the charismatic renewal seemed to promise the possibility of a retelling of the Christian story, a reconnection with the power of primitive Christianity, but somehow its locus in a Western evangelical and Pentecostal setting was too strong to remove its primary expression from a highly individualistic promise of ecstatic experience unrelated to the creation of community and cultural engagement. What was required was neither a renewalist theology that sought only to renew the institution of the church, nor a secular theology that called the church into the world. What was required was a public theology of radical cultural engagement that called the church to be constituted not for itself, nor even for the world in an abstract sense, but towards the remaking of human communities as deeply incarnational expressions of the church in mission.

This is still the challenge today. But to engage in such a mission will mean to take the Christian narrative much more seriously in terms of its world transforming possibilities. And that will require a very clear view of the difference between the gospel and the culture it seeks to transform. As Robert Jenson puts it:

> On a mission field, the church has to do its own work, and that means first of all that it has to know precisely what is *not* there in the culture, that it hopes to bring to it. Which is to say: it must know and cultivate its differences from that culture. All that talk a few years ago about the world setting the agenda, about seeing where God was at work in the world and jumping in to help, etc., was just a last gasp of the church's establishment in the West, of its erstwhile ability to suppose that what the culture nurtured as good had to be congruent with the good the church had to bring.[9]

We gain a sense of what that re-engagement might look like from Oliver O'Donovan's assertion that the task of the church is to point to the New Jerusalem as the future hope of the world:

> If the Christian community has as its *eternal* goal, the goal of its pilgrimage, the disclosure of the church as city, it has as its *intermediate* goal, the goal of its mission, the discovery of the city's secret destiny through the prism of the church.[10]

The distinctiveness of the church lies not in its life as an institution but in its founding story that calls the church to repentance just as it simultaneously calls the world to a new vision of its future. To truly engage the host culture the church has to learn how both to indwell that narrative and to reconfigure it around the key issues that the culture must see and hear for its own salvation (chapters 6 and 7).

The subversion of ideologies

To live counter-culturally will mean to confront rival ideologies and not to be subverted by them. As Francis Fukuyama points out, the collapse of communism means that the most potent ideology in the West is the consumer story as represented by the narrative of free-market capitalism.[11] In this story, happiness is measured in terms of economic success and by what we consume. In such a narrative everything, including people and values, are commoditized.

Free-market capitalism encourages a highly individualistic consumerism, and it is all too possible for that story to subvert the Christian story by attempting to turn Christianity into just another product – in this case a kind of spiritual self-help experience in which the believer is "ministered to." Such a subversion inevitably leads to a passivity that constantly demands to be fed and amused in order to be contented.

The willingness of the church to collude in the "marketing" of Christianity undermines all forms of genuine communitas. That in turn leads to an unqualified acceptance of the secularization story and the private/public split that has left many churches without any prophetic political mission at all. The Christian story should, instead, help us recover a deeper sense of personhood and identity which can then lead to the creation of genuine community. That can occur precisely because of the Christian insight that we cannot understand our own identity apart from an appreciation of the other. We will say more about this issue in the next chapter.

The nature of power and its redistribution

It is impossible to subvert the ideology of capitalism without facing the difficult issue of power, especially as it relates to leadership. The consumer story pretends to distribute power to those who are consuming. In reality, however, power is accrued by those who are busy selling us things. The Christian story is one that emphasizes team and mobilization, and one simply cannot have teambuilding and a widespread distribution of power in the form of a mobilized movement without thinking very hard about the nature and location of power.

Christianity does not have an easy history in relation to power, particularly in those periods where the emphasis was less on mission and more on the preservation and advancement of a complex institution in its relationship with secular powers. The emphasis on privilege, position, office, hierarchy and superiority, translated into the power of bishop, priest, pastor and preacher, has too often led to the abuse of power in all its manifestations – sexual abuse, emotionally and spiritually manipulative leaders, and authoritarian excesses like the Shepherding movement. This has sometimes been replicated in evangelical and charismatic leadership styles (which emphasize the notion of the "anointed leader") whenever the power issue is not faced.

In contrast, the Christian story reminds us that Jesus lays down his power for the sake of the world and the Holy Spirit redistributes power to the whole body of believers. The attractional model of church is sometimes based on old models of the powerful charismatic (usually male) leader – a model that does not lead to the creation of responsible mature human beings but tends to leave whole congregations in a state of infantile dependence.

Moreover, the power issue has never been adequately faced in the old form of seminary education. Men and women need a context in which to work together as equals, and the one-man band approach is perpetuated when you do not create a team environment where leaders simply have to learn to work together. If we are truly going to engage creatively as equals, then we need to be exposed at the training level to different theologies and different forms of being church. Similarly, underlying pathologies that will simply create insecure, temperamental, sarcastic or caustic leaders have to be faced and dealt with at this stage rather then being allowed to erupt and wreck congregations later.

It is difficult to imagine cultural engagement being undertaken by local churches operating in isolation. For cultural engagement to be adequately achieved, a trans-local context will be required. Perhaps the model adopted by doctors, to bring together general practitioners, all with their different skills and expertise, in urban health clinics where they are all responsible for the health of a whole community, has to be replicated in terms of the church. This will inevitably lead to what is already happening in towns and cities, namely the dismantling of the parish system, which can be notoriously territorial, personally limiting and isolating. To create missional leaders we have to create a context where community-wide cultural engagement is part of the job description. Without that context, leaders will fall back to the old pastor/counselor, preacher/evangelist or manager/administrator models, or simply abdicate leadership responsibilities altogether.

The reimagining of cultural identity

Zygmunt Bauman has offered some helpful insights by describing cultural identities as essentially fluid. He notes that at the height of modernity the entrepreneur/producer cultural identity was dominant and that in the context of postmodernity, with its over-aesthetic re-evaluation of life, it is not surprising that the sensations/seeker/gatherer model has emerged. This trend has been replicated in church life, with modernity-style mega-churches being dominated by the managerial economic model and postmodern churches occasionally being obsessed with the aesthetics of worship and lifestyle, with a focus on gathering around the production of artistic sensations or an appeal to seekers to come and consume. Indwelling the biblical story allows genuine fluidity in terms of identity, roles and ministries in the present context, but it also allows for constancy and stability in people and congregations.

Ministers and congregations become those who are immersed in the biblical background – their identities are defined by the story and the gospel they incarnate. As contemporary actors in the theatre of the gospel they are encouraged to improvise and experiment and not to allow ministry to stagnate. The gospel challenges them to embody the biblical story in their lives in community.

As we have already indicated, imagining and creating missional communities is difficult, not only because we are dealing with a Western culture that has been set on a different cultural trajectory from that of Christianity, but also because Western culture is itself in turmoil. The degree of difficulty is such that we may need to come up with resources and approaches that can offer additional assistance to beleaguered leadership teams struggling with issues of role and identity in a fast-changing landscape where change is disorienting because it is discontinuous.

In various parts of the Western world different kinds of missional order seem to be springing up. These are mostly lay orders, but the creative function of an abbot, the place of a mother house which can offer another space and place from which to find perspective, vows which are more than merely local commitments, and a set of nourishing disciplines which are stronger because they contain the possibility of external accountability, all offer a fresh stream of sustenance to leadership teams operating under stress.

Alan Roxburgh concludes his book *The Sky is Falling* with a very detailed proposition for the creation of a particular missional order. The precise details are, however, not as important as the key principle:

> This leadership *communitas* under the guidance of an Abbot/Abbess is more than an add-on to current congregational leadership. Questions about how to add this on to what leaders are already doing or about adding more staff to create a team miss the point. What is being proposed is a different perspective. The malaise of the church cannot be addressed through adjustment: it requires a change in the nature of leadership.[12]

Change of this degree of intensity really needs some external resources to help it along the way – not management consultants, but spiritual guides, men and women who will not give us answers, but will ask us the right questions. Individuals who, by their holy living and connectedness to a community of others committed to a rule of life, can help us, too, to create communitas.

The goal is movement and movements are unpredictable

The goal of all this activity is movement – not for its own sake but for the sake of the world. Movements require flat structures and are genuinely lay in their driving force. They tend to emphasize relationships, especially among leaders, and, rather like a virus, a successful movement will mutate many times to meet the local conditions that it finds. We should therefore expect the future to be shaped around highly flexible, relational networks that aim to build coalitions that can in turn impact society much more powerfully than a local congregation is able to do on its own.

Such networks facilitate quick and easy communication and deconstruct unnecessary and outmoded hierarchies of power and control. The new type of apostolic ministry which is most helpfully oriented toward the mission of the church finds a new role within the person-oriented efficacy of relational networking. Of course we need to be cautious even in the area of networks, because it is possible for leaders who emphasize the importance of networks to do so in terms of their own ministry and for the sake of the kudos that may come their way. If networks are there to serve the mission and expansion of the Christian church in a highly globalized world, then in terms of the gospel narrative and the example of Christ the relationships that leaders generate need to go deeper than purely functional ones.

Movement makers must actively look for the great surprises that reveal themselves in history as unexpected developments and outcomes. In that sense the future can more easily be imagined by looking at and adopting the themes of diaspora and exile. The elect community that learns to live in exile is the lean mean machine. Part of the experience of exile for Israel contained the injunction to seek the good of the community in which the people of Israel found themselves. To seek the good of others is unavoidably a social, political and moral act because by its very nature it seeks to answer the question, How do we live together such that the poor are aided and justice flows? This question (and any others that may flow legitimately from it) helps the community of God's people to become honed down to the bare essentials of mission and acts to create a deeply political (at least in the "public square" sense – see chapter 11) and prophetic community of grace and reconciliation. So we need to look for the church in exile if we want to understand the future. The church in exile is often the church on the margins which seeks to rebuild the structures of community in a world where the glue of community has come unstuck in the face of an unrelenting individualism. It is vital that the church that operates in this way does so for the sake of others and not in order to bolster its power and prestige. It is precisely this factor that disallows Christendom-type arrangements and allows the church to become a genuinely political movement in the sense of the questions that such activity inevitably raises.

The missional matrix – creative community living in the light of the story

The kind of church that is able to work creatively with the themes that we outlined above does not come into being by accident. There needs to be intentionality (even if it is an intuitive rather than a programmed intentionality) in the minds of leaders as they begin to imagine communities with sufficient spiritual confidence to embark on such a journey, and still more, to survive and thrive along the way. We can describe that intentionality as *imagination around a missional matrix*.

But before we come to the precise details of a "missional matrix" there is one other question that needs to be addressed. Alan Hirsch makes a powerful case for the rejection of "atttractional" models of church.[13] We agree with him, but are also aware (both from observing dynamic congregations and from our own experience of local church life) that there is a core difficulty here. Dynamic missional models are at least *attractive*, even if they do not *intend* to be *attractional*. There is a difference, and for us it is simply this: models that are purely attractional have a low expectation concerning the contribution of adherents. It is enough in an attractional model for people to attend and to give of their finances. But missional models that happen to be attractive are that way at least partly because they have a high threshold of expectation in terms of what members will do. In that sense adherents are not merely members, but both feel they are participants at a deeper level and, indeed, actually and objectively are so.

Now with reference to the missional matrix: we want to suggest that missional congregations need to work on five key areas over time. There is no priority in relation to these areas; they all need to be worked on simultaneously as leaders create the conditions for more imaginative engagements with culture.

The missional matrix that we want to discuss can be represented as follows:

The leadership team

In recent times there has come a significant interest in the subject of the ministry gifts referred to in Ephesians 4: apostles, prophets, evangelists, pastors and teachers. When describing these gifts some writers have used the phrase *apostolic team*,[14] since it is very clear that leadership and ministry in the New Testament operated substantially around one or other of the various apostolic bands that traveled widely and remained connected in loose networks. More particularly, it was the actual operation of leaders who called themselves apostles in the context of the emerging "house churches" (sometimes called "the new churches" or "new apostolic

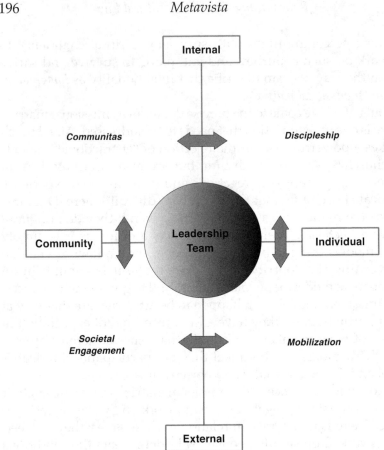

networks") that began an innovative discussion around the issue of the Ephesians 4 ministry gifts.[15]

It is abundantly clear that no matter how important each of the ministry gifts is, it is the apostolic gifting that draws the other gifts into a team relationship. Hirsch calls this process a part of "apostolic genius," and he makes the claim that the apostle is the "custodian of Apostolic Genius and of the gospel itself."[16] It is the job of the apostolic figure to create the team environment in which all of the various ministry gifts can flourish.

Of course there are difficulties as we try to engage with the concept and reality of an Ephesians 4 leadership team, which we might also simply call an *entrepreneurial* leadership team. There are at least three core problems. First, given that most churches have worked for a very long time with the gifts of pastor and teacher as defining the key leadership style, engineering a transition in which other gifts can be present is usually painful and disturbing. That is why many of those who have the entrepreneurial gifts associated with apostles, prophets and evangelists are usually to be found in congregations that they have either begun themselves or have led to such significant growth that those congregations have effectively become church plants.

Second, most situations where there is an apostolic team in operation have occurred organically and have not been engineered by the deliberate recruitment of appropriately gifted individuals. The founding leader or leaders have usually operated intuitively, adding to the team as they have seen needs, resources and opportunities appropriately matched. An awareness that we need a wider range of gifts beyond the purely pastoral and teaching functions helps us to develop the potential to think about leadership from the perspective of a wider horizon and so to deliberately create the kind of innovative leadership culture that is much more likely to reveal, cultivate and attract the entrepreneurial gifts required in such a team.

Third, entrepreneurs are not always team players. Actually producing healthy, functioning teams out of individuals who can often be difficult, high-order introverts – or extroverts – is a challenging exercise. Small wonder that congregations easily revert to the safe choice of a pastoral type to love and care for the flock, rather than embark on the white-knuckle, no-safety-belt ride that apostolic teams sometimes engender. Yet it is precisely in this somewhat dangerous environment that individuals who are currently outside the church find a challenge and then their calling and fulfillment.

What we are describing, therefore, is an organic process rather than a ready-to-go formula. The best apostolic teams will emerge over time as friendships of grace flow from a constant grappling, not just with the mechanics of the task but also with the profound application of the gospel both in the lives of those that the teams encounter and lead and in the team members themselves. Strong friendships bring flat leadership structures as love and respect flourish and grow. Success in building a team culture that clearly reflects the grace of the gospel itself is an essential, because it is precisely this type of team culture that creates the conditions for those cultural values to be represented in the rest of the congregation or movement that is being led.

Discipleship

All movements begin with high levels of expectation regarding the participation of their members. That participation or mobilization is not possible without a high threshold in terms of behaviors. That is a particular problem in the West because of the cultural context in which we find ourselves. A consumer culture in which little is expected of us except for consumption of various sorts, where we derive meaning through that which we consume, is not sympathetic to notions of Christian discipleship with the accompanying implication of personal disciplines.

In one sense discipleship is always a challenge. It was so in the time of Jesus – at least one young man was sent away sorrowful because of the cost of discipleship. Jesus did not design a discipleship that was easy to embrace – after all, it ultimately led him to the cross and his challenge to succeeding generations is also to pick up our cross in order to follow him.

But at least other generations have understood easily the need to work hard in order to survive. The generation born in the West since 1945 is probably unique in the history of the world in that the basic needs of life are guaranteed through the structures of the welfare state. Shelter, food, clothing, heat and light – the essentials of life – are not really in question for those fortunate enough to live in the West.[17] The employees of the welfare state may on occasion make mistakes, and sometimes those mistakes can be serious, but in general we do not have to worry about actual survival. The idea of discipline, of hard work, of taking responsibility for who we are and who we might become are more deeply counter-cultural now than probably at any other time in the history of the Western world.

Ironically it is not that any of this is bad in itself. It is commendable not to have large proportions of the population so poor that they are struggling to survive. It is good to be able to enjoy many consumer products – but the curious reality is that the order of the day is often not enjoyment but boredom. It is as if one needs a particular kind of discipline to deal with abundance and we have not yet found a society-wide means of inculcating that. A number of thinkers attribute the roots of this problem to an earlier association of happiness with economic well-being.

Commenting on the relationship of happiness to virtue one writer notes:

> You don't just arrive at a blissful destination and then stay there for the rest of your life. Happiness doesn't just happen; it must be prepared for, cultivated and sustained. Over and over again, the match must be refought and the victory gained anew.[18]

This problem is sufficiently deep in contemporary Western culture for us to have to address it in more detail. Essentially what we are referring to is the notion of discipleship as counter-cultural living, which, as Robert Bellah and his associates have noted, relies on fostering and developing new "habits of the heart."[19]

(1) Developing habits of the heart

The phrase *habits of the heart* is used to describe those core disciplines which are normally built deeply into the lives of individuals and communities and enable those individuals and communities to flourish. Bellah's thesis suggests that a rampant individualism, combined with a strong utilitarian approach to society, has undermined those habits to the detriment of individuals and community life. A related argument is made by Robert Putnam in his book *Bowling Alone*, in which he describes the importance of social capital in creating the kind of communities in which people desire to live.[20]

A similar conclusion flows from Joseph Ratzinger's analysis of Herman Hesse's novel *Steppenwolf*.[21] He suggests that Hesse presents the radical individual as the isolated individual and ultimately the lonely individual. That loneliness leads to boredom and hence to thrill-seeking and so to high-risk behavior. The ultimate thrill becomes death itself.

Larry Rasmussen picks up the concerns of John Dewey in relation to the "machine age" and its destruction of small communities and their values without ever arriving at the "Greater Community," by noting the tendency of modernity to depict persons in economic terms as always being autonomous creatures able to make and unmake relationships as a series of choices.[22] Such processes (the destruction of communities and the depiction of individuals as economically autonomous) dissolve not only communities but also any sense of a public good, or in Putnam's terms, social capital.

The construction of a vision of society in which individuals are only ever economic beings living in autonomous isolation has profound implications for the way in which we seek to be happy. For Ellen Charry the older tradition in which happiness was always connected to virtue was broken by modernity, and particularly by Kant's view of ethics which tended to see ethics as obedience to a set of known frameworks – we might even say obedience to a joyless duty.[23] Happiness and love were not part of the moral life, still less goals of such a life.

With such a crucial separation between happiness and goodness having been made, there was a strong sense in which Christians had to make a choice between a concern for happiness and an emphasis on goodness. Not surprisingly, given such a choice, Christians chose goodness over happiness. That choice was accelerated to some extent by the location of a concern for happiness in the secular, hedonistic and utilitarian theories of Bentham, Mill and Sidgwick. In such a setting pleasure is separated from goodness and located much more in material or economic well-being.

The separation of happiness from virtue is critical in the sense that before the Enlightenment most traditions of thought recognized that part of being happy involved learning to live one's life in good relationship with others, developing disciplines in a community context in order to cope better with the vicissitudes of life – suffering and its inevitable hardships. As Richard Schoch claims:

> We cannot find happiness in isolation. A certain amount of quiet and calm reflection is surely necessary just to understand what happiness means, but the activity of *becoming happy* is one that binds us to the world. Finding happiness means not despising the world but wanting to create a better one within it. We might say, then, that our happiness is nested in the world, for the world is where, over a

lifetime, we patiently build up the layers of a habitat – and the action of "habit" is crucial here – that we can proudly call good. [24]

What, then, are the "habits of the heart" that we need to cultivate?

In one sense these habits are culturally defined. In general we can say that people need to develop a capacity to be attentive to the needs of others as well as to their own needs, to develop attitudes towards honesty, integrity, fidelity and long-term goals that build personal resilience combined with sensitivity to a common good. The exercise of charity in the broader sense of acts of kindness and not just the giving of money helps to build communities that are worth belonging to. To some extent the precise content of appropriate "habits" needs to be discussed and agreed by the individuals and communities that are called to practice them.

(2) Spiritual disciplines

There is an important sense in which we need habits of the heart as a foundation for developing spiritual disciplines. Spiritual disciplines offer us a range of commitments and rhythms which build on other good habits, further reinforcing them but also moving us closer to a capacity to hear God and so develop a sense of direction in relation to our calling or vocation in the world. Key disciplines would include a commitment to daily times of prayer, to weekly worship and to regular times of retreat (say three times a year).

In all of this there are various resources that can help us. First, there are those who might act as spiritual directors for us. Their key function is not to tell us what to do but to ask us the right questions that will sensitize us to what God might want to say to us.

Then there are those people who might be mentors along the way. Mentors helps us to interact with goals that we might want set for our lives, they ask key questions about how we are doing in relation to those goals, and they help us to be accountable for our development as people in agreed areas of life.

Finally there are those who might coach us in specific skills that we need to develop. It is likely that we will want to draw on the abilities of a range of different people over time who can help us develop in a variety of areas.

The development of strong spiritual practices is crucial for us to sustain our lives in times when institutions are weak. In the past, we might have been able to rely on broader institutional structures to compensate for our own poor investment in this area. In times of cultural and institutional transition we need to ensure that we have developed our own resources. One study of church leaders in the West revealed that a majority of clergy have no personal spiritual disciplines at all.[25] The whole body of Christ needs to take responsibility for the cultivation of strong spiritual lives amongst the people of God.

Mobilization

The intention of a discipleship process is that it should lead to action. But we should not wait until a moment of graduation or completion before we act. On the contrary, discipleship assumes an action-reflection model. We note in the New Testament that Jesus sends out the disciples long before they might be considered fully-fledged completers of the Jesus School of Discipleship Training. They are fully involved participants in the mission as part of their training.

Of course the discipleship process is never completed – as followers of Jesus we remain lifelong learners. But it is also the case that there comes a time when as individuals we accept responsibility for the calling we have been given and begin to experiment with a specific ministry to serve others. Every Christian has a vocation that needs to be exercised.

At its best, Christianity is a movement of lay people gifted, called and empowered to participate in the mission that God has given to his whole church. The role of laypeople is not simply to support the clergy in their vocation as though ministry belongs to the clergy and the support of ministry to the laity. Certainly there is a place for those who have particular callings within the life of the church, but it might be better to say that the calling of the clergy is to empower and support the laity in their ministry to the world in which they live. The laity are never called by Jesus Christ to be passive audiences, consumers of grace, forever ministered to.

The appropriate task of a leadership team is to create a culture in which all expect, as the norm, to be active, mobilized ministers. In fact, one might go so far as to say that the single most important measure of their effectiveness as a team should be the extent to which they succeed in this task.

The growth of a given congregation or movement critically depends on its ability to generate a fully mobilized workforce. Of course, it is possible to run an institution – even a very successful one – without such a radical mobilization, but the inevitable focus of such a body will be its own well-being with little focus on the external world except mission as a program – one small part of what the church does, but not its raison d'être.

Societal engagement

The mobilization of many individuals requires a social context in which the ministries that mobilization produces can be exercised. Most Christians will engage with the world within a relatively small distance from their home and workplace. Of course, for some people the workplace can be a huge distance from the home and that raises particular challenges for those individuals – but again, most people wish for some kind of engagement with the community of people where they worship, where they have friends, where their children go to school, and where they play sport or socialize with others.

The call that comes to the missional church is to exegete the community in which it is located – to engage in what some call *ethnography*, such that the stories that make up a given community are well understood. The members of a given congregation need to be helped to see how their personal stories interact with the various community narratives. As this process develops it gradually becomes clear how the missional church can engage with its community to bring transformation to it.

We need to be very clear about this point. It is not about finding opportunities for evangelistic outreach, nor is it just a matter of healing the hurts of a given community. Both of these activities may form part of a transformational agenda and encounter, but the *key* issue becomes: How can the church, working with a gospel of grace, help to create transformed communities? With this go questions like what partnerships need to be developed, what problems need to be overcome, what resources will be required, and how can prayer and a creative reimagining of what a community could look like begin to create a new reality?

Communitas

Both Alan Hirsch and Alan Roxburgh[26] draw on the idea of communitas developed by the anthropologist Victor Turner who was describing rites of passage among some African people groups. Roxburgh had earlier produced a book which drew on Turner's related concept of liminality. The point that both authors make is that in concentrating on _community_ there is often a tendency to drive a given congregation towards an unhelpful preoccupation with the quality of community life such that the outside world becomes an inconvenient interruption. Mission becomes something we were going to do once we have established a high quality of community. Strangely, though, the day when we finally feel satisfied with our community life never arrives – paradoxically, an exclusive concern for community does not help with the very creation of the quality of community life that we seek.

By contrast, _communitas_ describes a group of people bound together by both the disorientation of an unfamiliar situation (the rites of passage) and a task that needs to be undertaken (to become adults).

Thus: while community is inwardly focussed, _communitas_ is outwardly focussed, but uses the community as a resource.

There is a clear application of this concept for mission. It is the developed community – developed from the insights of the personal disciplines of discipleship, but also from the experience of profound friendships – that is able to engage society in transformational activities. The experiences of transformational engagement can help a healthy community to sense and clarify the missional journey on which it has embarked. The creation of these kinds of communities will require both a healthy congregational life and also the experiences of community in smaller groups. These smaller groups might be a combination of cell groups, small prayer groups (possibly triplets) and even accountability groups where the journey of discipleship interacts with actual participation in a small group setting. But whatever the precise formulation of the smaller group, the actuality of participation is a key ingredient in the overall process of creating a missional community.

The art of missional lift-off

It should now be very obvious why the establishment of this type of church cannot be a linear process where any single element of the missional matrix takes priority over any other but why all the elements have to be tackled simultaneously. The various ingredients in this process critically depend on one another for their effectiveness.

Those who have tried to produce congregational cultures of this type report that one can work for a long time without anything much seeming to happen, and then suddenly it all seems to "take off." One person who was in a congregation in the process of "take-off" described it as "being in the zone." What he meant was that they had worked hard enough and long enough on the process to have placed themselves in the zone where God by his Spirit could intervene and things just seemed to happen. They happen when you are "in the zone," but creating the conditions for the zone takes a great deal of hard work.

It is rather like a ship in a dry dock. Once the repairs are completed it is time for the ship to float, but a great deal of water must be pumped in before the ship actually floats. Then, suddenly, there comes a particular moment when the ship does float. There is nothing special about the last few gallons of water; it is just that they came on top of all the other gallons.

To some extent what we are describing can be thought of in terms of expectancy theory. As people begin to have experiences of God, expectation is raised and the more people expect things to happen the more they do. But creating the conditions for all that to happen is an art form; there is not the certitude of empirical method or engineering production.

Assuming that we can create the kind of confident missional communities that we describe above we now have to begin to imagine how such communities might construct a broader engagement with Western culture such that the culture itself takes a new turn – or occupies a new metavista.

11

Towards a Hermeneutic of Imagination

"The engagement of the religious citizen with a democratic regime is perhaps best captured under the notion of "pilgrim citizenship'. Recognizing the penultimate character of the public realm, believers will not seek their final resting place in this sphere of power and persuasion. Nonetheless, people of faith will often find the public realm to be a place of genuine hospitality and fulfilment, a place in which their own deepest convictions and beliefs are tested, criticized, confirmed, and reformed."

(R.F. Thiemann)[1]

The idea that religion in general and Christianity in particular should reappear on the public scene in the West is as disturbing to some as it is surprising and welcome to others. There are many threads in such a development, and while this is not the place to give a comprehensive overview we need to note at least some of them.

The relationship between religion, or faith, and the Enlightenment project has not been an altogether happy one. The deeply embedded notion of Enlightenment thought that it is essential to maintain "a prejudice against prejudice" often tacitly assumed that religion was the greatest representative of prejudice and therefore necessarily must be resisted. Simultaneously, the Enlightenment tradition also valued freedom and therefore religious belief had to be permitted as one of those freedoms. But freedom of religious practice was variously understood either as freedom *from* religion (the French tradition), or as freedom *for* religion (the North American tradition). More recently it has tended to be the former that has predominated in Western democratic debate.

In recent decades this approach has been experienced by faith groups as an attempt to marginalize religion to the point where religion is simply not permitted to make a contribution to public life. There is even a suggestion that religion is harmful and not something that children should be exposed to (as was depicted, for example, in the film documentary *Jesus Camp*, which highlighted what amounts to a form of fundamentalist religious abuse of children in the US). In short, secularization, or the triumph of reason, will not be complete until religion is finally eradicated both in the private and the public sphere. The irony of the religious nature of this kind of secularizing crusade has not been lost on some observers:

> The news of modernity's death has been greatly exaggerated. The Enlightenment project is alive and well, dominating Europe and increasingly North America, particularly in the political drive to carve out "the secular" – a zone decontaminated of the prejudices of determinate religious influence. In Europe, this secularizing project has been translated, ironically but not unsurprisingly, into a *religious* project with increasing numbers of devotees of "secular transcendence" – all the while marginalizing forms of determinate religious confession as "dogmatic." In the United States, the march of the secular finds its expression in the persistent project to neutralize the public sphere, hoping to keep this pristine space unpolluted by the prejudices of concrete religious faith.[2]

In the US the greatest reaction to this secular crusade has been that of the Religious Right, which has not only given the impression of taking over the Republican Party, but has forced the Democratic Party to reassess its recent view of religion.[3] As many have noted, the Religious Right has chosen to fight the onslaught of modernity with the weapons of modernity at the very time when all of those weapons are under new scrutiny.[4]

In Europe it has often seemed as if the fight has long been settled in favor of a secular establishment:

> Up until recently there had, at least, been something of an ad hoc resolution in Britain. The role of religion in public life was widely thought to have been satisfactorily settled, in practice, if not in theory. There was, as Sunder Katwala, Director of the Fabian Society, has written, a:
>
>> "Largely absent minded maintenance of an established Church, whose leaders' public moderation often bordered on agnosticism

within a society which thought of itself as increasingly secular."

That arrangement was itself relatively harmless. Indeed, when considered alongside the various remaining ceremonial and cultural links between church and state, it was possibly even positive, at least for reasons of social cohesion and tourism. There may have been a few mopping up exercises remaining – bishops in the Lords, blasphemy laws, perhaps even disestablishment – but these were little more than the finishing touches to a newly deconsecrated public square.[5]

The rather gentlemanly and polite British solution described above actually masks a much more aggressive European approach towards Christianity of which the British settlement is a part. Joseph Weiler, a South African secular Jew, has offered a penetrating analysis of the recent denial of the positive contribution of Christianity in European history under the heading of "Christophobia." In a summary of his views by George Weigel we read:

The issue of historical memory is not a matter of interest to historians alone. Historical memory, Joseph Weiler insists, is essential for moral community. And there can be no free political community without the foundation of a moral community, a community of shared moral commitments.[6]

Curiously, it has been precisely in the wake of the apparent victory of secular forces over religious ones that faith has made an unexpected re-entry on to the public stage. This *re-entry* is by no means unambiguous and the term re-entry could certainly be contested as an assessment of what has happened in recent years, but there are some good reasons for believing that a new dialogue is opening up between faith groups and the wider Western society.

Why the rapprochement?

What has occasioned these recent beginnings of a rapprochement between those who are inside faith traditions and those who are outside those traditions who have a shared concern for the future of our world?

In truth there are many tributaries that contribute to this new stream of thought, but three are important for our immediate context.

The limitations of modernity

First, the limitations of modernity have become increasingly evident:

> The claims of contemporary sciences, both natural and human, are a good deal more modest, seeking neither to deny nor to explain away the contingency of things.[7]

That same contagion of modesty has impacted politicians as they have grappled with new uncertainties regarding how society might actually be framed. The old ideologies around which political parties have functioned for much of the modern period have largely disappeared and new ways of thinking about political life are being sought. The twin dates of 1989 (the fall of the Berlin Wall) and 2001 (the attack on the Twin Towers) signaled the end of an era in terms of political certainties concerning the shape of our world. Even the assumption that the job of politicians is only to expand for ever the GNP of every nation state is up for examination.

The real contribution of faith communities

Second, faith communities, however debilitated in terms of national institutional strength, have proved to be more durable at a local level than some expected.[8] The role of religion in the collapse of communism, and specifically the role of the Pope in the demise of the communist regime in Poland, was never anticipated. The sight of thousands of shipyard workers in Gdansk kneeling in the open air as they prayed together caused bemusement among some in the West.

The governments of many Western nations have come to recognize the potency of faith in the provision of social care, even to the point of recognizing that faith communities often do a better job than government agencies.[9]

Similarly, the prominent role of faith groups in campaigns against third world debt (the Jubilee Campaign), and against poverty more widely (Make Poverty History), has earned the respect of many government ministers for the positive contribution of religious commitment. In a curious way the public square has opened up to religion before faith groups have demanded any particular place in it. Indeed, the invitation to participate has sometimes led to a degree of confusion as Christian leaders have wondered how to respond to this unexpected attention.

Doing public theology

Third, despite the relative unpreparedness of many Christian leaders for a dialogue about public theology, a good deal of thinking has been taking place over the past 40 years in academic circles about a Christian involvement in the public space. The thinkers that we have in mind fall into two categories. Those in the first category are sometimes referred to as the new traditionalists – writers such as Hauerwas, MacIntyre and Milbank. Those in the second category are also conservative from a theological perspective but are more progressive in terms of their political thought. These would be thinkers such as Wolterstorff and Hunsinger.[10] (These are by no means the only thinkers in this field; one could also add luminaries such as Oliver O'Donovan.) Since we examined the important contribution of all these current thinkers to political theology in chapter 7, suffice to say at this juncture that it is the new traditionalists who tend to be the persons who have operated in a combative debate with an older liberal, secular tradition which has seemed to want to keep faith out of the public square. Their work has offered a new generation of graduates a means of engaging with public life that moves beyond an older liberal churchmanship without wishing to operative reactively in the manner of the Religious Right.

We could also add to this scholarship a body of work emanating particularly from thinkers in the field of sociology who are exploring the role of social capital (Robert Putnam, Peter Berger and Jeffrey Stout) and additional understandings of community.

This academic reflection, along with the growing credibility of faith groups locally and nationally, creates the possibility of a new creative imagination about how we might live together and order our shared world differently from the way a secular liberal establishment has been doing it while excluding religion as a contributor.

Imagining our future differently

As we prepare to reflect on the contribution of a new, creative imagination we need to be clear about what we mean by certain key words and phrases that are part of the currency of this debate.

Defining our terms

The term *secular* we take in its original Christian meaning to refer to the things of this age. In this sense, as we noted in chapter 4, Christian thinkers offered the term secular as a Christian contribution both to limit the power of the church in terms of the things of this world, and also to limit the power of the state by reminding secular rulers that this age will be judged by the world to come.

By *secularized* we mean the somewhat more hostile removal of the sacred from any influence in this world and in this sense to refer to a program to see the world as rightfully operating without the need for a sacred canopy.

The phrase *the public square* was used by Richard Neuhaus and others to describe the place where debate and decisions take place. As an image it harks back to eighteenth-century small-town squares, which usually contained all the major social, government and business institutions in physical form. Town hall, law court, chamber of commerce, church, and places of entertainment would all be found in the main square. This was the public space in which public life was enacted and it was referred to as the *commons*. We now use the term *public square* to denote not so much a physical place, but rather a metaphorical space for mutual acknowledgement and ongoing public debate.

The term *civil society* was first coined by Hegel to denote a new reality that was neither the state nor the family nor the church, but the economy as shaped by the growing business community and later by charities and other institutions that came into being partly in response to these new economic power centers.[11] Some have come to use the term to describe the space between rulers and the ruled and so to restrict its meaning to only the space occupied by charitable and welfare organizations.[12] Writers like Habermas have used the term to describe a much more complex set of interactions between what he calls the "lifeworld" and public life in the shape of politics, the media and the marketplace. It is in the arena of civil society that public opinion is courted and shaped:

> The core of civil society comprises a network of associations that institutionalizes problem-solving discourses on questions of general interest inside the framework of organized public spheres.[13]

Public theology, therefore, is that thinking that we do in the public square about civil society, but also more widely about secular society, of which Christians are also fully a part.

The forces of secularization in general and secular humanism in particular resist such public theology on the grounds that Christians have a set of private beliefs which inform their public theology and that the views of Christians about public life make no sense unless one shares those "sectarian" commitments. Since most people do not share those private beliefs, it would be better for Christians not to engage in public theology but to restrict themselves to debates about doctrine, ecclesiology and other theological speculations which are unrelated to public life of any kind.

This argument completely misses the significance of what we call *fiduciary frameworks*, which apply to everyone contributing to public debate. Such frameworks, or plausibility structures, honestly accept that we all have traditions of belief, opinions and faith presuppositions which we bring to public life and that indeed it is in such public debate that these prior commitments are tried out and tested.

The way ahead

So how can and should Christians engage in public theology?

Three options need to be rejected outright. First, we are not engaged in an attempt to create Christendom by stealth. An appeal to a Christian heritage, while helpful in some respects, does not by itself have sufficient intellectual content to be sustainable as an option.

Second, we are not seeking to use the government to be a public enforcer of private morals. While it is undoubtedly the case that private actions have public consequences, it is essential that the views of society as a whole are changed, not merely those of the government. To go down that road would be to make the same mistakes as the Religious Right in the UK and the US.[14]

Third, identifying Christianity in terms of its various ethnic expressions, while tempting as an option in the inner city, will serve only to confirm the accusation by secularizers that Christianity is the private truth of particular cultures.

All these approaches that we are rejecting are essentially appeals to the past, and while Christianity does have a history and a tradition, it is not a static faith, but is continually being reshaped by an eschatological imagination and hope.

The incarnation, by its cosmic significance, seeks to connect past, present and future in an unfolding and unfinished narrative. Now as postmodern philosophers remind us, most metanarratives, if not all of them, contain reference, both implicitly and explicitly, to the question of power and its uses. The incarnation narrative, too, crucially includes many implicit and explicit perspectives on the use of power, and it is to the issue of power that we must, therefore, now turn.

Learning to be a creative minority

To talk about the public square is partly to talk about power and its uses. Christians have been accustomed to exercising a good deal of power in the public square. In the context of Christendom that power was well established, not only legally and constitutionally but, more importantly, in terms of the imaginative force of the story which Christianity told. The certainty that it was better to be good than evil, that human life was intrinsically valuable, that we have a responsibility towards one another – these and many other foundational ideas underpinned the operation of the public square. But the establishing of these ideas as the core ingredients of a whole culture did not come about easily, and certainly not by means of legislation.

During the period that we now call the Dark Ages, when Christianity was struggling to make its message known in the context of a Western world that had been invaded by largely pagan peoples dominated by a warrior class, Christians had to live for a time as a creative minority. The most obvious expression of this creative minority was that of the monastery. It was here that the message was both told and lived. In many ways, the living of the story was more important than its verbal proclamation. For example, one of the great contributions of the monks in this time of liminality was to affirm the dignity of work, which we referred to in the previous chapter, but also to promote the value of education and the arts as sources of social imagination.

The coming of a warrior class, largely illiterate, tribal in structure and rural in nature, stood in complete contrast to an earlier age which had been urban, had valued learning and education and in which economic life was well ordered and provided the basis for the creation of wealth. Warrior classes do not value education and the fine arts as much as the martial arts. Societies do not become stable, just, or wealthy on the basis of such force. It was as the monks demonstrated their capacity to work hard, not only to provide for themselves so that they would not be a burden to others, but also to offer generous hospitality to the needy, and space in which learning and artistic play could function, that a new value system gradually became established. Telling the story was not nearly as important as indwelling and living it.

In times of liminality, such as the one that the West is presently passing through, it is more important to live as creative minorities than to live either as coercive minorities or as ineffective majorities. Pope Benedict XVI makes the powerful point that even though in some senses Christians technically constitute majorities in most Western nations, that does not help to construct a new civil society, because in the very places where these majorities are to be found – the old confessional churches – there has come a loss of vitality. Speaking particularly of Europe, rather than the West as a whole, he says:

> So how can Europe attain a Christian civil religion that over-comes the boundaries between denominations and gives voice to values that sustain society rather than console the individual? Such a religion can obviously not be built by experts, since no committee or council, whoever its members, can possibly generate a global ethos. Something living cannot be born except from another living thing. Here is where I see the importance of creative minorities. Christians are still clearly the majority in much of Europe ... Even the existing majorities, however, have grown weary and disenchanted ...

There is nothing sectarian about such creative minorities. Through their persuasive capacity and their joy, they reach other people and offer them a different way of seeing things.

Therefore my first thesis is that a civil religion that truly has the moral force to sustain all people presupposes the existence of convinced minorities that have "discovered the pearl" and live it in a manner that is also convincing to others.[15]

Living as creative minorities is very different from living as compliant majorities. Recently one of us was in discussion with some church leaders from Sweden who were rejoicing in their recent cataclysmic decline in church membership. Why was this an occasion for rejoicing? They explained to me that they had been proud for many years of their standing in Swedish society. Despite the much vaunted advent of Sweden as a deeply secular society the percentage of the population that were married in church, had their children baptized, were buried in a Christian ceremony and paid their church tax remained above ninety percent. But further inquiry revealed that most Swedes believed little or nothing of the Christian story, and indeed in many cases knew nothing of its essential content. Being members of the church did not constitute membership of the Christian church so much as it signified an essential component of Swedish citizenship.

Once the Swedish state church was disestablished in the year 2000, the connection between Swedish citizenship and church membership was decisively broken and significant numbers of the population severed their connection with the church. Church leaders expect that within the next few years the number of Swedes who adopt formal membership in the church of Sweden will fall even further, to below fifty percent. The church will become a clear minority.

Interestingly, but perhaps not surprisingly, the impact on those who have remained is noticeable.

Church leaders report an increase in commitment on the part of those who do attend, a growth of interest in the distinctive message of the church, and a growing commitment to mission within Sweden. Church planting, with its associated concern for mission, is on the agenda for a church which previously felt that its parish system was sufficiently comprehensive for such a concern to have little or no value. In speaking with church leaders one senses a growth in excitement for the future of a church which will inevitably need to find a different role as a minority group. The essential difference between operating as a creative minority and living as an ineffectual majority is that while operating as a majority the church has tended to adapt the message of the gospel to the dominant narrative of a very secular society. As soon as the church becomes a minority it is able to consider afresh ways in which the Christian narrative offers a constructive critique to the secular narrative. While such an outcome is not inevitable, it is at least a possibility.

What does it mean, then, to operate as a creative minority?

We have already referred to Pope Benedict's observation that the great confessional churches in the West appeared tired – worn out by the struggle of attempting to work with the tide of secularism only to discover, eventually, that secularism is not a partner but an assassin.[16] The final realization that Western culture has not only departed from its roots but is intent on denying them at all costs has produced what might be described as a collective anaphylactic shock on the part of the church.

Missional thinking and the imagining of the future

In such a situation, the call of the church is not to recover the past but to recover spiritual confidence in order to reshape tomorrow. In grappling with this task, we need a hermeneutic which is deeply missional.

James Brownson points to the deeply missional character of his own attempt to imagine a biblical hermeneutic. His conviction is that running through the Bible there is a core dialectic, of which he says:

> This dialectic between our common humanity and our cultural particularity – a dialectic that lies at the heart of a missional hermeneutic – is itself grounded in the narratives of scripture.[17]

He then proceeds to tease out this dialectic which seeks both the blessing of a particular people (Israel – a cultural particularity) and, through them, the good of the whole world (common humanity). Moreover, he points out that the New Testament embrace of the

Gentiles moves God's blessing in a missionary embrace of all cultures as well as all humanity.

This all takes place in the context of another tension – that between the commonality of the text and the diversity of interpretation. Brownson sees this tension as a necessary conversation because of the various voices contained within the text of Scripture itself. A missional hermeneutic, which Brownson attempts to articulate, helps us to approach three key questions which together form the horizon of the future – a metavista from which we might operate; we look at each in turn.

Human flourishing

There are a number of contemporary issues which take us to the frontiers of human endeavor and imagination which must be addressed by a missional theology if we are to understand human flourishing. Issues around fertility control and genetic engineering raise questions about the boundaries of human life. The nature of our personhood comes into focus as we deal with complex issues of sexuality, gender and even difficult questions around death and dying.

Looking back on previous ages Christians can point to an honorable record in creatively shaping compassionate approaches to many of these questions, for example in the hospice movement with respect to death, and also, in many periods of Christian engagement with society, with respect to the advancement of women.

Unfortunately, the recent record of the church in this latter area, particularly because of the painful debate about the role of women in ministry (settled decades ago in many nonconformist denominations), has given an impression of a conservatism that does not accord with the biblical narrative. Would it be possible for Christians to play a part in reimagining a new relationship between women and men in the coming century, one in which the war of the sexes is replaced by a new partnership made possible by more flexible patterns of work? Apart from any other consideration, it is becoming abundantly clear that children flourish in the emotional security of strong parental partnerships.

Questions relating to how children develop – spiritually, ethically, emotionally as well as physically – have come to the fore in recent times. What does it mean to be a child? How might the transition to adulthood be managed more effectively? Are children becoming sexualized at too early an age? Is that sexualization part of a broader view of children either as consumers or (worse still) as fashion accessories, mere commodities in the good life?[18]

We are perhaps not accustomed to debating these questions in our missiology classes, and yet if we are to develop a theology that engages in a significant dialogue with our culture then we must learn such skills.

Forming community

The debate about human flourishing takes a particular turn when we consider how it might be possible to live in relationship with others.

There is a powerful political dimension to this debate. As John Franke points out, "The autonomous self is understood by many contemporary observers as the primary context in which the social and political structures of American culture have taken shape."[19] In this tradition, community is neither possible, nor indeed necessary for human flourishing and identity. Franke refers to Robert Bellah (see chapter 10) thus: "[F]or most Americans, the meaning of life is 'to become one's own person, almost to give birth to oneself'."[20]

The tradition of the strong individual has been dominant until relatively recently. (We have undertaken our own strong critique of this tradition in chapter 4.)

The research of Robert Putnam suggests people want to live in communities that have high social capital, and that occurs only when community is fostered by strong traditions that foster a sense of kindness and the common good. It seems, paradoxically, that the cult of the individual actually functions well only in the context of a vibrant inheritance that emphasizes community. In that sense, the strong individual, while apparently needing no one else, is actually operating parasitically. The reality, therefore, is not that the individual needs no one else, but only that he or she contributes little to others.

Franke describes the revitalization, through the work of thinkers such as Alasdair MacIntyre, Michael Sandel, and Charles Taylor – the new communitarians – of a tradition that emphasizes the social nature of humanity. From there, he describes the commonality between two traditions:

[R]ecent years have seen a degree of convergence in the liberal-communitarian debate, leading many social theorists to conclude that "the concepts of individualism and community are interdependent. Each needs the presence of the other to be able to reach its highest level. In other words, the phenomenon of human experience is always, simultaneously and inextricably, both social and individual. There is no human being apart from the social group in which he or she participates, and there is no group apart from the individual members who constitute that group." Seyla Benhabib typifies thinkers who see value in both positions. She borrows the communitarian thesis that traditions, communities and practices shape our identities. At the same time, she advances the liberal concern for maintaining reflective distance, on the basis that it facilitates the ability to criticize, challenge, and question the content of these identities and the practices they prescribe.[21]

We have already appropriated the thinking of Paul Ricoeur with regard to understanding, recognizing and living oneself as another which deconstructs the arrogant and aggressive individualism of the modern era.

The discussion about the nature of individuals in relation to community is critical for shaping a discussion about our common future. A missional theology will want to explore a theology of the church as individuals in community. It is precisely at this point that the constitutive narrative of Scripture, which gives meaning to the past in order to interpret the present in relation to a new future, becomes so vital.[22] Living as a creative minority means to inculcate a viable life as communities of hope.

Christians have not merely inherited a founding document containing a narrative; they themselves are also actually part of that narrative, or story, with "practices of commitment" that enable strong bonds of community to be forged that can, where necessary, withstand enormous pressures from the rest of the world. The resilience of the people of God must be accompanied by joy and hope, because these enable a future to be created which is sustaining of identity and ultimately of human flourishing.

Creating community in society

It is one thing for Christians to create viable communities – even attractive, hospitable, welcoming and growing communities; it is another thing to say that the community of Christians also exists for those who have no desire to belong to such a community of faith. It is one thing to claim that this story is true for the Christian community; it is another to claim that the truth it conveys has a vital contribution to make in refounding the future of human society. Christians must certainly believe that such is true, but in order to tell the story in such a way that the wider world is able to drink from that same well of reason and wisdom and truth requires a much greater degree of imagination than Christians have managed in recent times.

But the signs are encouraging. Increasingly, as we noted earlier in this chapter, coalitions of Christians, whether internationally, nationally or locally, are beginning to grasp the practical import of the Christian narrative in terms of the exercise of compassion – sometimes in campaigning for justice, sometimes in offering practical help. These broad coalitions are able to have a greater impact than any single group or denomination.

This collaboration is sometimes occasioned because politicians recognize the capacity of faith groups in general to motivate and mobilize large numbers of people. What they don't easily grasp is that the capacity to mobilize volunteers is not just some strange ability that can be called upon from time to time when it is convenient to do so, but that, rather, the ability of Christians to build community as well as care about the wider society flows from the conviction that the Christian story "offers good news and hope for our situation, good news that must be lived out and proclaimed with courage and wisdom."[23]

What is of crucial importance, however, is that this conviction depends critically on a notion that the Christian story is public truth and not merely private truth. The tendency of a public sphere dominated by a tradition of the individual to relegate Christians to the realm of the private has had devastating consequences for both faith and for society. As James Brownson puts it:

Religion in general, and Christian faith in particular, has been relegated to the private realm, where truth claims are immaterial and where disputes are not resolved but simply massaged into docility by psychological and sociological analysis. As a result, the public sphere is increasingly stripped of any moral framework (those are private issues), and society as a whole more and more resembles some giant machine gone amok, driven by rapidly expanding economic and technological powers, but devoid of any sense of purpose, or even a clear sense of the common good.[24]

In welcoming religion into the public square, politicians must not make the mistake of thinking that they are simply co-opting willing volunteers to improve society to a degree. The story that motivates action comes along with the involvement of Christians, and that story cannot remain docile indefinitely. A missional theology will want to tell the story in the public square. This can sound alarming to those who have lived with the arrogance of Enlightenment thought for so long that they have ceased to see its totalitizing brutality. But they can take comfort from the reality that the Christian narrative, contrary to secular suspicions, in fact tends towards tolerance, reciprocity and mutuality.

Perhaps we could urge one another to see that what we need in a missional theology is a reconciling enterprise, and not so much enlightenment as illumination. We do not wish to say farewell to reason, but we would like to countenance an Age of Imagination which connects reason to faith and which humbly seeks mutual illumination – a great communal light to shine on our future. The metavista we seek will require the efforts of all – those with faith convictions supplied by the great religions of our world and those with faith convictions from other philosophical traditions.

If the twentieth century can teach us anything it is that it will require significant humility in order for us not to be devoured by forces and powers that easily wreak havoc. To quote Stanley Hauerwas:

> We live in a world of powers that are not our creation and we become determined by them when we lack the ability to recognize and name them. The Christian story teaches us to regard truthfulness more as a gift than a possession and thus requires that we be willing to face both the possibilities and threats a stranger represents. Such a commitment is the necessary condition for preventing our history from becoming our fate.[25]

Christians wish to offer their story with humility – not merely as a story that they possess, but as a gift that comes to us all from both the past and the future. "The true light that illumines every man was coming into the world" (John 1:9).

12

Conclusion and Beyond

"A growing number of scholars, journalists, politicians, and development practitioners are focussing on the role of cultural values and attitudes as facilitators of, or obstacles to, progress. They are the intellectual heirs of Alexis de Tocqueville, who concluded that what made the American political system work was a culture congenial to democracy; Max Weber, who explained the rise of capitalism as essentially a cultural phenomenon rooted in religion; and Edward Banfield, who illuminated the cultural roots of poverty and authoritarianism in Southern Italy, a case with universal applications. Cultural studies and emphasis on culture in the social sciences were in the mainstream in the 1940's and 1950's. Interest then dropped off. But a renaissance in cultural studies has taken place during the past 15 years that is moving toward the articulation of a new culture-centered paradigm of development, of human progress."

(L.E. Harrison and S.P. Huntington)[1]

The movie *Babel*, which was a contender for best picture in this year's (2007) Oscar nominations, tells a sprawling, kaleidoscopic and intriguing story of the reality of inter-cultural globalization. Three stories represent three cultural traditions which, despite all their acute differences, are linked by what we might call the bizarre and chaotic interconnectivity of the global world we presently inhabit. Modern secular Japan, Islamic Morocco and Catholic Mexico all come together due to a chance encounter that connects unwitting individuals from all three countries in a series of dramatic events of which no one participant is ever actually fully aware. In the middle of this collision of cultural narratives, playing the role of both victim and imperial outsider, is modern America, represented by actors Brad Pitt and Kate Blanchett. In the end it is America that has to adjust painfully and exhaustingly to the reality of the global world it helped to create but which now holds it, and indeed the whole of the so-called developed West, in the maelstrom of its own interconnected destiny.

This is the reality of the metavista world we have tried hard throughout this book both to describe and imaginatively to anticipate. No one cultural story or tradition dominates amidst this densely reconfigured collision of cultural histories. At one and the same time we find ourselves continually both victim of our own exhausted story and imperial intruder in the story of others. This also entails that the old cultural procedures of blame and shame are no longer applicable or even desirable. Time has moved on and new inter-disciplinary studies are posing a new set of issues and questions.[2]

It once seemed appropriate to blame the failed experiments of colonialism and developmentalism in Africa and Latin America on the cynical and ruthless business and trade agreements of the rich, developed West. The realities of UNESCO, UNAIDS, the various international symposiums on climate change and world poverty plus countless other independent studies and initiatives have shown that it is in fact a much more complicated situation than such blame and shame tactics allow. It is time to address the wider socio-political realities of shared national values, cultural attitudes toward change, development and prosperity, and habits of the heart that hold a nation in the thrall of past verities rather than future transformational possibilities.[3]

These are sensitive issues and in no way do we want to revisit the racist, ideological and imperial history of the past that couched these variables in terms of the economic, cultural and political superiority of the West. A global world means a multicultural, pluralist, interdependent and interconnected world in which we will all be constantly and profoundly affected by new developments in information and communication technology, by the continued democratization of knowledge, practical skills and generally available know-how, and by internationally operative business, managerial and organizational techniques.

This is not a world to be feared; it is simply one that will be continually reimagined – and it is time for the Christian church also to look afresh to its internal culture, its construal of the biblical narrative, and its supposedly gospel-oriented prophetic role in the contemporary world. Only by doing that can the Christian church move out beyond the decaying and collapsed structures of Christendom, forestall its persistent refusal to indwell the biblical story, and overcome its lack of political and ecumenical capital and cogency in a fast-changing world. Only in this way will the church become suitably skilled and equipped to negotiate a new role for itself in the new metaspace, or metavista, that is opening up before us.

In this chapter we want to conclude our deliberations and investigations by offering a manifesto to the contemporary church suggesting how she might more confidently move into this new metavista world and so cease to be an anachronistic relic of past and outmoded cultural traditions.

A new manifesto

Living adventurously at the interface

First and foremost (and indeed as *Babel* suggests), *the church has to learn to live adventurously at the intersection of three different and at times competing cultural narratives.* They are:

(1) the creational two-testament narrative of unity and diversity which the Bible recounts

(2) the narrative of historical Christianity within which each and every individual church should stand

(3) the wider cultural narratives which a truly global world makes freely available to us all.

These three closely inter-related realities can be represented by the diagram in Figure 1.

It should be clear by now that we have defined *culture* in such a way that the older notions of the centrality of reason, experience, praxis (and now also imagination) are taken up within the wider cultural narrative. Similarly, if we look at this model as a dynamic one and imagine spinning the outer wheel or perimeter at colossal speed, then the distinct points represented by Scripture, Tradition and Culture, where the triangle intersects the outer perimeter, will eventually collide. This is similar to what takes place at the subatomic level of reality. Each atom is made up of a number of

Figure 1

Putting it all together

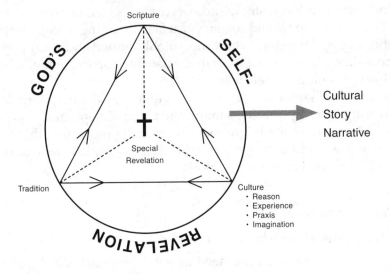

vibrating and agitated particles: neutrons, protons and electrons that all collide. It is from the collision of such particles that energy is released. This analogy applies to the fundamental hermeneutical reality of radical cultural engagement.

To live this kind of counter-cultural life the church has to "risk" living at the interface of the collision of all three narratives. Why? Because only then will the energy of the divine Spirit be released to make us the exile community, or the *diaspora* community, of love, trust, hope, reconciliation, repentance, suffering and witness that can offer to the world the transformational vision of the coming kingdom of God. Within a dynamic, organic, interconnected and multidimensional world such a collision of narrative identities is going on all the time. Why should it be any different in the church? It is in fact the collision of all three narratives that creates a new story and releases a new ecumenical vision or "fiduciary framework" of the kingdom life.

Without such a collision of narratives we simply cannot (i) indwell the multivalent story of the biblical narrative; (ii) understand and appropriate the tradition of historic Christianity from which we originated; and (iii) avoid either cultural accommodation or withdrawing into the ghetto of a culturally myopic and insular church. It has never been a safe option to live a genuinely counter-cultural Christian life, because such a life deconstructs old cultural verities and ignites new habits of the heart. It invites old men to dream dreams and young men to have visions. Indeed, as both the liberation and feminist theologians have demonstrated, it deconstructs old alienating paradigms and thrusts us into the new reality of a "discipleship of equals" where we can no longer afford to ignore the global intercultural reality of the Christian church.

One refinement of Figure 1 is to realize that God's self-revelation is given to us in the collision of all three narrative traditions. God, it appears, was the first narrative theologian! Indeed, the utterly central reality of this kind of collision is nowhere more iridescently revealed than in the death and resurrection of Jesus the Messiah. Jesus comes to grief precisely because he is caught in the intersection of three contending narratives: (i) the narrative of the biblical story, which is now receiving its central reconfiguration in the preaching and praxis of the suffering servant of God; (ii) the competing traditions of a divided second temple Judaism; and (iii) the powerful representatives of the story of the Graeco-Roman Empire. Jesus' resurrection and enthronement as the divine Son of the eternal God blows apart – indeed, ruptures and renders impotent – the first-century configuration of all three narratives.[4] Jesus' predictions of a new world being reconfigured through his own death and resurrection were soon to come to pass.[5] All three previous narratives were taken up and transformed by the new kids on the block (the *ecclesia*) who lived and died because Jesus alone was *Kyrios* and Lord.

This does not in any way imply an anti-Semitic rhetoric of supersessionism. As modern exegetes of John's Gospel[6] and those scholars exploring later second-century works are discovering, it seems as if ecclesia and synagogue co-existed as divided members of one family well into the third century.[7] What in fact brokered a much more decisive and structural separation and led to the baleful history of anti-Semitism that reached its nadir in twentieth-century Nazi Germany was, in fact, the arrival of Christendom when the

Emperor Constantine embraced the Christian faith as the new "plausibility structure"[8] for the Holy Roman Empire.

The role of tradition

It is time now to look more closely at the role of tradition in the schema we have been outlining.

Our refusal to follow Alasdair MacIntyre and valorize tradition as that which holds cultural narratives intact does not in any way mean that we seek to diminish or undermine the importance of tradition either in the Christian church or in the wider world of cultural and religious dialogue. We have opted, instead, for Michael Polanyi's notion of a "fiduciary framework" because it seems to us at least to bring the role of tradition into proper association with other plausibility structures, the tacit dimensions of belief and knowledge, and the explanatory role of wider cultural stories.

The narrative of the Christian tradition is quite crucial for the continued identity and credibility of the Christian church. There are four historical traditions within the overlapping trajectories of the one, holy, catholic and apostolic church. They are the Orthodox, Catholic, Protestant and Pentecostal traditions. The latter two are, to our minds, best understood as evangelical reform movements within the broader streams of the other two traditions.[9] The catholic and ecumenical reality of the wider Christian church is maintained by the fact that all four streams of historical Christianity have a common creed and a common biblical narrative (notwithstanding the addition of the Apocrypha in the Catholic Bible), and share adherence to the doctrinal formulations of the ecumenical councils. In other words, we all live by the *regula fidei* (the rule of faith) that should keep us answerable and accountable to one another. The fact that it often does not do so – either in theory or in practice – is cause for grave concern. A "generous orthodoxy"[10] lives and breathes within the collision of all three narratives we have been considering. A sectarian heterodoxy or – what is worse – a schismatic cult or sect-like version of the Christian faith which sometimes labors under the somewhat elusive identity of non-denominational or new church Christianity, has often simply lost touch with its connections to one of the four brands of historic Christianity. In so doing it often manifests its identity in terms of a culturally accommodated brand of consumer religion, the gospel of which is a patently obvious version of ideological, authoritarian and fundamentalist culture religion.

Yet again this takes place because the narrative the Bible tells is depoliticized, and some other very important ingredients are also surrendered – for instance (i) the recognition that the Christian church (the ecclesia) is a new manifestation of the community life of Israel that should not disconnect itself from its ancestral home; and (ii) a common liturgy that recites the historical creeds and re-enacts the sacraments of baptism and the Eucharist. And surrendered for what? A culturally accommodated triumphalist glory-train that leads to disingenuous fantasy and further dismembers the already wounded body of Christ.

Introducing a new kind of ecumenical initiative

The old ecumenism began with Vatican II and the refreshing winds of the new *aggiornamento* (literally: "bringing up to date") that finally brought the Roman Catholic Church into the twentieth century.[11] This movement took subsequent shape in a fascinating release of theological energy that sought to find real confessional and doctrinal unity between the divided streams of Christendom.

This initiative foundered because Christendom was dying on its feet and the historic churches were in a radical state of what some viewed as terminal decline. The later ecumenism that surfaced among the acolytes of the World Council of Churches around the 1970s was directed toward a new outward focus of unity aimed at the integrity of creation and justice among the nations and was, in fact, a lively response to the newly birthed reality of globalization. Both, however, were top-down initiatives that failed to recognize the arrival of the postmodern world with its very jaundiced attitude to any form of authority or program planning that operated from above.

A new program of ecumenism

In accordance with the rules of engagement for the new metavista world we outlined in chapter 3 and further developed in chapter 9 we offer a new program of ecumenism that can take root only in bottom-up planning earthed in communities from below.

It must be an interchurch initiative

As we have hinted already, radical cultural engagement can really work successfully only as an interchurch movement or a coalition of likeminded, outwardly focussed local churches that understands, indwells and seeks to communicate the Christian gospel to the particular cultural traditions of which it is an important and decisive part. Let us learn from the medical and artistic communities that have discovered that a radical engagement with contemporary cultural realities demands shared resources, shared ideas, shared community initiatives and shared traditions of belief and practice. Accordingly, despite the mega-churches' propensity to go it alone, the focussed unity of the Christian church will find expression not in a divided Christendom but in a new, reoriented metavista community of shared faith and resources, a community that will creatively and imaginatively get out of the ghetto and rediscover the original meaning of *ecumenical*. Thankfully there is already a lot of evidence that this kind of interchurch initiative is actually taking place

Where possible it should endeavor to include interfaith dialogue

In a world of international terrorism generated by ideological interpretation and affiliation to competing religious narratives, modern ecumenism at the local level should include what has previously be referred to as "interfaith dialogue." All religions are oriented towards competing truth claims and different foundational texts and often pastors and preachers are ill-equipped to enter into this kind of hermeneutical interchange. However, like all dialogue, it is based on friendship, mutual respect, trust and understanding, and openness to the radical challenge of the other. In the present highly dangerous international situation such dialogue is even more necessary and should be oriented to understanding one another's holy Scriptures more thoroughly and working for peace, justice and mutual understanding in our respective communities.[12]

It must develop a new kind of seminary education

A new kind of interdisciplinary seminary education needs to be invented. Certainly we still require seminaries that will equip men and women for pastoral, liturgical, sacramental and homiletical ministry (although we are not nearly so sure whether such training should continue to be organized and orchestrated in denominational silos). The difficulty with our traditional seminary education is that it rarely seems to produce public intellectuals who understand that radical cultural engagement requires a portfolio of knowledge and skills brokered through interdisciplinary exposure to public theology. Our experience of mainstream ministerial theological education (at least in the Protestant tradition) is that it is continually short on funding and so tries to produce candidates for ministry in as short a time as possible. Unfortunately, low investment in rigorous theological education usually yields low results in terms of radical cultural engagement. Cultural engagement is a highly imaginative exercise that, like a good wine, requires maturation and nurturing in the theological mainstream before going public (a reality that some Roman Catholic orders like the Jesuits appear to recognize).

Public intellectuals who can hold their own in the public domain and are skilled at the interdisciplinary task of public theology are very different people from closeted academics, overworked and underpaid pastors, or freewheeling charismatic preachers and evangelists. The former remain in the ivory tower of academia, the second are often close to burnout, and the latter are, unfortunately, frequently courted by the media-driven entertainment business that masquerades as public discourse in present democratic societies.

Karl Barth, Reinhold Niebuhr, Karl Rahner, Jean Luc Marion, Henri de Lubac, Hans Urs Von Balthasar, Paul Ricoeur, Wolfhart Pannenberg, Jürgen Moltmann, Lesslie Newbigin, Raimond Pannakar, Rosemary Radford Reuther, Luce Irigaray, Martha Craven Nussbaum and Julia Kristeva – to name but a few – all developed into public intellectuals because their particular theological and philosophical positions were crafted through exposure to interdisciplinary work and study. Can our present, largely denominational seminaries, oriented as they are toward pastoral and ministerial education, actually produce such gifted intellectuals?

The evidence is, unfortunately, not encouraging. A new type of seminary, more interdisciplinary in orientation, needs to be invented. The curriculum of such a seminary would have to be much more oriented toward biblical theology (which is not the same as biblical studies, in that it requires integration with broader theological and philosophical movements), ethics, political theology, systematics and aesthetics, with the latter including philosophy and cultural studies. In other words, public theology requires an integrated vision of the good, the true and the beautiful.

We need to emphasize the importance of biblical theology, which comes into its own the moment we take seriously the world "in front of the text," or radical cultural engagement. The idea that biblical theology somehow died a death in the 1970s when Langdon Gilkey, Brevard Childs and James Barr suddenly uncovered its methodological disarray is a greatly overrated myth and no longer seems nearly as convincing as it did in the heyday of the historical-critical methodologies.[13] Ireneaus, Augustine, Aquinas, Calvin, Luther and Barth were all biblical theologians because they all, in their different ways, knew how to indwell the biblical narrative and how to reconfigure that narrative around the changing church traditions and cultural parameters operative in their day.

It should embrace and integrate globalization
Globalization understood not just in the aggressive economic sense, but as intercultural, contextualized thinking and theology is here to stay and should be embraced and realistically integrated into every seminary and local church program. The saying that the poetic motion of a butterfly's wings in an English garden creates a tornado in the US graphically describes the phenomenon of global interconnectivity, a reality that global warming has also brought to everyone's attention. The prophetic call of Bono and other such artists within the movie and popular music industries, as well as the political campaigning of Jim Wallis, the Sojourners community and others to make poverty history and to end the worldwide HIV/AIDS pandemic, should be an agenda embraced by every local church and parachurch agency. That is simply because the Christian church is already a worldwide intercultural movement and we in the West have much to gain from exposure to new forms of contextualized theologies and new ways of counter-cultural living being explored and developed in the Two-Thirds World (or "majority world') often in situations where shared human capital and funding are in short supply.

Indwelling a counter-cultural story

Counter-cultural living requires indwelling a counter-cultural story.

Let us return briefly to Callum Brown, who documented the rise of a deep-seated form of secularization as something that confronted the church in Britain somewhere around 1963. His point was that the moral and lifestyle revolutions of the 1960s eventually overwhelmed the cogency and appeal of the evangelical narrative of individual conversion and sanctification to those outside the traditional churches. Many would find that quite a contentious claim to make, particularly when we look at the subsequent growth of evangelicalism in the church both in the US and in Britain from the 1960s to the present day, although Brown offers some telling and convincing evidence based on actual interviews with those outside the Christian churches.

Let us therefore put the issue rather differently. A Jesuology centered solely on individual faith and allegiance to Jesus, backed up by a bibliolatry that destroys the narrative flow of the biblical story, which then leads to an ecclesiology that is all but non-existent, is a drastically truncated version of the story the Bible tells and cuts no ice when it comes to radical cultural engagement. We repeat: there are four stories – creation, Israel, Jesus the Messiah and the church – which together make up the biblical narrative. All are interlinked; indeed, each story is recapitulated, reconfigured, re-envisioned and replayed in the others. By recognizing this reality we learn to indwell the whole biblical narrative. Israel is a God given response to the problem of violence and the despoiling of the creation blessing; Jesus the Christ is *the* ultimate response to the election, exile and idolatry of Israel; the church is another divine initiative to how the gospel of the crucified and risen Christ can be imaged and incarnated in the diaspora people of God and the good news declared to the nations.

The biblical wisdom literature is a responsive practical ethic to show how the elected people of God can live a counter-cultural life. The gospel that we need to share and creatively live out in the twenty-first-century world, wracked as this world is by radical religious conflict, grotesque poverty, ecological collapse and renewed nuclear proliferation,[14] must:

(1) embrace the integrity and stewardship of creation

(2) understand the cultural significance of the biblical nation of Israel as a model for the kingdom life of the church

(3) exalt Jesus the Messiah as the representative of humanity who broke down the binary opposition between the individual and community and lived his life as another

(4) embrace the mission of the church, which, like Israel, seeks to bring healing, righteousness and shalom to the nations.

Living in this kind of comprehensive narrative, creatively improvising on the original script, and at the same time revisiting the socio-political ramifications of the whole story renders the old Christendom divisions between liberals and evangelicals not only superfluous but more than a little self-serving. To a certain extent the new theological movements, like radical orthodoxy, post-liberalism, some of the new Catholic and Reformed theological repositionings, and those reappropriating the theology of Karl Barth in a postmodern context, have all left that outmoded dichotomy behind. The same applies to the movement we have called radical cultural engagement. It is, indeed, an irony that the first theologian of the modern era to really try and outline the role and importance of culture in theological enquiry was Paul Tillich.[15] His subsequent theological method of correlation was, however, another attempt to subvert the theological veracity of the whole biblical narrative.[16]

To live and move and have our being at the interface of the collision of the story the Bible tells, the tradition of historical Christianity from which we were honed, and the intercultural reality of contested global narratives is a wholly different way both to do theology and to live a counter-cultural form of discipleship. We hope this book will awaken a vision for a new generation of Christians to embrace that form of missional endeavor.

If that is to take place, then, as Walter Brueggemann suggests, we will also have given a new song to the presently voiceless and empowered those who are presently oppressed:

The key to public issues in our society, as in every society, concerns access to power and the processes of decision making. It is obvious that a monopoly of access exists and that many are voiceless and excluded from decision making. Access is characteristically arranged in the interest of certain notions of order and merit. In the public conversation, against such a destructive commitment to an order which opposes egalitarianism in politics and economics, the Bible powerfully insists that questions of justice, questions of abundant life for the marginal, and questions of social access, social goods, and social power cannot be silenced.[17]

Notes

Preface

[1] After a spell as General Secretary of the United Bible Societies, Mr. Crosbie is now CEO of SGM-Lifewords, a Bible agency committed to similar strategies of biblical and cultural engagement to those that will be outlined in this book. His constant practical support, encouragement and thoughtful companionship are reflected in much that is described here.

[2] This sentiment was frequently expressed at the many road shows held throughout Britain that accompanied the relaunch of the BFBS as a campaigning organization in 2001.

Introduction

[1] C.S. Lewis, "Introduction", in *Athanasius: The Incarnation of the Word of God.*

[2] Tertullian, *The Prescription Against Heretics*, chap. 7.

[3] Cf. C.J.D. Greene, *Christology in Cultural Perspective*, chap. 10.

[4] Tertullian, *The Prescription Against Heretics*, chaps. 20 and 21.

[5] See the review of Brown's book by Colin Greene in *The Bible in TransMission*, Autumn (2001), 18/19, available online at {www.biblesociety.org.uk}.

[6] C.G. Brown, *The Death of Christian Britain*, 13.

[7] For an informative and interesting analysis of the differences between Islam and Christianity in this regard see A. Shanks, *God and Modernity*, chap. 12.

[8] See Greene, "Theology, Culture and the End of Religion," in S. Holmes (ed.), *Public Theology and Cultural Engagement.*

[9] In Britain the success of the project known as *Faithworks*, which originated with the Evangelical Alliance, would bear testimony to his trend.

[10] The Alpha network claims to have achieved over one million people attending such faith-based groups with over 250,000 new professions of faith.

[11] We will examine the variegated strands of the secularization story in much more detail in chapter 9. In this regard see also R. Gill, *The Myth of the Empty Church.*

[12] Similar sentiments were expressed in Britain around the same time that Brown's book appeared by the Roman Catholic Archbishop of Westminster, Cormac Murphy O'Connor, at the National Conference of Priests in Leeds, UK, Sept 2001 – remarks that gained much media coverage.

[13] A counter example to such thinking is contained in Graham Cray's *Mission-Shaped Church: Church Planting and Fresh Expressions of Church in a Changing Context* which documents how the Church of England is seeking out more diverse expressions of church life in intriguing and innovative ways.

[14] See, e.g., G. Davie, *Europe*.

[15] This trend is not evident in the whole of the US. So, for instance, Seattle and the Pacific North West generally exhibit church attendance figures almost identical to those in Britain.

[16] Cf. P.L. Berger, *The Noise of Solemn Assemblies*. It is quite astonishing to see how Berger's analysis of American Christianity, which was published in 1969, still stands over 35 years later.

[17] This analysis would be borne out by the statistics released by the Barna Research Survey, which is notably pessimistic about the future of Christianity in the US.

[18] In this regard, Dietrich Bonhoeffer's perceptive analysis of the secularization of the American church still stands more than 70 years later: "Much of the secularization of American Christianity derives from the fact that in practice the church often adopts a highly secular role to the neglect of other matters and from the enthusiastic claim of the church to universal influence on the world." Quoted in G. Hunsinger, *Disruptive Grace*, 72.

[19] Some would argue that what remains of Christendom in the US is more than remnants, but even so, the mainline denominations are presently in danger of sleep-walking toward the precipice in a cultural situation that is becoming increasingly postmodern and pluralistic.

[20] Much of this work was documented between 1997 and 2003 in the highly appreciated publication *The Bible in TransMission*, which is sent out three times a year to over 50 percent of the clergy in England and Wales of every denominational affiliation.

[21] For an accessible and interesting historical analysis of this key period in the history of the BFBS see S. Batalden, K. Cann and J. Dean (eds.), *Sowing the Word*. See also the review of that book by D.W. Bebbington in *The Bible in TransMission*, Spring 2005, 18/19.

[22] The phrase *societal imagination* was adapted from a comment by W. Brueggemann, "that in the NT the expression 'the kingdom of God' was the most powerful metaphor for the renewal of societal imagination." In his book *Cultural Transformation and Religious Practice* (132, 154–55) Graham Ward describes culture as a shared "social imaginary"; he explains the phrase and the role of the imagination in the following way: "What imagination does is glimpse the new possibilities for meaning that metaphor provokes ... to glimpse alternative and perhaps better possibilities ... to fashion different social imaginaries ... [to] open up new possibilities, new relationships ... new ways to perceive, desire, interpret and rethink the world,"

[23] Cf. L. Newbigin, *The Other Side of 1984* and his other works listed in the Bibliography. For an ecumenical analysis of Newbigin's work see T.F. Foust et al. (eds.), *A Scandalous Prophet*; G.R. Hunsberger, *Bearing the Witness of the Spirit*; and G. Wainwright, *Lesslie Newbigin*.

[24] An understanding of culture in this sense developed from the semiotic theory of Ferdinand de Saussure (1857–1913) and Charles Sanders Pierce (1839–1914) and is enshrined in the work of Jacques Derrida.

[25] This the basic thesis of R. Williams's fascinating study, *Lost Icons*.

[26] A good example of a pop icon who has exploited the iconic structure of cultural engagement in a constant attempt at redefinition is Madonna.

[27] The fruit of our joint labors was showcased in three significant national and international conferences: "Mission to our culture in the light of Scripture and the Christian tradition" in 1990, "Freedom and Truth in a Pluralist Society" in 1991; and "The Gospel as Public Truth" in 1992. Arguably this partnership was instrumental in providing The Gospel and our Culture movement with a much higher profile in Britain and Europe.

[28] A good example of this would be the partnerships the BFBS developed with Jeremy Begbie and Cambridge University called "Theology through the Arts" and the Biblos Project with Exeter University School of Education. Both of these projects could not have either begun or survived without the significant funding provided by the BFBS.

[29] Cf. B. O'Connor (ed.), *The Adorno Reader*, Part iv, and S. Jarvis, *Adorno*, chap. 4.

[30] Cf. P. Ricoeur, *Time and Narrative*, Vol. 1.

[31] We do, however, agree with Graham Ward that "Cultures are polyphonic, hybrid and fragmentary, always being composed and recomposed. They are sites of displacement and newly fashioned affiliation. They are dialogic entities, in the way that Mikhail Bakhtin understands 'dialogic'. They are not monolithic and homogenous, though some cultures and views of the social are often more officially legitimated than others" (*Cultural Transformation*, 6). As we will illustrate in chapter 2, however, legitimation is now a real problem in a postmodern society. Nevertheless, Bakhtin is a good example of what we mean by hermeneutical dialogical activity, which, to our mind, is the basic meaning of cultural engagement. Cf. M.M. Bakhtin, *Problems of Dostoevsky's Poetics; Rabelais and His Word*; and *The Dialogic Imagination*.

[32] We will concentrate on the importance of globalization in today's world in more detail in chapters 1 and 4.

[33] Cf. A. Shanks, *God and Modernity*, chap. 12.

[34] V. Ramachandra, "Learning from Modern European Secularism: A View from the Third World Church," *European Journal of Theology*, Vol. 12, No. 1, 2003, 35–48.

[35] Cf. F. Jamison, *Postmodernism or the Cultural Logic of Late Capitalism*.

[36] Cf. M. Horkheimer and T.W. Adorno, *The Dialectic of Enlightenment*; also Adorno, *Against Epistemology a Metacritique*. For a helpful analysis of Adorno's insights in this regard see C. Hearfield, *Adorno and the Modern Ethos of Freedom*.

[37] G. Loughlin, *Telling God's Story: Bible, Church and Narrative Theology*.

Chapter 1

[1] J. Thornhill, *Modernity*, 129.

[2] R.N. Bellah et al., *Habits of the Heart* and *The Good Society*.

3   Bellah et al., *Habits*, 50.
4   J. Moltmann, *The Way of Jesus Christ*, 56.
5   See also Greene, *Christology*, chap. 3.
6   J. Stout, *Democracy and Tradition*, 289–90. Cf. also A.C. MacIntyre, *After Virtue; Whose Justice? Which Rationality?* and *Dependent Rational Animals*.
7   Stout, *Democracy*, 290: "Yet I see no good reason to suppose that modernity, even as we know it in the West, is the expression of a single project, the career of a single ambition. There is more to modernity than that. There is a life, a complicated network of practices and institutions and goods and evils to be taken in."
8   J.F. Lyotard, *The Postmodern Condition*.
9   Quoted in D. Marquand and A. Seldon (eds.), *The Ideas that Shaped Post-war Britain*.
10 J.Z. Muller, *Adam Smith in his Time and Ours*.
11 A. Smith, *An Inquiry into Nature and the Causes of The Wealth of Nations*, Book iv, chap. ii.
12 H.W. Schneider (ed.), *Adam Smith's Moral and Political Philosophy*.
13 Cf. D.C. Korten, *When Corporations Rule the World*.
14 In this regard see the helpful discussion of the debates and disputes between Paine and Burke in Stout, *Democracy*, chap. 9. John Adams a life-long friend of Paine remarked in 1805, "I know not whether any man in the world has had more influence on its inhabitants or affairs for the last 30 years than Tom Paine."
15 E. Burke, *Reflections on the Revolution in France*, 76.
16 T. Paine, *The Rights of Man*, Part 1, see www.ushistory.org/paine or eBooks@ Adelaide, 2004.
17 Paine, *Rights*, Part 2.
18 In this regard see Thornhill, *Modernity*, 129–75.
19 T. Paine, *The Age of Reason*.
20 MacIntyre, *After Virtue* and *Whose Justice?*
21 S. Hauerwas, *After Christendom; Dispatches from the Front*, chap. 4; and *A Better Hope*.
22 Stout, *Democracy*. See also his *Ethics after Babel*.
23 J.A. Secord, *Victorian Sensation*, Introduction.
24 See B.G. Worrall, *The Making of the Modern Church*.
25 Cf. M. Polanyi, *Personal Knowledge*.
26 T. Friedman, *The Lexus and the Olive Tree*, xvii.
27 Friedman, *Lexus*, xix.
28 R. Bauckham, *Bible and Mission*, 3.
29 This is the argument put forward by Bauckham in *Bible and Mission*: "By economic globalization I refer to the global spread of consumerist individualism, all dominated by the multi-national corporations with their bases in the United States and other western countries." 94. The problem here is that Bauckham and others conflate globalization with Americanization. Friedman, on the other hand, distinguishes them, recognizing (as we do as well) that the world wide web is in fact more democratic than this, allowing

other nations and global markets which do not answer to American and Western corporatism, to thrive. See also A. Giddens, *Runaway World*.

30 Friedman, *Lexus*, xx.

31 L.E. Harrison and S.P. Huntington (eds.), *Culture Matters*.

32 Friedman, *Lexus*, 44–72.

33 Friedman, *Lexus*, 327–47.

34 I. Kant, *Beantwortung der Fruge*. Cf. Greene, *Christology*, 85.

35 S. Best and D. Kellner, *Postmodern Theory*, 219.

36 Cf. J. Ellul, *The Technological Bluff* and *The New Demons*. M. Heidegger, *The Question Concerning Technology*; cf. also M. Zimmerman, *Heidegger's Confrontation with Modernity: Technology, Politics and Art*.

37 Best and Kellner, *Postmodern Theory*, 221.

38 T.W. Adorno, *Negative Dialectics*.

39 T.W. Adorno, "The Actuality of Philosophy", 120

40 J. Habermas, "Modernity Versus Postmodernity" in *New German Critique*, 22.

Chapter 2

1 G. Steiner, *Real Presences*, 3.

2 R. Appignanesi and C. Garrett, *Postmodernism for Beginners*, 19.

3 Z. Bauman, *Intimations of Postmodernity*, x.

4 Much of the standard literature on postmodernity documents this process of development, good examples of which are S. Connor, *Postmodernist Culture*; Best and Kellner, *Postmodern Theory*; C. Jencks, *Postmodernism*; J.W. Bertens, *The Idea of the Postmodern*; Z. Bauman, *Postmodernity and its Discontents*.

5 Review article in *The Times*, May 15, 2003.

6 *The Times*.

7 Other examples of films from this genre would be David Lynch's *Blue Velvet* (1986), Yvonne Rainer's *The Man Who Envied Women* (1985) and Quentin Tarantino and Roger Avary's *Pulp Fiction* (1994).

8 M. Featherstone, *Consumer Culture and Postmodernism*, 126.

9 Featherstone, *Consumer Culture*, 45.

10 M. Poster, "Introduction" to *Jean Baudrillard, Selected Writings*. See also in this regard J. Baudrillard, *In the Shadow of the Silent Majorities* and *Simulacra and Simulations*.

11 Poster, "Introduction".

12 Cf. J. Baudrillard, *Le Systeme des Objets; La Société de Consommation* and *Pour une Critique de l'Economie Politique du Sign*. See also D. Keller, *Media Culture*.

13 Baudrillard, *La Société* and *Critique*, quoted in Bertens, *Idea*, 147.

14 The continual diet of media-induced so-called reality shows seems to bear out this analysis.

15 Tori Amos, in her most recent CD, *American Doll Posse*, makes this point forcibly in the track "Digital Ghost."

16. The increasing popularity of internet simulations such as *Second Life*, where individuals can construct their own avatars and create another simulated existence in community with others, deconstructs the boundaries between what we previously understood as the "real world" in favor of the indicing simulacra.

17. S. Lash, *Sociology of Postmodernism*.

18. Much the same argument can be found in Horkheimer and Adorno, *The Dialectic of Enlightenment*.

19. Lash, *Sociology*, 79, quoted in Bertens, *Idea*, 218.

20. G. Deleuze and F. Guattari, *Anti-Oedipus*.

21. J.F. Lyotard, *Economie Libidinale*.

22. Lash, *Sociology*, 100. Quoted in Berten, *Idea*, 219.

23. R. Descartes, *Discourse on Method*.

24. R. Descartes, *Meditations on First Philosophy*.

25. I. Kant, *The Critique of Pure Reason*.

26. R. Rorty, *Philosophy; and the Mirror of Nature*.

27. Rorty, *Philosophy*, 171.

28. Lyotard, *Postmodern Condition*, 31–37.

29. J. Habermas, *The Theory of Communicative Action*.

30. D.J. Herman, "Modernism versus postmodernism: towards an analytic distinction." Quoted in Bertens, *Idea*, 127.

31. First published in *L'échange symbolique et la mort*.

32. Bertens, *Idea*, 150.

33. Baudrillard, *Simulations* and *Shadow*.

34. M. Ryan, "Postmodern Politics," in *Theory, Culture and Society* 5, 576. Quoted in Bertens, *Idea*, 188.

35. Ryan, "Postmodern Politics."

36. Bertens, *Idea*, 191.

37. MacIntyre, *After Virtue* and *Whose Justice?*

38. E. Laclau, and C. Mouffe, *Hegemony and Socialist Strategy*, 37.

39. Best and Kellner, *Postmodern Theory*, 243.

40. G. Bassham, "The Religion of the Matrix and the Problems of Pluralism," 111–12.

41. R. Corliss, "Popular Metaphysics."

Chapter 3

1. A.G. Amsterdam and J. Bruner, *Minding the Law*. Part of the opening quote of W. Brueggemann, *An Introduction to the Old Testament*.

2. Cf. J. Millbank, C. Pickstock and G. Ward (eds.), *Radical Orthodoxy*.

3. R. McCloughry and W. Morris, *Making a World of Difference*, 14, quoting P. Coleridge, *Disability, Liberation and Development*, 43–44.

4. McCloughry and Morris, *World*, 15.

5. R. Carey, BBC Information {http://www.bbc.co.uk/pressoffice/pressreleases/stories/2002/03_march/26/bbconeident.shtml}

6. Disability Rights Commission website {http://www.drc-gb.org}

7   Two films which have also treated the issue of disability sensitively and imaginatively are *Four Weddings and a Funeral* (1994) and much more recently, *Babel* (2006). In both films the issue of deafness is a key ingredient in the resolution of the respective plots.

8   Cf. Lyotard, *Postmodern Condition*.

9   This has been the essence of A.C. MacIntyre's claim about the importance of tradition in his recent publications: *After Virtue*; *Whose Justice?*; *Three Rival Versions of Moral Enquiry*; and *Dependent Rational Animals*.

10 Polanyi, *Personal Knowledge*, 266. In this regard we are following L. Newbigin who first noted the potential of Polanyi's description of fiduciary frameworks in his book *The Other Side of 1984*.

11 V. Harrison, "Putnam's Internal Realism and von Balthasar's Epistemology."

12 Ward, *Cultural Transformation*, 81.

13 This more comprehensive vision of life and knowledge may also lie behind the apostle Paul's injunction to the Philippians to strive to attain whatever was true, honorable, just, pure, pleasing, and commendable, rather than what appeared philosophically certain, scientifically plausible or historically probable (Phil. 4:8).

14 J. Morris, *Pride Against Prejudice*, 192.

15 Cf. W. Brueggemann, *Theology of the Old Testament*; D.L. Petersen, *The Prophetic Literature*; and R. Mason, *Propaganda and Subversion in the Old Testament*.

16 It was for this reason that the BFBS formed an innovative storytelling partnership with the Northumbria Community called *The Telling Place*, which performed various forms of storytelling in numerous venues around Britain.

17 B.J. Walsh and S.C. Keesmaat, *Colossians Remixed* and N.T. Wright, *Paul*.

18 Walsh and Keesmaat, *Colossians*, 74–75.

19 P. Ricoeur, *Lectures on Ideology and Utopia*.

20 D.R. Stiver, *Theology after Ricoeur*, 152–53.

21 Gottwald was heavily influenced by George E. Mendenhall, "The Hebrew Conquest of Palestine," but parted company with Mendenhall by utilizing Marxist sociological categories. In the wake of Gottwald's work there followed a veritable explosion of sociological analysis of the Old Testament. See, e.g., R.R. Wilson, *Prophecy and Society in Ancient Israel*.

22 M. Foucault, *The Archaeology of Knowledge* and other works of his listed in the bibliography.

23 M. Foucault, *Power/Knowledge*, 117.

24 M. Foucault, *The History of Sexuality*, 49.

25 Best and Kellner, *Postmodern Theory*, 70.

26 Cf. P. Ricoeur, *Oneself as Another* and *Time and Narrative*, 3 vols.

27 M. Merleau-Ponty, *Phenomenology of Perception*, 82.

28 See G. Loughlin, *Telling God's Story*, 139–52.

29 M. Heidegger, *Being and Time*.

30 Bauman, *Discontents*, 179–80.

31 Cf. N. Postman, *Amusing Ourselves to Death*.

32 Cf. Azar Nafisi, *Reading Lolita in Tehran*.
33 D. Bonhoeffer, *The Cost of Discipleship*.
34 Gottwald, *Tribes*. See also his *The Hebrew Bible in its Social World and in Ours*.
35 In conversation with W. Shenk, the American Mennonite missiologist who for a time was seconded to help with the *Gospel and our Culture movement* in Britain.

Chapter 4

1 J.D. Caputo, *On Religion*, 51–52.
2 T. Capote, *In Cold Blood*: "Until one morning in mid-November of 1959, few Americans – in fact, few Kansans – had ever heard of Holcomb. Like the waters of the river, like the motorists on the highway, and like the yellow trains streaking down the Santa Fe tracks, drama, in the shape of exceptional happenings, had never stopped there" (Introduction). See also Irving Malin (ed.), *Truman Capote's In Cold Blood* and M.T. Inge and T. Capote, *Truman Capote: Conversations*.
3 D.J. Bosch, *Believing in the Future*, 10.
4 See O. O'Donovan, *The Desire of the Nations*, 193–226. For a fuller discussion of the theological debate that still surrounds the validity or otherwise of the Christendom experiment see Greene, *Christology*, 43–51 and 60–63.
5 Cf. S. Murray, *Post-Christendom: Church and Mission in a Strange New World*, 75–82.
6 D.J. Hall, *Confessing The Faith*, Vol. 3, 205.
7 J. Moltmann, *The Coming of God*, 164. Oh, that the Christian right in the US would read more church history and see that they are in danger of repeating the same mistake.
8 Hall, *Confessing*, Vol. 3, 208.
9 Hall, *Confessing*, Vol. 3, 208.
10 In *The Next Christendom* Philip Jenkins contends that a new Christendom has now taken shape in Africa, Southeast Asia, and Latin America as a direct result of that missionary expansion and the astounding numerical growth of new adherents of the Christian faith. Christianity is again enjoying majority status in the Two-Thirds World, but this is a very different form of Christianity from that found in the West. Jenkins draws a lot of his inspiration from the clash of civilizations theory advanced by Samuel Huntington, according to which the revival of religion, particularly Christianity and Islam, in the Two-Thirds World is a direct result of the destabilizing influence of rapid globalization and is viewed as a search for meaning and identity in the midst of the homogenizing effects of the global market. The future, he contends, will inevitably become an increasingly religious contest between Christianity, Judaism, and Islam. We are about to see the crusades revisited. But Jenkins's thesis suffers from the same endemic weaknesses and defects as that of Samuel Huntington (see chapter 1). Sheer numerical strength and the undoubted vibrancy of the Roman Catholic, Protestant, and Pentecostal churches in the

Two-Thirds World does not constitute another version of Christendom and in that sense Jenkins makes a profound category mistake.

11 Cf. Murray, *Post-Christendom*, 145–310.

12 Cf. S. Kierkegaard: "Christendom has done away with Christianity, without being quite aware of it. The consequence is that, if anything is to be done, one must try again to introduce Christianity to Christendom." (*Training in Christianity and the Edifying Discourse Which "Accompanied" It*, 39; cf. F. Nietzsche, *The Gay Science* and *Thus Spoke Zarathustra*.

13 M. Heidegger, *The Question Concerning Technology and Other Essays*, 64.

14 D. Bonhoeffer, *Letters and Papers from Prison*.

15 Not surprisingly, we refer here to the Death of God theology, or secular theology of the 1960s, that followed John A.T. Robinson's much maligned and misunderstood book *Honest to God*.

16 L.B. Mead, *The Once and Future Church*, 18.

17 This happened when the Darwinian theory of evolution began to assert its influence on the public imagination of people in Europe especially, and when social Darwinism offered an alternative to the Christian worldview of God's providential guidance and direction.

18 In his *Post-Christendom* Murray skillfully outlines what the reality of the Post-Christendom situation actually is for those Christians who are truly aware of the demise of Christendom as a cultural garment of Christianity.

19 Cf. M.A. Noll, *The Old Religion in a New World*, 37–71.

20 Berger, *Noise*, 13, quoted in Hall, *Confessing*, 230–31.

21 Berger, *Noise*, 13, in Hall, *Confessing*, 229.

22 Berger, *Noise*, 19, in Hall, *Confessing*, 230.

23 S. Hauerwas, and W.H. Willimon, *Resident Aliens*; Hauerwas and Willimon, *Where Resident Aliens Live*; and Hauerwas, *After Christendom*.

24 W. Brueggemann,, *The Prophetic Imagination*; *Hopeful Imagination*; and *Like Fire in the Bones*.

25 Hunsinger, *Disruptive Grace*.

26 A profound and depressing example of this tendency is Richard Neuhaus's book *Naked Public Square*, which extols the virtues of some vague notion called "religion" to endorse America's grandiose ambitions and interventions in world politics.

27 D. Bonhoeffer, "Protestantism without Reformation" in Edwin H. Robertson (ed.), *No Rusty Swords*: "American theology and the American church as a whole have never been able to understand the meaning of 'criticism' by the Word of God and all that signifies. Right to the last they do not understand that God's 'criticism' touches every religion, the Christianity of the churches and the sanctification of Christians, and that God has founded his church beyond religion and beyond ethics" (p. 113).

28 Cf. R.T. Hughes, *Myths America Lives By*.

29 Moltmann, *Coming*, 175–76.

30 See R. Jewett and J. Shelton Lawrence, *Captain America and the Crusade against Evil*.

31 Cf. Bellah et al., *Habits*: "The American dream is often a very private dream of being the star, the uniquely successful and admirable one, the one who stands

out from the crowd of ordinary folk who don't know how. And since we have believed in that dream for a very long time and worked very hard to make it come true, it is hard for us to give it up, even though it contradicts another dream that we have – that of living in a society that would really be worth living in" (p. 285).

32 Bono, National Prayer Breakfast in the White House, 2006 {http://www.usa today.com/news/washington/2006–02–02-bono-transcript_x.htm, 2 February, 2006}

33 It is interesting that with just a little stretch of the imagination it could be claimed that John Millbank has constructed a whole theology upon this premise!

34 See, e.g., S. Wellman, *David Livingstone* and M. Buxton, *David Livingstone*.

35 A. Schweitzer, *The Quest of the Historical Jesus*, 401.

36 Moltmann, *Coming*, 168.

37 The term was first used in regard to post-colonial literature that sought to identify the socio-political and cultural legacies of the colonial era. It is said to have come into use with E. Said's *Orientalism*. Cf. also E. Said, *Culture of Imperialism*. Other important texts are Frantz Fanon, *Black Skin, White Masks*; and *The Wretched of the Earth*; B. Ashcroft, *The Empire Writes Back*; R.J.C. Young, *Postcolonialism*; and U. Narayan, *Dislocating Cultures*.

38 Cf. L. Sanneh, *Whose Religion is Christianity?*

39 R.S. Sugirtharajah, "Postcolonial Biblical Interpretation," 67.

40 Peter Piot, "Responding to the HIV/AIDS Epidemic: Prospects for near and distant futures."

41 Cf. Greene, *Christology*, chap. 7. In this respect my own analysis was simply following that of the early liberation theologians some of whom have subsequently moved on beyond the old developmental and dependency theories.

42 Harrison and Huntington (eds.), *Culture Matters*, xx

43 Cf. Greene, *Christology*, 74–95.

44 Greene, *Christology*, 249–82.

45 J. Derrida, *Of Grammatology*.

46 L. Wittgenstein, *The Blue and Brown Books*. See also *Tractatus Logico-Philosophicus* and *Philosophical Investigations*. For an excellent biography of Wittgenstein see R. Monk, *Ludwig Wittgenstein*.

47 J.F. Lyotard, *The Differend*. See also A. Benjamin (ed.), *The Lyotard Reader*.

48 Deleuze and Guattari, *Anti-Oedipus*.

49 Stiver, *Theology*, 161.

50 Stiver, *Theology*, 162.

51 G. Lakoff and M. Johnson, *Philosophy in the Flesh*, 3, quoted in Stiver, *Theology*, 160. We agree with Stiver that the sentiments expressed in this quotation are rather overstated and that two millennia of philosophy will not be so easily dismissed!

52 Stiver, *Theology*, 160.

53 "The embodied and embedded nature of the self undergirds the entire hermeneutical project because it suggests that we ourselves are not transparent

texts whose meaning is to be read off univocally. We are more like a rich poetic text, full of allusions and depth. It is not just that others must interpret us – we must interpret ourselves. We are as much riddles to ourselves as we are to others. The interactive nature of the self, with all its subterranean passages, means that the hermeneutical task will never be finished" (Stiver, *Theology*, 161).

54 Stiver, *Theology*, 172.
55 Ricoeur, *Oneself*, 121.
56 Cf. Ricoeur, *Oneself*, 140–240.

Chapter 5

1 T. Work, *Living and Active*, 6–7.
2 This research took place between 1998 and 1999.
3 See "The Use of the Bible in Pastoral Practice" on the website of the School of Religions and Theological Studies, University of Cardiff: {http://www.cardiff.ac.uk/relig/research/researchprojects/previousprojects/index.html}.
4 Paul Ballard and Steve Holmes (eds.), *The Use of the Bible in Pastoral Practice*; G. Oliver, *Human Bible, Holy Bible*; and S. Pattison, M. Cooling and T. Cooling, *Using the Bible in Christian Ministry*. See also N.T. Wright, *Scripture and the Authority of God*.
5 An excellent example of this kind of helpful literature is E.F. Davis and R.B. Hayes, *The Art of Reading Scripture*.
6 One obvious example of a publication in this regard is the phenomenally successful *The Da Vinci Code*, which blandly disseminated such erroneous views as the following: "The Bible is a product of man, my dear, not of God. The Bible did not fall magically from the clouds. Man created it as a historical record of tumultuous times, and it has evolved through countless translations, additions and revisions. History has never had a definitive version of the book … the fundamental irony of Christianity! The Bible, as we know it today, was collected by the pagan Roman emperor Constantine the Great" (p. 231).
7 One of the reasons the BFBS started the publication *The Bible in TransMission* was to make it possible for issues like these to be debated in an open and thoughtful fashion.
8 See J. Barr, *Fundamentalism* and D.G. Bloesch, *Holy Scripture* (especially chaps. 2 and 4).
9 See J.P. White, *Scripture Alone*; also V.E. Bacote, L.C. Migueliz and D.L. Okholm (eds.), *Evangelicals and Scripture*; K.A. Mathison, *The Shape of Sola Scriptura*; and J. Barton, *The Cambridge Companion to Biblical Interpretation*.
10 Brueggemann, *Theology*, 11–12.
11 See also Greene, *Christology*, chap. 5, and R.A. Harrisville and W. Sundberg, *The Bible in Modern Culture*, chaps. 3–5.
12 Brueggemann, *Theology*, 12.
13 See Greene, *Christology*, chap. 5.

[14] The fact that Brueggemann chooses to take this route in his own *Theology of the Old Testament* is, for some, sufficient evidence that he is simply espousing a rhetorical version of the old liberalism.

[15] This is often the way modern fiction treats the Bible; once again cf. *The Da Vinci Code* as an example.

[16] See R. Holloway, *Godless Morality* and *Doubts and Loves*.

[17] To a certain extent this is the way all those who espouse the label *post-liberal* use the Bible in their respective systems.

[18] Murray, *Post-Christendom*, 119.

[19] J.H. Yoder, *The Politics of Jesus*.

[20] See L. Newbigin, *Foolishness to the Greeks*.

[21] Harrisville and Sundberg, *Modern Culture*, chap. 2.

[22] Harrisville and Sundberg, *Modern Culture*, 39.

[23] J. Smart, *The Strange Silence of the Bible in the Church*.

[24] See C.E. Braaten and R.W. Jenson (eds.), *Reclaiming the Bible for the Church*; S.E. Fowl, *Engaging Scripture*; and R.W.L. Moberly, *The Bible, Theology and Faith*.

[25] Greene, *Christology*, chap. 6. To put the matter succiently: in essence the biblical story was supplanted by the Enlightenment metanarrative coupled with an unremitting scholarly vigilance against authority and tradition; a prejudice in favor of a thinly veiled false objectivity; a search for the universal norms of reason; and a reading of history as evolutionary progress.

[26] Wright, *Scripture*.

[27] Cf. A.C. Thiselton, *New Horizons in Hermeneutics* and Kevin J. Vanhoozer, *Is there a Meaning in this Text?*

[28] P. Ricoeur, "The Model of the Text."

[29] Brueggemann, *Theology*, 57–58.

[30] Ricoeur, "Model."

[31] Cf. P. Ricoeur, *Figuring the Sacred*, Part Three. See also M. Coleridge, "Life in the Crypt or Why Bother with Biblical Studies?."

[32] W. Wink, *The Bible in Human Transformation*, 1.

[33] This is one of the primary reasons the BFBS and the University of Gloucester began the groundbreaking series of interdisciplinary consultations and publications referred to as the *Scripture and Hermeneutics Seminar*, which has now finished its work as a ten-year project and has published eight volumes. See the SAHS published by Paternoster/Zondervan.

[34] J. Goldingay, *Models of Scripture*.

[35] In what follows I am much indebted to G. Loughlin's fine and eloquent study *Telling God's Story*, which has done much to revive a sensitive and critical narrative approach to the Scriptures.

[36] K. Barth, *Church Dogmatics*, 1/1. See also Hunsinger, *Disruptive Grace*, chap. 9.

[37] The same conviction is frequently voiced by J. Derrida – cf. *On Grammatology*.

[38] E. Auerbach, *Mimesis*.

[39] It is this view of the Bible that Lesslie Newbigin also endorsed (see his *The Gospel in a Pluralist Society*, chap. 8). Newbigin was also influenced in this

regard by the writings of Wolfhart Pannenberg, e.g. in Pannenberg et al., *Revelation as History*.

40 See Loughlin, *Telling*, 36–37, 41–43, 70–73.

41 G.A. Lindbeck, *The Nature of Doctrine*.

42 See, also by Frei, *The Identity of Jesus Christ* and a collection of his essays in G. Hunsinger and W.C. Placher (eds.), *Theology and Narrative*. Also see S. Hauerwas and L. Gregory Jones (eds.), *Why Narrative?*

43 Loughlin, *Telling*, 37.

44 See Frei, *Eclipse*.

45 C.H.H. Scobie, *The Ways of Our God*, 11.

46 See Lindbeck, *Nature*, final chapter.

47 Loughlin, *Telling*, 43.

48 B.E. Daley, "Is Patristic Exegesis still Usable?", in *The Art of Reading Scriptures*.

49 Lindbeck, *Nature*, final chapter, reproduced in full in J. Webster and G.P. Schner (eds.), *Theology After Liberalism*. See also D.H. Kelsey, *The Uses of Scripture in Recent Theology*.

50 Auerbach, *Mimesis*, 12, quoted in Loughlin, *Telling*, 71.

51 See Brueggemann, *Introduction*.

52 See the temptation narratives in the synoptic gospels (Matt. 4:1–11, Mark 1:12–13, Luke 4:1–12).

53 Loughlin, *Telling*, 74.

54 Ricoeur, *Time*, Vol. 1.

55 N.T. Wright, *The New Testament and the People of God*, 359–69.

56 Wright, *Scripture*, 89–93.

57 In a brief but useful textbook for students, C.G. Bartholomew and M. Goheen have taken Wright's schema and added the sixth act; see *The Drama of Scripture*.

58 Wright, *People*, 359–69.

59 H.G. Gadamer, *Truth and Method*.

60 See Greene, *Christology*, chap. 12.

61 A.N. Wilder, "Story and Story-World."

Chapter 6

1 Barach Obama, *The Audacity of Hope: Thoughts on Reclaiming the American Dream*, excerpt reprinted in *Time*, 15 October 2006, 54.

2 This movie was originally made for television and subsequently released in DVD format. It is a six-hour performance.

3 {http://us.imdb.com/title/tt0318997}

4 Cf. Vanhoozer, *Meaning*.

5 Cf. Flannery O'Connor, *Everything that Rises must Converge: The Complete Stories* and *The Habit of Being*.

6 In this regard see T. Hart, "Imagination and Responsible Reading," in C.G. Bartholomew et al. (eds.), *Renewing Biblical Interpretation*.

7 Steiner, *Presences*, 11.

8   K.J. Vanhoozer, *First Theology*, 15–41.

9   D. Kelsey, *The Uses of Scripture in Recent Theology*, 167–68.

10 Vanhoozer, *First Theology*, 29.

11 Cf. Barth, *Church Dogmatics*, 1/1 and 1/2.

12 Cf. R. Bultmann, *Existence and Faith*. See also W. Schmithals, *An Introduction to the Theology of Rudolf Bultmann*.

13 Vanhoozer, *First Theology*, 159–203.

14 Vanhoozer, *First Theology*, 173. See also N. Wolterstorff, *Divine Discourse*. Speech acts (or communicative action) may be locutionary, illocutionary, perlocutionary and interlocutionary. The first term refers simply to what is stated; the second is what the author intended to state; the third involves an array of intended or unintended actions that might take place due to what was said. The fourth refers to the covenant of discourse – the fact that communicative action aims toward creating covenant relationships based on promises.

15 See the series of essays on speech act theory in C.G. Bartholomew et al. (eds.), *After Pentecost*. If we look at N.T. Wright's construal of the relationship between God and Scripture it appears as if something similar is taking place. Wright appears to keep the notion of narrative central to how he understands both the biblical text and the way the church indwells the text. According to Wright, Scripture is a unified narrative configured into five acts or subplots. "When we read Genesis 1–2, we read it as the first act in a play of which we live in the fifth. When we read Genesis 3–11, we read it as the second act in a play of which we live in the fifth. When we read the entire story of Israel from Abraham to the Messiah (as Paul sketches it in Gal. 3 or Rom. 4), we read it as the third act. When we read the story of Jesus, we are confronted with the decisive and climactic fourth act, which is not where we ourselves live – we are not following Jesus around Palestine, watching him heal, preach and feast with the outcasts, and puzzling over his plans for a final trip to Jerusalem – but which, of course, remains the foundation upon which our present (fifth) act is based" (*The Last Word*, 124). Clearly, if this is the case, then again the nature of a narrative which does include the ability to indwell every aspect of the story has, in fact, been replaced by diachronic historical sequencing and description.

16 This aspect of literary theory and critique is often not taken sufficiently into consideration by biblical scholars. Cf. Steiner, *Presences*.

17 Cf. Vanhoozer, *Meaning*, 367–453.

18 N.T. Wright, *The Last Word*, 124.

19 Loughlin, *Telling*, 190–91.

20 Loughlin, *Telling*, 194.

21 Cf. R. Putnam, *Bowling Alone*.

22 P. Ricoeur, "Metaphor and the Central Problem of Hermeneutics." In J.B. Thompson (ed.), *Hermeneutics and the Human Sciences*.

23 Stiver, *Theology*, 58.

24 C. Westermann, *Genesis, An Introduction*.

25 Cf. W. Brueggemann, *Genesis* (Interpretation Series).

26 Barth, *Church Dogmatics*, 3/1.
27 Cf. Newbigin, *Gospel*, chap. 7, for a similar critique.
28 Cf. Wright, *People*.
29 W. Brueggemann, *Old Testament Theology*, 74.
30 See G. Von Rad, *Old Testament Theology 2*, 118.
31 See Bartholomew and Goheen, *Drama*. See also Psalm 105 and 106 for two different answers to this dilemma.
32 See G. Von Rad, *Wisdom in Israel*; R.E. Murphy, *The Tree of Life*.
33 Wright, *People*, 243. See also Bartholomew and Goheen, *Drama*.
34 Wright, *People*, 180–214.
35 W. Pannenberg, *Systematic Theology*, Vol. 2, 282.
36 Cf. B. Walsh and S. Keesmatt, *Colossians Remixed*; N.T. Wright, *Paul*; R.A. Horsley (ed.), *Paul and Empire*; *Paul and Politics*; and *Paul and the Roman Imperial Order*.

Chapter 7

1 Hunsinger, *Disruptive Grace*, 68–69. The reference is to Istvan Deak, "How Guilty Were the Germans?."
2 Interestingly enough, Hunsinger notes in his Introduction (p. 6) that no essay he has ever written received so much comment both in favor of and against as this one. See also T.J. Gorringe, *Karl Barth* and F. Jehle, *Ever Against the Stream*.
3 It is this naïve yet seemingly undiminished belief in the so-called special friendship between modern America and Britain that contributed, at least in part, to the demise of both prime ministers.
4 See M. Schuchardt, "The Radiation Sickness of the Soul."
5 *Disruptive Grace*, 92. Hunsinger is quoting from Robert C. Batchelder, *The Irreversible Decision*, 181.
6 Richard J. Neuhaus, *The Naked Public Square*. See also Stout, *Democracy*, 159–61.
7 W. Wink, *The Powers That Be*.
8 W. Stringfellow, *An Ethic for Christians and Other Aliens in a Strange Land*, 21, quoted in C. Rowland, "The Apocalypse and Political Theology."
9 See E. Jungel, *Christ, Justice and Peace*, Introduction, for a full and recent translation of the Barmen Declaration.
10 See Hunsinger, *Disruptive Grace*, 89–113.
11 Stout, *Democracy*, 104.
12 Stout, *Democracy*, 105.
13 Stout, *Democracy*, 118–61.
14 S. Hauerwas, and D. Burrell, "From System to Story." See Stout, *Democracy*, 142.
15 This has been the force of A.C. MacIntyre's trenchant criticism of the tradition of modern liberal democracy, particularly in *After Virtue* and *Whose Justice? Which Rationality?*

[16] J.H. Yoder's *The Politics of Jesus* became something of a publishing phenomenon as far as recent theological books are concerned, selling nearly 90,000 copies between 1972 and 1996. The reason, claims Craig Carter, is that Yoder teaches us how to live Christianly in a post-Constantinian and Post-Enlightenment age (C.A. Carter, *The Politics of the Cross*, 15–16).

[17] S. Hauerwas, *A Community of Character* and *The Peaceable Kingdom*.

[18] O'Donovan, *Desire*, 276.

[19] S. Hauerwas, *Against the Nations and Dispatches*.

[20] The decisive influence of MacIntyre on Newbigin first became apparent with the publication of *Foolishness*.

[21] P.L. Berger, *The Homeless Mind*.

[22] Stout, *Democracy*, 149.

[23] S. Hauerwas, *Performing the Faith*, 215–41.

[24] Stout, *Democracy*, 156–61.

[25] Stout, *Democracy*, 183–224.

[26] See O. O'Donovan, *Resurrection and Moral Order* and *Desire*.

[27] O'Donovan voices this criticism of Liberation Theology, which he refers to as the Southern School, in *Desire*, 16.

[28] O'Donovan, *Desire*, 15.

[29] O'Donovan, *Desire*, 19 and 30–32.

[30] O'Donovan, *Desire*, 20.

[31] O'Donovan, *Desire*, 22.

[32] O'Donovan, *Desire*, 45–46.

[33] O'Donovan, *Desire*, 45–46.

[34] The first three in *Desire*, 46–47, and the remainder on pp. 65, 72, 80. See also C.G. Bartholomew, "Introduction" to *A Royal Priesthood?*

[35] O'Donovan, *Desire*, 133.

[36] O'Donovan, *Desire*, 211–12.

[37] A. Leftwich, *What is Politics?*

[38] A. Heyword, *Key Concepts in Politics*.

[39] See Kate Millett, *Sexual Politics*.

[40] O'Donovan, *Desire*, chap. 6, especially the section "The Legacy of Christendom." For an illuminating analysis and critique of O'Donovan's defense of the victory of Christ in the legacy of Christendom see J. Chaplin, "Political Eschatology and Responsible Government," and O'Donovan's response in Bartholomew et al. (eds.), *A Royal Priesthood?*

[41] See O. O'Donovan and J. Lockwood O'Donovan, *Bonds of Imperfection*.

[42] O'Donovan, *Desire*, chap. 7, especially the section "The Menace of Modernity."

[43] J.H. Yoder, *The Christian Witness to the State*, 9. See also Carter, *Politics*, 145–50.

[44] Yoder, *Witness*, 10.

[45] J.H. Yoder, "The Otherness of the Church" in M. Cartwright (ed.), *The Royal Priesthood*, quoted in Carter, *Politics*, 148.

[46] Cf. Yoder, "The War of the Lamb," in his *The Politics of Jesus*.

47 K. Barth, *The Knowledge of God and the Service of God*, 214. See the excellent and revealing discussion of these and other issues in regard to Barth's political theology in Jehle, *Ever*.

48 Jehle, *Ever*, 60.

49 Such an interpretation of the kingdom seems to me to be implied in Isaiah 65:17–25 and endorsed by Revelation 21. This is not, therefore, a secular modernist reinterpretation of these themes but a genuine attempt at imaginative hermeneutical application.

50 A.I. Solzhhenitsyn, *The Gulag Archipelago*, 34.

Chapter 8

1 C.G. Brown, "The secularisation decade: What the 1960s have done to the study of religious history," in H. McLeod and W. Ustorf (eds.), *The Decline of Christendom in Western Europe, 1750–2000*, chap. 2.

2 J. Cox, "Master-narratives of long-term religious change."

3 What Cox does outline are the ways in which a master narrative works to convince an audience of its basic truth without being required to demonstrate it is actually truth. In the case of the secularization story, the image of continual decline or a downward sloping graph is constantly invoked, whereas the reality is far more complex. Cox, "Master-narratives," 207.

4 M. Midgeley, *Science as Salvation*.

5 Cox, "Master-narratives," 201.

6 Cox, "Master-narratives," 201.

7 Cox, "Master-narratives," 208.

8 Davie, *Europe*, ix.

9 Davie, *Europe*, 8.

10 Davie, *Europe*, 19.

11 Cox, "Master-narratives," 201.

12 Brown, *Death*, 1.

13 Brown, *Death*, 1.

14 Brown, *Death*, 9–10.

15 Davie, *Europe*, 21.

16 This case is made in H. Schlossberg, *The Silent Revolution and the Making of Victorian England*.

17 Brown, *Death*, 14.

18 Brown, *Death*, 14–15.

19 G. Himmelfarb, "From Clapham to Bloomsbury."

20 Davie, *Europe*, 142.

21 W. Ustorf, "A Missiological Postcript," in H. McLeod and W. Ustorf (eds.), *The Decline of Christendom in Western Europe, 1750–2000*.

22 L. Woodhead, "The turn to life in contemporary religion and spirituality," in U. King (ed.), *Spirituality and Society in the New Millennium*.

23 Davie, *Europe*, 147.

24 G. Weigel, *The Cube and the Cathedral*.

Chapter 9

[1] A. Roxburgh, *The Sky is Falling*, 89.

[2] These figures are taken from *The English Church Census 2005* {www.christian-research.org.uk/intro.htm}. There is some dispute about their accuracy, but they still show a huge gap between stated affiliation and actual attendance.

[3] "Black people now account for 10% of all churchgoers in England ... This is most obvious in Inner London, where 44% of churchgoers are now black, 14% other non-white, and only 42% white." Press release for *Pulling out of the Nose Dive: 2005 English Church Census* {http://www.christian-research.org.uk/intro.htm}.

[4] D. Hay, and K. Hunt, *Understanding the Spirituality of People who don't go to Church*. Some of this work is described in D. Hay, "Spirituality and the Unchurched."

[5] Davie, *Europe*, 147.

[6] G. Davie, *Religion in Britain since 1945*, 192.

[7] S. Toulmin, *Cosmopolis: The Hidden Agenda of Modernity*, 13.

[8] Toulmin, *Cosmopolis*, 16.

[9] Newbigin's first book on this topic, *The Other Side of 1984*, was quickly followed by *Foolishness to the Greek* and *The Gospel in a Pluralist Society*; all three deepened the analysis concerning Enlightenment thought.

[10] Newbigin's thinking, by his own admission, was deeply rooted in an analysis of modernity – he gave little thought in the first phase of his thinking to the postmodern condition. But the extent to which he exposed the faith dimension of modernity such that it will never be possible to look at modernity again without seeing its faith dimension, was remarkable.

[11] J. Munson, *The Nonconformists*.

[12] R. Wuthnow, *Christianity in the 21st Century*, 127: "The liberal identification with progress does have a certain appeal even today. We can look to the wonders of modern medicine and say that some things have surely gotten better ... It is nice to have religionists on board the ship of progress, helping to steer it through the uncharted waters of new moral challenges ... Beyond that, liberalism has difficulty even in claiming the future for itself, because that future, the one envisioned by the progressives, is still very much in the hands of the scientists and the rational technocrats. They are the true bearers of progress, guiding the ship with up-to-date navigational equipment, the religionists are only the chaplains, offering ceremonial prayers each morning and evening" (p. 127).

[13] G. Wainwright, *Lesslie Newbigin*, 11.

[14] Wainwright, *Lesslie Newbigin*, 12.

[15] A. Hirsch, *The Forgotten Ways*, 128.

[16] Newbigin, *Other Side*.

[17] Roxburgh, *Sky*, 22.

[18] Roxburgh, *Sky*, 23.

[19] Roxburgh, *Sky*, 53.

Chapter 10

[1] N. Boyle, *Who Are we Now?*, 80.

[2] Sanneh, *Whose Religion*, 22.

[3] Alan Roxburgh, in an article on the Allelon website entitled "Emergent Church: taking shape within polar opposites," March 11, 2006, quotes parts of a blog by Anna Dodridge: "so, now, we hang out together … we are families … and that's it. No alt services, no small group meetings, we just get on with our lives, we pray together, we give and receive prophecy, we worship God in service actions and conversations. We learn and teach the Bible by our everyday conversation and circumstances" {http://emergingchurch.info/ stories/annadodridge/index.htm}.

[4] Sanneh, *Whose Religion*, 3.

[5] See, e.g., R. Warren, *Building Missionary Congregations* and M. Robinson, *Winning Hearts, Changing Minds*.

[6] See, e.g., M. Depree, *Leadership Jazz*.

[7] L.B. Mead, *Transforming Congregations for the Future*.

[8] "Leaders now require adaptive skills to anticipate, create, and revise their institutional cultures. The pastoral skills in which they were trained are important, but no longer sufficient to handle all they will face" (Roxburgh, *Sky*, 64).

[9] Robert W. Jenson, "What is a Post-Christian?," 30.

[10] O'Donovan, *Desire*, 286.

[11] F. Fukuyama, *The End of History and the Last Man*.

[12] Roxburgh, *Sky*, 183.

[13] Hirsch, *Forgotten*, 123.

[14] See, e.g., D. Devenish, "Mission structures in the New Testament."

[15] In his book *Restoring the Kingdom*, Andrew Walker describes the Ephesians 4 ministries as practiced by House Church leaders; see especially pp. 161ff. Eddie Gibbs and Ian Coffey amplify the theme in *Church Next* as they describe significant apostolic networks as part of the shape of the church to come.

[16] Hirsch, *Forgotten*, 153.

[17] The problem of the unpreparedness of populations in the West for dealing with this newfound wealth was discussed as long ago as the late 1950s by John Kenneth Galbraith in *The Affluent Society*.

[18] Richard Schoch, *The Secrets of Happiness*, 17.

[19] Bellah et al., *Habits*.

[20] Putnam, *Bowling Alone*.

[21] See Charles Moore, "Pope Benedict has a sense of history" at www.telegraph. co.uk (20 April, 2005).

[22] L.L. Rasmussen, *Moral Fragments and Moral Community*, 37.

[23] This material is taken from the annual Stob lecture given by Ellen Charry in 2005. See {http//www.calvinseminary.edu.continuingEd/stob/pastLectures. php}.

[24] Schoch, *Secrets of Happiness*, 17.

[25] Pat Keifert of Church Innovations in Minneapolis St Paul makes this claim as a consequence of significant consultancy interaction with clergy over several decades.

[26] Hirsch, *Forgotten*, 205 and Roxburgh, *Sky*, 102.

Chapter 11

[1] R.F. Thiemann, *Religion and Public Life: A Dilemma for Democracy*, 169.

[2] J.K.A. Smith, *Introducing Radical Orthodoxy*, 31f.

[3] J. Wallis, *God's Politics*.

[4] Smith, *Introducing Radical Orthodoxy*, 32. But also see the self-critique of the right in C. Thomas and E. Dodson, *Blinded by Might*.

[5] N. Spencer, "Doing God".

[6] Weigel, *Cube*, 69.

[7] S. Toulmin, *Return to Reason*, 209f.

[8] The impact of local congregations in the US is extensively documented by N.T. Ammerman, *Pillars of Faith*. "The work congregations do in the world requires a wide range of partners. Almost no one works alone. Only 3 percent of the congregations we encountered were completely without networks of partners."

[9] Spencer, "'Doing God'," 43, quotes many statistics from English regions that demonstrate the attempts of local government to assess the financial value of faith communities' volunteer time.

[10] For an overview of their thinking see Stout, *Democracy*.

[11] For a brief account of Hegel's use of this term see G. Simpson, *Critical Social Theory*, 103.

[12] See, e.g., Spencer, "'Doing God'", 40.

[13] Habermas is quoted (as part of a longer explanation of his thinking about civil society) in Simpson, *Critical*, 122.

[14] Curiously, the Clapham Sect began its public life by attempting to bring prosecutions against those they deemed to be acting immorally in public. They failed and soon saw that they needed to campaign to win hearts and minds on much bigger issues than the narrow ones they had attempted to bring to the law courts. Using government and the law courts to enforce views on morality that have not first been widely accepted by society as part of a greater public good will almost certainly fail as a strategy.

[15] J. Ratzinger, and M. Pera, *Without Roots*, 120.

[16] The hostility to Christian roots and heritage can be clearly seen in the debate about whether or not to include any mention of Christianity in the proposed European constitution. See Weigel, *Cube*, 56ff.

[17] J.V. Brownson, "Living the Truth in Love: Elements of a Missional Hermeutic," 484.

[18] See, e.g., the ideas of Rowan Williams in *Lost Icons*.

[19] J. Franke, *The Character of Theology*, 168.

[20] Franke, *Character*, 168.

21 Franke, *Character*, 171.

22 This is why Newbigin was so interested in the work of Polanyi, who was so important in describing how knowledge requires tradition and communities. Franke explores the same territory, citing Polanyi.

23 Brownson, "Speaking," 479.

24 Brownson, "Speaking," 479.

25 Hauerwas, *Community*, 10.

Chapter 12

1 Harrison, and Huntington (eds.), *Culture*, xxi–xxii. While this book breaks new ground in its analysis of the centrality of cultural values and dispositions in determining a nation's orientation towards certain goals it does so by rehabilitating a very American and Eurocentric notion of economic progress which in our present context we should regard with some understandable suspicion.

2 See Harrison and Huntington (eds.), *Culture*, particularly the chapters by Harrison and Huntington themselves.

3 This is, in fact, what the Harvard Academy for International and Area Studies {http://www.wcfia.harvard.edu/academy} is endeavoring to promote.

4 Cf. Greene, *Christology*, chap. 12.

5 Matt. 24:1–51; Mark 13:1–27; Luke 21:5–36.

6 A. Lincoln, *Truth on Trial*.

7 Cf. J. Lieu, *Christian Identity in the Jewish and Graeco-Roman World*; D. Boyarin, *Dying for God*; and P.C. Finney, *The Invisible God*.

8 An expression coined by Peter L. Berger in *The Heretical Imperative*.

9 In that respect we adopt a position similar to the way G. Lindbeck views his own appropriation of his native Lutheranism – see J.J. Buckley (ed.), *The Church in a Postliberal Age*.

10 A phrase taken up and turned into a provocative book of that title by Brian McClaren. As far as I am aware the phrase originated with W. Brueggemann.

11 See G. Lindbeck, "Reminiscences of Vatican II."

12 Despite Stanley Hauerwas's jaundiced attitude to such language we do not as yet know where an alternative language is to be found!

13 Cf. B. Childs, "On Reclaiming the Bible for Christian Theology." Also see C. Bartholomew, "Biblical Theology and Biblical Interpretation," and F. Watson, *Text and Truth*, 18–28.

14 Alan Hirsch describes our present, twenty-first-century context in similar terms: "The truth is that the twenty-first century is turning out to be a highly complex phenomenon where terrorism, paradigmatic technological innovation, an unsustainable environment, rampant consumerism, discontinuous change, and perilous ideologies confront us at every point" (*Forgotten*, 16).

15 P. Tillich, *Theology of Culture*.

16 Cf. Greene, *Christology*, chap. 4, part two.

17 W. Brueggemann, *The Book That Breathes New Life*, 13.

Bibliography

Adorno, T.W., *Against Epistemology a Metacritique: Studies in Husserl and the Phenomenological Antinomies* (trans. W. Domingo). MIT Press, 1984.

Adorno, T.W., "The Actuality of Philosophy." Inaugural Lecture 1931. In Hearfield, C., *Adorno and the Modern Ethos of Freedom.* Ashgate New Critical Thinking in Philosophy. Aldershot: Ashgate Publishing, 2004.

—, *Negative Dialectics.* Translated by E.B. Ashton. New York, NY: Seabury Press, 1978; London: Routledge, 1990.

Ammerman, N.T., *Pillars of Faith: American Congregations and their Partners.* London: University of California Press, 2005.

Amsterdam, A.G. and J. Bruner, *Minding the Law.* Cambridge: Harvard University Press, 2000.

Appignanesi, R. and C. Garrett, *Postmodernism for Beginners.* Cambridge: Icon Books, 1995.

Ashcroft, B., *The Empire Writes Back: Theory and Practice in Post-Colonial Literature.* London: Routledge, 1990.

Auerbach, E., *Mimesis: The Representation of Reality in Western Literature.* Translated by Willard R. Trask. 50th anniversary edition. Oxford: Princeton University Press, 2003.

Bacote, V.E., L.C. Migueliz and D.L. Okholm (eds.), *Evangelicals and Scripture: Tradition, Authority and Hermeneutics.* Downers Grove, IL: Inter-Varsity Press, 2004.

Bakhtin, M.M., *Problems of Dostoevsky's Poetics.* Edited and translated by Caryl Emerson. Minneapolis, MN: University of Michigan Press, 1984.

Bakhtin, M.M., *Rabelais and His World*. Translated by Hélène Iswolsky. Bloomington, IN: Indiana University Press, 1993. [Written 1941, 1965]

—, *Speech Genres and Other Late Essays*. Translated by Vern W. McGee. Austin, TX: University of Texas Press, 1986.

—, *The Dialogic Imagination: Four Essays*. Edited by Michael Holquist. Translated by Caryl Emerson and Michael Holquist. Austin: University of Texas Press. 1981. [Written during the 1930s]

—, *Toward a Philosophy of the Act*. Edited by Vadim Liapunov and Michael Holquist. Translated by Vadim Liapunov. Austin: University of Texas Press, 1993.

Ballard, P. and S. Holmes (eds.), *The Bible in Pastoral Practice: Readings in the Place and Function of Scripture in the Church*. Grand Rapids, MI: Eerdmans, 2005.

Barr, J., *Fundamentalism*. 2nd edn. London: SCM Press, 1995.

Barth, K., *The Knowledge of God and the Service of God According to the Teaching of the Reformation, Recalling the Scottish Confession of 1560*. Translated by J.L.M. Haire and Ian Henderson. Gifford Lectures 1937–1938. New York, NY: AMS Press, 1979.

—, *Church Dogmatics*. Edited by Bromley, G.W. and T.F. Torrance. 1/1. *Doctrine of the Word of God: Prolegomena to Church Dogmatics*; 1/2. *The Doctrine of God: The Election of God; The Command of God*; 3/1. *The Doctrine of Creation: The Work of Creation*. Edinburgh: T&T Clark, 1956–1977.

Bartholomew, C.G. and M. Goheen, *The Drama of Scripture: Finding Our Place in the Biblical Story*. Grand Rapids, MI: Baker Academic, 2004.

Bartholomew, C.G., "Biblical Theology and Biblical Interpretation." In Healy, Mary et al. (eds.), *Out of Egypt: Biblical Theology and Biblical Interpretation*. SAHS Vol. 5. Milton Keynes/Grand Rapids: Paternoster/Zondervan, 2004.

Bartholomew, C.G. et al. (eds.), *After Pentecost: Language and Biblical Interpretation*. SAHS Vol. 2. Carlisle: Paternoster, 2001.

—, *A Royal Priesthood?: The Use of the Bible Ethically and Politically. A Dialogue with Oliver O'Donovan*. SAHS Vol. 3. Carlisle/Grand Rapids, MI: Paternoster/Zondervan, 2002.

Barton, J. (ed.), *The Cambridge Companion to Biblical Interpretation.* Cambridge: Cambridge University Press, 1998.

Bassham, G., "The Religion of the Matrix and the Problems of Pluralism." In William Irwin (ed.), *The Matrix and Philosophy: Welcome to the Desert of the Real.* Chicago, IL: Open Court, 2002.

Batalden, S., K. Cann and J. Dean (eds.), *Sowing the Word: The Cultural Impact of the British and Foreign Bible Society.* Sheffield: Sheffield Phoenix, 2004.

Batchelder, R.C., *The Irreversible Decision: 1939–1950.* Boston, MA: Houghton Mifflin, 1962.

Bauckham, R., *Bible and Mission: Christian Witness in a Postmodern World.* Grand Rapids, MI/Carlisle: Baker Academic/Paternoster, 2003.

Baudrillard, J., *In the Shadow of the Silent Majorities, or, the End of the Social, and other Essays.* Translated by Paul Foss, John Johnston and Paul Patton. New York, NY: Semiotext(e), 1983.

—, *L'échange symbolique et la mort.* Paris: Gallimard, 1976.

—, *La Société de Consommation.* Paris: SGPP, 1970.

—, *Le Système des Objets.* Paris: Gallimard, 1968.

—, *Pour une Critique de L'Economie Politique du Sign.* Paris: Gallimard, 1972.

—, *Simulacra and Simulation.* First published 1981. Translated by S. Glaser. Ann Arbor, MI: University of Michigan Press, 1994.

Bauman, Z., *Intimations of Postmodernity.* London: Routledge, 1992.

—, *Postmodernity and its Discontents.* Cambridge: Polity, 1987.

—, *Modernity and the Holocaust.* New York, NY. Cornell University Press, 2000.

Bellah, R.N. et al., *Habits of the Heart: Individualism and Commitment in American Life.* Berkeley, CA: University of California Press, 1985.

Bellah, R.N., *The Good Society.* New York, NY: Random House, 1991.

Berger, Peter L., *The Heretical Imperative: Contemporary Possibilities of Religious Affirmation.* Garden City, NY: Anchor Press, 1979.

—, *The Homeless Mind: Modernization and Consciousness.* New York, NY: Random House, 1973.

Berger, Peter L., *The Noise of Solemn Assemblies: Christian Commitment and the Religious Establishment in America*. Garden City, NY: Doubleday, 1961.

Bertens, J.W., *The Idea of the Postmodern: a History*. London: Routledge, 1995.

Best, S. and D. Kellner, *Postmodern Theory: Critical Interrogations*. London: Macmillan, 1991.

Bloesch, D.G., *Holy Scripture: Revelation, Inspiration and Interpretation*. Carlisle: Paternoster, 1994.

Bonhoeffer, D., "Protestantism without Reformation" in *No Rusty Swords: Letters, Lectures, and Notes from the Collected works [of] Dietrich Bonhoeffer*. Edited and introduced by Edwin H. Robertson. London: Fontana, 1970.

—, *Letters and Papers from Prison*. Edited by Eberhard Bethge. Translated by Reginald H. Fuller. London: SCM Press, 1953.

—, *The Cost of Discipleship*. Translated by Reginald H. Fuller. London: SCM Press, 1959.

Bosch, D.J., *Believing in the Future: Toward a Missiology of Western Culture*. Leominster: Gracewing, 1995.

Boyarin, D., *Dying for God: Martyrdom and the Making of Christianity and Judaism*. Stanford, CA: Stanford University Press, 1999.

Boyle, N., *Who Are we Now? Christian Humanism and the Global Market from Hegel to Heaney*. Edinburgh: T&T Clark, 1998.

Braaten C.E. and R.W. Jenson (eds.), *Reclaiming the Bible for the Church*. Grand Rapids, MI: Eerdmans, 1995.

—, *The Strange New Word of the Gospel: Re-evangelizing in the Postmodern World*. Grand Rapids, MI: Eerdmans, 2002.

Brown, C.G., *The Death of Christian Britain*: London: Routledge, 2001.

Brown, D., *The Da Vinci Code*. London: Corgi Books, 2004.

Brownson, J.V., "Speaking the Truth in Love: Elements of a Missional Hermeneutic." *International Review of Mission* (2006): 484.

Brueggemann, W., *Like Fire in the Bones: Listening for the Prophetic Voice of Jeremiah*. Minneapolis, MN: Fortress Press, 2006.

—, *Old Testament Theology: Essays on Structure, Theme, and Text*. Edited by P.D. Miller. Minneapolis, MN: Fortress Press, 1992.

Brueggemann, W., *The Prophetic Imagination*. 2nd edn. Minneapolis, MN: Fortress Press, 2001.

—, *Theology of the Old Testament: Testimony, Dispute, Advocacy*. Minneapolis, MN: Fortress Press, 1997.

—, *An Introduction to the Old Testament: The Canon and Christian Imagination*. Louisville, KY: Westminster John Knox Press, 2003.

—, *Genesis: A Bible Commentary for Teaching and Preaching*. Atlanta, GA: John Knox Press, 1982.

—, *Genesis*, "Interpretation". Atlanta, GA: John Knox Press, 1982.

—, *Hopeful Imagination: Prophetic Voices in Exile*. Minneapolis, MN: Fortress Press, 1986.

—, *Israel's Praise: Doxology Against Idolatry and Ideology*. Philadelphia, PA: Fortress Press, 1988.

—, *The Book that Breathes New Life: Scriptural Authority and Biblical Theology*. Philadelphia, PA: Fortress Press, 2004.

Buckley, J.J. (ed.), *The Church in a Postliberal Age* (Radical Traditions). A collection of G. Lindbeck's essays. London: SCM Press, 2002.

Bultmann, R. *Existence and Faith: Shorter Writings of Rudolf Bultmann*. Selected, translated, and introduced by Schubert M. Ogden. New York, NY: Meridian Books, 1960.

Burke, E., *Reflections on the Revolution in France: And on the Proceeding in Certain Societies in London Relative to That Event in a Letter Intended to Have Been Sent to a Gentleman in Paris. 1790*. Harvard Classics Vol. 24, Part 3. New York, NY: Bartleby.com, 2001.

Buxton, M., *David Livingstone*. Basingstoke: Palgrave, 2001.

Capote, T., *In Cold Blood: A True Account of a Multiple Murder and its Consequences*. New York, NY: Random House, 1965.

Caputo, J.D., *On Religion*. London: Routledge, 2001.

Carter, Craig A., *The Politics of the Cross: The Theology and Social Ethics of John Howard Yoder*. Grand Rapids, MI: Brazos Press, 2001.

Cartwright, M. (ed.), *The Royal Priesthood: Essays Ecclesiological and Ecumenical*. Grand Rapids, MI: Eerdmans, 1994.

Chaplin, J., "Political Eschatology and Responsible Government: Oliver O'Donovan's Christian Liberalism." In *A Royal*

Priesthood?: the Use of the Bible Ethically and Politically: a Dialogue with Oliver O'Donovan. Edited by C.G. Bartholomew et al. SAHS Vol. 3. Carlisle: Paternoster 2002.

Childs, B., "On Reclaiming the Bible for Christian Theology." In *Reclaiming the Bible for the Church*. Edited by C.E. Braaten and R.W. Jenson. Grand Rapids, MI: Eerdmans, 1995.

Coleridge, M., "Life in the Crypt or Why Bother with Biblical Studies?." *Biblical Interpretation* 2 (1994): 139–51.

Coleridge, P., *Disability, Liberation and Development*. Oxford: Oxfam Academic, 1993.

Connor, S., *Postmodernist Culture: An Introduction to Theories of the Contemporary*. Oxford: Blackwells, 2001.

Corliss, R., "Popular Metaphysics." In *Time*, 19 April 1999.

Cox, J., "Master Narratives of long-term religious change," in *The Decline of Christendom in Western Europe, 1750–2000*. H. McLeod and W. Ustorf (eds.). Cambridge: Cambridge University Press, 2003, 201.

Cray, Graham, *Mission-Shaped Church: Church Planting and Fresh Expressions of Church in a Changing Context*. London, Church House Publishing, 2004.

Curry, T.J., *Farewell to Christendom: The Future of Church and State in America*. Oxford: Oxford University Press, 2001.

Daley, B.E., "Is Patristic Exegesis still Usable?: Some Reflections on Early Christian Interpretation of the Psalms." In *The Art of Reading Scripture*. Edited by Davis, E.F. and R.B. Hays. Grand Rapids, MI: Eerdmans, 2003.

Dancer, A., *William Stringfellow in Anglo-American Perspective*. Burlington, VT: Ashgate Publishing, 2005.

Davie, G., *Europe: The Exceptional Case. Parameters of Faith in the Modern World*. London: Darton Longman & Todd, 2002.

—, *Religion in Britain since 1945: Believing Without Belonging*. Oxford: Blackwell, 1994.

Davis, E.F. and R.B. Hays (eds.), *The Art of Reading Scripture*. Grand Rapids, MI: Eerdmans, 2003.

Deak, I., "How Guilty Were the Germans?," *New York Review of Books* 31, no. 9 (May 31, 1984), 37–42.

Deleuze, G. and F. Guattaro, *Anti-Oedipus: Capitalism and Schizophrenia*. London: Athlone, 1984.

Depree, M., *Leadership Jazz*. New York: Currency Doubleday, 1992.

Derrida, J., *Of Grammatology*. Translated by Gayatri Chakravorty Spivak. London: Johns Hopkins University Press, 1976.

Descartes, R., *Discourse on Method*. Translated by Donald A. Cress. Indianapolis, IN: Hackett, 1998.

—, *Meditations on First Philosophy*. Edited by Stanley Tweyman. Ann Arbor, MI: Caravan Books, 2002.

Devenish, D., "Mission structures in the New Testament: Supplementary comments on part 1 of 'Field governed mission structures'." *International Journal of Frontier Missions* 18 (2001): 67–68.

Ellul, J., *The New Demons*. Translated by C. Edward Hopkin. New York, NY: Seabury Press, 1975.

—, *The Technological Bluff*. Translated by G.W. Bromiley. Grand Rapids, MI: Eerdmans, 1990.

Fanon, F., *The Wretched of the Earth*. London: MacGibbon & Kee, 1961.

—, *Black Skin, White Masks*. New York, NY: Grove Press, 1967.

Featherstone, M., *Consumer Culture and Postmodernism*. London: Sage, 1990.

Finney, P.C., *The Invisible God: The Earliest Christians on Art*. New York, NY: Oxford Press, 1994.

Foucault, M., "Human Nature: Justice versus Power." In F. Elders (ed.), *Reflexive Water: The Basic Concerns of Mankind*. London: Souvenir Press, 1974.

—, *The Birth of the Clinic: An Archaeology of Medical Perception*. Translated by A. M. Sheridan Smith. London: Tavistock, 1973.

—, *The Order of Things: An Archaeology of the Human Sciences*. New York, NY: Vintage Books, 1970.

—, *Discipline and Punishment: The Birth of the Prison*. Translated by Alan Sheridan. 2nd edn. New York, NY: Vintage Books, 1995.

—, *Madness and Civilization: A History of Insanity in the Age of Reason*. Translated by Richard Howard. New York, NY: Vintage Books 1965.

Foucault, M., *The History of Sexuality*. Translated by Robert Hurley. New York, NY: Vintage Books, 1985.

—, *The Archaeology of Knowledge*. Translated by A.M. Sheridan Smith. London: Routledge, 2002.

—, *Power/Knowledge: Selected Interviews and Other Writings, 1972–1977*. Edited and translated by Colin Gordon. New York, NY: Pantheon Books, 1980.

Foust, T.F. et al. (eds.), *A Scandalous Prophet: The Way of Mission after Newbigin*. Grand Rapids, MI: Eerdmans, 2002.

Fowl, S.E., *Engaging Scripture: A Model for Theological Interpretation*. Challenges in Contemporary Theology. Oxford: Blackwell, 1998.

Franke, J., *The Character of Theology: An Introduction to its Nature, Task and Purpose*. Grand Rapids, MI: Baker, 2005.

Frei, H.W., *The Eclipse of the Biblical Narrative: A Study in 18th century and 19th century hermeneutics*. London: Yale University Press, 1974.

—, *The Identity of Jesus Christ: the Hermeneutical Bases of Dogmatic Theology*. Philadelphia, PA: Fortress Press, 1975.

—, *Theology and Narrative: Selected Essays*. Edited by George Hunsinger and William C. Placher. New York, NY: Oxford University Press, 1993.

Friedman, T.L., *The Lexus and the Olive Tree*. Rev. edn. New York, NY: Farrar, Straus, and Giroux, 2000.

—, *The World is Flat: a Brief History of the Twenty-First Century*. Rev. edn. New York, NY: Picador, 2007.

Fukuyama, F., *The End of History and the Last Man*. London: Penguin, 1993.

Gadamer, H.G., *Truth and Method*. London: Sheed & Ward, 1975.

Galbraith, J.K., *The Affluent Society*. London: Hamish Hamilton, 1958.

Gibbs, E. and I. Coffey, *Church Next: Quantum Changes in Christian Ministry*. New edn. Leicester: Inter-Varsity Press, 2001.

Giddens, A., *Runaway World: How Globalization is Reshaping our Lives*. New York, NY: Routledge, 2000.

Gill, R., *The Myth of the Empty Church*. London: SPCK, 1993.

Goldingay, J., *Models of Scripture*. Carlisle: Paternoster Press, 1994.

Gorringe, T.J., *Karl Barth: Against Hegemony*. Oxford: Oxford University Press, 1999.

Gottwald, N., *The Hebrew Bible in its Social World and in Ours*. Atlanta, GA: Scholars Press, 1993.

—, *The Tribes of Yahweh: a Sociology of the Religion of Liberated Israel, 1250–1050 B.C.E.* Maryknoll, NY: Orbis, 1979.

Greene, C.J.D., *Christology in Cultural Perspective: Marking Out the Horizons*. Grand Rapids, MI/Carlisle: Eerdmans/Paternoster, 2004.

Habermas, J., *The Theory of Communicative Action*. Translated by Thomas McCarthy. Boston, MA: Beacon Press, 1984.

—, "Modernity Versus Postmodernity". *New German Critique* 22 (1981), 3–14.

Hall, D.J., *Confessing the Faith: Christian Theology in a North American Context*. Minneapolis, MN: Fortress Press, 1996.

Harper, M., *Let My People Grow!: Ministry and Leadership in the Church*. London: Hodder & Stoughton, 1977.

Harrison L.E. and S.P. Huntington (eds.), *Culture Matters: How Values Shape Human Progress*. New York, NY: Basic Books, 2001.

Harrison, V., "Putnam's Internal Realism and von Balthasar's Epistemology." *International Journal for Philosophy of Religion* 44 (1998): 67–92.

Harrisville, R.A. and W. Sundberg, *The Bible in Modern Culture: Baruch Spinoza to Brevard Child*. 2nd ed. Grand Rapids, MI: Eerdmans, 1995.

Hart, T., "Imagination and Responsible Reading." In *Renewing Biblical Interpretation*. Edited by Craig Bartholomew, Colin Greene, and Karl Müller. SAHS Vol. 1. Grand Rapids, MI/Carlisle: Zondervan/Paternoster, 2000.

Hastings, A., *A History of English Christianity 1920–1990*. London: SCM Press; 1991.

Hauerwas, S. and D. Burrell, "From System to Story: An Alternative Pattern for Rationality in Ethics." In S. Hauerwas and L.G. Jones (eds.), *Why Narrative? Readings in Narrative Theology*. Grand Rapids, MI: Eerdmans, 1989.

Hauerwas, S. and L.G. Jones (eds.), *Why Narrative? Readings in Narrative Theology*. Grand Rapids, MI: Eerdmans, 1989.

Hauerwas, S. and W.H. Willimon, *Resident Aliens: Life in the Christian Colony*. Nashville, TN: Abingdon Press, 1989.

—, *Where Resident Aliens Live; Exercises for Christian Practice*. Nashville, TN: Abingdon Press, 1996.

Hauerwas, S., *After Christendom?: How the Church is to Behave If Freedom, Justice and a Christian Nation Are Bad Ideas*. Nashville, TN: Abingdon Press, 1991.

—, *Against the Nations: War and Survival in a Liberal Society*. Notre Dame, IN: University of Notre Dame Press, 1992.

—, *A Better Hope: Resources for a Church Confronting Capitalism, Democracy and Postmodernity*. Grand Rapids, MI: Brazos Press, 2000.

—, *Dispatches from the Front: Theological Engagements with the Secular*. Durham: Duke University Press, 1994.

—, *Performing the Faith: Bonhoeffer and the Practice of Nonviolence*. Grand Rapids, MI: Brazos Press, 2004.

—, *The Peaceable Kingdom: A Primer in Christian Ethics*. Notre Dame, IN: University of Notre Dame Press, 1983.

—, *A Community of Character: Toward a Constructive Christian Social Ethic*. Notre Dame, IN: University of Notre Dame Press, 1981.

Hay, D., "Spirituality and the Unchurched." *The Bible in TransMission*, Summer (1999). {http://www.biblesociety.org.uk/exploratory/articles/hay99.doc}

Hay, D. and K. Hunt, *Understanding the Spirituality of People who don't go to Church: A Report on the Findings of the Adult's Spirituality Project at the University of Nottingham*. Nottingham: University of Nottingham, 2000.

Hearfield, C., *Adorno And The Modern Ethos of Freedom*. Ashgate New Critical Thinking in Philosophy. Aldershot: Ashgate, 2004.

Heidegger, M., *The Question Concerning Technology, and other Essays*. Translated by William Lovitt. New York, NY: Harper & Row, 1977.

—, *Being and Time*. Oxford, Blackwells, 1962.

Heywood, A., *Key Concepts in Politics*. New York, NY: St. Martin's Press, 2000.

Himmelfarb, G., "From Clapham to Bloomsbury: a Genealogy of Morals." In G. Himmelfarb (ed.), *Marriage and morals among the Victorians and other essays*. London: Tauris, 1989. {www.facingthechallenge.org/himmelfarb.htm} (http://www.facingthechallenge.org/himmelfarb.htm.)

Hirsch, A., *The Forgotten Ways: Reactivating the Missional Church*. Grand Rapids, MI: Brazos Press, 2006.

Holloway, R., *Doubts and Loves: What is Left of Christianity*. Edinburgh: Canongate Books, 2002.

—, *Godless Morality: Keeping Religion out of Ethics*. Edinburgh: Canongate Books, 1999.

Holmes, S.R., *Public Theology in Cultural Engagement*. Milton Keynes: Paternoster, 2008.

Horkheimer, M. and T.W. Adorno, *The Dialectic of Enlightenment*. Translated by John Cumming. New York, NY: Herder & Herder, 1972.

Horsley, R.A. (ed.), *Paul and Empire: Religion and Power in Roman Imperial Society*. Harrisburg, PA: Trinity Press International, 1997.

—, *Paul and Politics: Ekklesia, Israel, Imperium, Interpretation: Essays in Honor of Krister Stendahl*. Harrisburg, PA: Trinity Press International, 2000.

Horsley, R.A., *Paul and the Roman Imperial Order*. Harrisburg, PA: Trinity Press International, 2004.

Hughes, R.T., *Myths America Lives By*. Urbana, IL: University of Illinois Press, 2003.

Hunsberger, G.R., *Bearing the Witness of the Spirit: Lesslie Newbigin's Theology of Cultural Plurality*. Grand Rapids, MI: Eerdmans, 1998.

Hunsinger, G., *Disruptive Grace: Studies in the Theology of Karl Barth*. Grand Rapids, MI: Eerdmans, 2000.

Inge, M.T. and T. Capote, *Truman Capote: Conversations*. Mississippi, MS: Mississippi University Press 1987.

Irwin, W. (ed.), *The Matrix and Philosophy: Welcome to the Desert of the Real*. Chicago, IL: Open Court, 2002.

Jamison, F., *Postmodernism and the Cultural Logic of Late Capitalism*. London: Verso, 1991.

Jarvis, S., *Adorno: A Critical Introduction*. New York, NY: Routledge, 1998.

Jehle, F., *Ever Against the Stream: The Politics of Karl Barth 1906–1968*. Grand Rapids, MI: Eerdmans, 2002.

Jencks, C., *Postmodernism: The New Classicism in Art and Architecture*. New York, NY: Rizzoli, 1987.

Jenkins, P., *The Next Christendom: The Coming of Global Christianity*. New edn. Oxford: Oxford University Press, 2007.

Jenson, R.W., "What is a Post Christian," in *The Strange New World of the Gospel*. C.E. Braaten and R.W. Jenson (eds.). Grand Rapids, MI: Eerdmans, 2002.

Jewett R. and J.S. Lawrence, *Captain America and the Crusade against Evil*. Grand Rapids, MI: Eerdmans, 2003.

Jungel, E., *Christ, Justice and Peace: Toward a Theology of the State*. Edinburgh: T&T Clark, 1992.

Kant, I., *Beantwortung der Frage: Was ist Aufklärung?* Neu-Isenburg: Edition Tiessen, 1987.

—, *The Critique of Pure Reason*. Translated by Werner S. Pluhar. Cambridge: Hackett, 1996.

Keller, D., *Media Culture: Cultural Studies, Identity and Politics between the Modern and the Postmodern*. London: Routledge, 1995.

Kelsey, D., *The Uses of Scripture in Recent Theology*. Harrisburg, PA: Trinity Press International, 1999.

Kierkegaard, S., *Training in Christianity and the Edifying Discourse Which "Accompanied" It*. Translated with introduction by W. Lowrie. London: Oxford University Press, 1941.

Korten, D.C., *When Corporations Rule the World*. 2nd edn. San Francisco, CA: Berrett-Koehler Publishers, 2001.

Laclau, E. and C. Mouffe, *Hegemony and Socialist Strategy: Towards a Radical Democratic Politics*. London: Verso, 1985.

Lakoff, G. and M. Johnson, *Philosophy in the Flesh: The Embodied Mind and Its Challenge to Western Thought*. New York, NY: Basic Books, 1993.

Lash, S., *Sociology of Postmodernism*. London: Routledge, 1990.

Leftwich, A., *What is Politics? The Activity and its Study*. Cambridge: Polity Press, 2004.

Lewis, C.S., "Introduction," in Athanasius, *The Incarnation of the Word of God: Being the Treatise of St. Athanasius De Incarnatione Verbi Dei*. London: The Macmillan Company, 1946.

Lieu, J., *Christian Identity in the Jewish and Graeco-Roman World*. Oxford: Oxford University Press, 2004.

Lincoln, A.T., *Truth on Trial: The Lawsuit Motif in the Fourth Gospel*. Peabody, MA: Hendrickson, 2000.

Lindbeck, G., "Reminiscences of Vatican II." In J.J. Buckley (ed.), *The Church in a Postliberal Age (Radical Traditions)*. Grand Rapids, MI: Eerdmans, 2003.

—, *The Nature of Christian Doctrine: Religion and Theology in a Postliberal Age*. Louisville, KY: Westminster John Knox Press, 1984.

—, *The Church in a Postliberal Age*. Collection of Lindbeck's essays edited by J.J. Buckley. London: SCM Press, 2002.

Loughlin, G., *Telling God's Story: Bible, Church and Narrative Theology*. Cambridge: Cambridge University Press, 1996.

Lyotard, J.F., *The Differend: Phases in Dispute*. Minneapolis, MN: University of Minnesota Press, 1988.

—, *Economie Libidinale*. Paris: Seuil, 1974.

—, *The Lyotard Reader*. Edited by Andrew Benjamin. Oxford: Basil Blackwell, 1989.

—, *The Postmodern Condition: A Report on Knowledge*. Theory and History of Literature Vol 10. Translated by G. Bennington and B. Massumi. Manchester: Manchester University Press, 1984.

MacIntyre, A.C., *After Virtue: A Study in Moral Theory*. London: Duckworth Press, 1985.

—, *Dependent Rational Animals: Why Human Beings Need the Virtues*. Paul Carus Lectures. Illinois, IL: Carus, 1999.

—, *Three Rival Versions of Moral Enquiry: Encyclopedia, Genealogy and Tradition*. Indiana, IN: University of Notre Dame Press, 1990.

—, *Whose Justice? Which Rationality?* Indiana, IN: University of Notre Dame Press, 1988.

Malin, I. (ed.), *Truman Capote's In Cold Blood: A Critical Handbook*. Belmont, CA: Wadsworth, 1968.

Marquand, D. and A. Seldon (eds.), *The Ideas that Shaped Post-War Britain*. London: Fontana Press, 1996.

Mason, R., *Propaganda and Subversion in the Old Testament*. London: SPCK, 1997.

Mathison, K.A., *The Shape of Sola Scriptura*. Moscow, ID: Canon Press, 2001.

McLeod, H. and W. Ustorf (eds.), *The Decline of Christendom in Western Europe, 1750–2000*. Cambridge: Cambridge University Press, 2003.

McCloughry, R. and W. Morris, *Making a World of Difference: Christian Reflections on Disability*. London, SPCK, 2002.

McLaren, B., *A Generous Orthodoxy: Why I am a Missional, Evangelical, Post/Protestant, Liberal/Conservative, Mystical/Poetic, Biblical, Charismatic/Contemplative, Fundamentalist/Calvinist, Anabaptist/ Anglican, Methodist, Catholic, Green, Incarnational, Depressed-yet-Hopeful, Emergent, Unfinished Christian*. Grand Rapids, MI: Zondervan, 2004.

Mead, L.B., *Transforming Congregations for the Future*. Bethesda, MD: Alban Institute, 1994.

—, *The Once and Future Church*. Washington DC, WA: Alban Institute, 1991 reprinted 1994.

Mendenhall, G.E., "The Hebrew Conquest of Palestine," *Biblical Archaeologist* 25 (1962): 66–87.

Merleau-Ponty, M., *Phenomenology of Perception*. London: Praeger, 2004.

Midgeley, M., *Science as Salvation: A Modern Myth and Its Meaning*. London: Routledge, 1992.

Millbank, J., C. Pickstock and G. Ward (eds.), *Radical Orthodoxy: A New Theology*. London: Routledge, 1999.

Millett, K., *Sexual Politics*. New York, NY: Doubleday, 1970.

Moberly, R.W.L., *The Bible, Theology and Faith: A Study of Abraham and Jesus*. Cambridge: Cambridge University Press, 2000.

Moltmann, J., *The Coming of God: Christian Eschatology*. London: SCM Press, 1996.

—, *The Way of Jesus Christ: Christology in Messianic Dimensions*. London: SCM Press, 1990.

Monk, R., *Ludwig Wittgenstein: The Duty of Genius*. London: Jonathan Cape, 1990.

Morris, J., *Pride Against Prejudice*. London: The Women's Press, 1994.

Muller, J.Z., *The Mind and the Market: Capitalism in Western Thought*. New York, NY: Alfred A. Knopf, 2002.

—, *Adam Smith in his Time and Ours: Designing the Decent Society*. Princeton, NJ: Princeton University Press, 1995.

Munson, J., *The Nonconformists: In Search of a Lost Culture*. London: SPCK, 1991.

Murphy, R.E., *The Tree of Life: An Exploration of Biblical Wisdom Literature*. Grand Rapids, MI: Eerdmans, 2002.

Murray, S., *Post-Christendom: Church and Mission in a Strange New World*. Milton Keynes: Paternoster Press, 2004.

Nafisi, A., *Reading Lolita in Tehran: a Memoir in Books*. London: Fourth Estate, 2003.

Narayan, U., *Dislocating Cultures: Identities, Traditions and Third World Feminism*. Thinking Gender. London: Routledge, 1997.

Neuhaus, R.J., *The Naked Public Square: Religion and Democracy in America*. Grand Rapids, MI: Eerdmans, 1984.

Newbigin, L., *A Proper Confidence: Faith, Doubt and Certainty in Christian Discipleship*. Grand Rapid, MI: Eerdmans, 1995.

—, *Foolishness to the Greeks: The Gospel and Western Culture*. London: SPCK, 1986.

—, *The Gospel in a Pluralist Society*. London: SPCK, 1989.

—, *The Other Side of 1984: Questions for the Churches*. London: Church House, 1990.

Nietzsche, F., *The Gay Science* (trans.) W. Kaufman. NY: Vintage Book Editions, 1974.

—, *Thus Spoke Zarathustra: A Book for All and None*. NY: Random House Inc, 1995.

Noll, M.A. *The Old Religion in a New World: The History of North American Christianity*. Grand Rapids, MI: Eerdmans, 2002.

O'Connor, B. (ed.), *The Adorno Reader*. Oxford: Blackwell Publishing, 2000.

O'Connor, F., *Everything That Rises Must Converge*. Farrar, Straus, and Giroux, 1965.

—, *The Complete Stories*. 33rd edn. Farrar, Straus, and Giroux, 1971.

O'Connor, F., *The Habit of Being*. Farrar, Straus, and Giroux, 1988.

O'Donovan, O. and J. Lockwood O'Donovan. *Bonds of Imperfection: Christian Politics Past and Present*. Grand Rapids, MI: Eerdmans, 2004.

O'Donovan, O., *Resurrection and Moral Order: An Outline for Evangelical Ethics*. 2nd edn. Leicester: Apollos, 1994.

O'Donovan, O., *The Desire of the Nations: Rediscovering the Roots of Political Theology*. Cambridge; Cambridge University Press, 1996.

Obama, B., *The Audacity of Hope: Thoughts on Reclaiming the American Dream*. New York, NY: Random House, 2006. Excerpt reprinted in *Time*, 15 October 2006.

Oliver, G., *Human Bible, Holy Bible: Questions Pastoral Practice Must Ask*. London: Darton Longman & Todd, 2006.

Paine, T., *Collected Writings*. Edited by T. Foner. New York, NY: Library Classics of the United States, 1995.

—, *The Age of Reason*. 1796. New York, NY: BiblioBazaar, 2007.

Pannenberg, W. (ed.), *Revelation as History: A Proposal for a More Open, Less Authoritarian View of an Important Theological Concept*. New York and London: Macmillan, 1968

—, *Systematic Theology*. 3 Vols. Transated by G. Bromiley. Edinburgh: T&T Clark, 1991–98.

Pattison, S., M. Cooling and T. Cooling, *Using the Bible in Christian Ministry*. London: Darton, Longman & Todd, 2007.

Petersen, D.L., *The Prophetic Literature: An Introduction*. Louisville, KY: Westminster John Knox Press, 2002.

Piot, P., "Responding to the HIV/AIDS Epidemic: prospects for near and distant futures." Speech delivered at the London School of Economics, February 2005. {http://www.lse.ac.uk/collections/LSEPublicLecturesAnd Events/events/2005/20041216t1723z001.htm}

Polanyi, M. *Personal Knowledge: Towards a Post-Critical Philosophy*. 2nd edn. Chicago, IL: University of Chicago Press, 1977.

Poster, M. (ed.), *Jean Baudrillard, Selected Writings*. Stanford, CA: Stanford University Press, 1988.

Postman, N., *Amusing Ourselves to Death: Public Discourse in an Age of Show Business*. New York, NY: Penguin Books, 1986.

Putnam, R., *Bowling Alone: The Collapse and Revival of American Community.* New York, NY: Simon & Schuster, 2001.

Ramachandra, V., "Learning from Modern European Secularism: A View from the Third World Church," *European Journal of Theology,* Vol. 12, No. 1, 2005.

Rasmussen, L.L., *Moral Fragments and Moral Community: A Proposal for Church in Society.* Minneapolis, MN: Fortress Press, 1993.

Ratzinger, J. and M. Pera, *Without Roots: The West, Relativism, Christianity, Islam.* Translated by Michael F. Moore. New York, NY: Basic Books, 2006.

Ricoeur P., *Lectures on Ideology and Utopia.* Edited by G.H. Taylor. New York, NY: Columbia University Press, 1986.

—, *Oneself as Another.* Translated by K. Blamey. Chicago, IL: University of Chicago Press, 1994.

—, "The Model of the Text: Meaningful Action Considered as a Text." In P. Ricoeur. *Hermeneutics and the Human Sciences: Essays on Language, Action and Interpretation.* Translated and edited by J.B. Thompson. Cambridge: Cambridge University Press, 1981.

—, "Metaphor and the Central Problem of Hermeneutics." In P. Ricoeur. *Hermeneutics and the Human Sciences: Essays on Language, Action and Interpretation.* Translated and edited by J.B. Thompson. Cambridge: Cambridge University Press, 1981.

—, *Figuring the Sacred: Religion, Narrative and Imagination.* Translated by D. Pellauer. Edited by M.I. Wallace. Minneapolis, MN: Fortress Press, 1995.

—, *Time and Narrative.* Translated by K. McLaughlin and D. Pellauer. 3 vols. Chicago, IL: Chicago University Press, 1984–88.

Robinson, J.A.T., *Honest to God.* London: SCM Press, 1963.

Robinson, M. and S. Christine, *Planting Tomorrow's Churches Today: a Comprehensive Handbook.* London: Monarch Books, 1992.

Robinson, M. *Winning Hearts, Changing Minds.* London: Monarch Books, 2001.

Rorty, R., *Philosophy and the Mirror of Nature: Consequences of Pragmatism.* Oxford: Blackwells, 1980.

Rowland, C., "The Apocalypse and Political Theology." *In A Royal Priesthood? The Use of the Bible Ethically and Politically: a dialogue with Oliver O'Donovan.* Edited by C. G. Bartholomew et al. SAHS Vol. 3. Carlisle: Paternoster, 2002.

Roxburgh, A., *The Sky is Falling: Leaders Lost in Transition.* Eagle, ID: Allelon, 2006.

Ryan, M., "Postmodern Politics," in *Theory, Culture and Society* 5 (1988): 559–76.

Said, E., *Orientalism.* New York, NY: Vintage Books, 1979.

—, *Culture and Imperialism.* New York, NY: Vintage Books, 1994.

Sanneh, L., *Whose Religion is Christianity? The Gospel Beyond the West.* Grand Rapids, MI: Eerdmans, 2003.

Schlossberg, H., *The Silent Revolution and the Making of Victorian England.* Columbus, OH: Ohio State University, 2000.

Schmithals, W., *An Introduction to the Theology of Rudolf Bultmann.* Translated by J. Bowden. London: Solle, 1968.

Schneider, H.W. (ed.), *Adam Smith's Moral and Political Philosophy.* First published 1948. New York, NY: Hafner, 1948.

Schoch, R., *The Secrets of Happiness: Three Thousand Years of Searching for the Good Life.* London: Profile Books, 2006.

Schuchardt, R.M., "The Radiation Sickness of the Soul." The Bible in TransMission, Summer (2002). {www.biblesociety.org.uk/exploratory/articles/schuchardt02.pdf}

Schweitzer, A., *The Quest of the Historical Jesus: A Critical Study of its Progress from Reimarus to Wrede.* London: A&C Black, 1968.

Scobie, C.H.H., *The Ways of Our God: An Approach to Biblical Theology.* Grand Rapids, MI: Eerdmans, 2003.

Secord, J.A., *Victorian Sensation: The Extraordinary Publication, Reception and Secret Authorship of Vestiges of the Natural History of Creation.* Chicago, IL: University of Chicago Press, 2000.

Selby, P. and R.S. Sugirtharajah, *Voices from the Margin: Interpreting the Bible in the Third World.* New York, NY: Orbis, 2006.

Shanks, A., *God and Modernity: A New and Better Way to Do Theology.* London: Routledge, 2000.

Simpson, G., *Critical Social Theory: Prophetic Reason, Civil Society and Christian Imagination.* Minneapolis, MN: Fortress Press, 2002.

Smart, J., *The Strange Silence of the Bible in the Church: A Study in Hermeneutics*. Philadelphia, PA: Westminster Press, 1970.

Smith, A., *An Inquiry in the Natures and Causes of The Wealth of Nations*. First published 1786. Chicago, IL: University of Chicago Press, 1977.

Smith, J.K.A., *Introducing Radical Orthodoxy: Mapping a Post-secular Theology*. Grand Rapids, MI: Baker, 2004.

Song, Choan-Seng, *Jesus, the Crucified People. The Cross in the Lotus World* Vol 1. Minneapolis, MN: Fortress Press, 1996

—, *Theology from the Womb of Asia*. Maryknoll, NY: Orbis Books, 1986.

—, *Third-Eye Theology: Theology in Formation in Asian Settings*. Maryknoll, NY: Orbis Books, 1979.

Spencer, N., "Doing God:" A Future for Faith in the Public Square." *Theos*, 2006, 17.

Steiner, G., *Real Presences*. Chicago, IL: University of Chicago Press, 1991.

Stiver, D.R., *Theology after Ricoeur: New Directions in Hermeneutical Theology*. Louisville, KY: Westminster John Knox Press, 2001.

Stout, J., *Democracy and Tradition*. Princeton, NJ: New Forum Books, 2004.

—, *Ethics After Babel*. Princeton/Oxford: Princeton University Press, 2001.

Stringfellow, W., *An Ethic for Christians and Other Aliens in a Strange Land*. Waco, TX: Word Books, 1973.

Sugirtharajah, R.S., "Postcolonial Biblical Interpretation." In Selby, P. and R.S. Sugirtharajah, *Voices from the Margin: Interpreting the Bible in the Third World*. New York, NY: Orbis, 2006, 67

Tertullian, *The Prescription Against Heretics*. Kila, MT: Kessinger Publishing, 2004.

Thiemann, R.F., *Religion and Public Life: A Dilemma for Democracy*. Washington, DC: Georgetown University Press, 1996.

Thiselton, A.C., *New Horizons in Hermeneutics*. Carlisle: Paternoster, 1992.

Thomas, C. and E. Dodson, *Blinded by Might: Can the Religious Right Save America?* Grand Rapids, MI: Zondervan, 1999.

Thornhill, J., *Modernity: Christianity's Estranged Child Reconstructed*. Grand Rapids, MI: Eerdmans, 2000.

Tillich, P. and R.C. Kimball, *Theology of Culture*. Oxford: Oxford University Press, 1959.

Toulmin, S., *Cosmopolis: the Hidden Agenda of Modernity*. Chicago, IL: University of Chicago Press, 1990.

—, *Return to Reason*. London: Harvard University Press, 2001.

Ustorf, W., "A Missiological Postcript." In H. McLeod and W. Ustorf (eds.), *The Decline of Christendom in Western Europe, 1750–2000*. Cambridge: Cambridge University Press, 2003.

Vanhoozer, K., *First Theology: God, Scripture and Hermeneutics*. Leicester: Apollos, 2002.

—, *Is There a Meaning in This Text? The Bible, The Reader, and the Morality of Literary Knowledge*. Leicester: Apollos, 1998.

Von Rad, G., *Old Testament Theology*. Translated by D.M.G. Stalker. 2 Vols. Edinburgh: Oliver & Boyd, 1962 and 1965.

—, *Wisdom in Israel*. Norcross, GA: Trinity Press International, 1993.

Wainwright, G., *Lesslie Newbigin: A Theological Life*. Oxford: Oxford University Press, 2000.

Walker, A., *Restoring the Kingdom: The Radical Christianity of the House Church Movement*. London: Hodder & Stoughton, 1985.

Wallis, J., *God's Politics: Why the American Right Gets It Wrong and the Left Doesn't Get It*. New York, NY: Lion Hudson, 2006.

Walsh, B.J. and S.C. Keesmaat, *Colossians Remixed: Subverting the Empire*. Downers Grove, IL: Inter-Varsity Press, 2004.

Ward, G., *Cultural Transformation and Religious Practice*. Cambridge: Cambridge University Press, 2005.

Warren, R., *Building Missionary Congregations*. Board of Mission Occasional Paper. London: Church House, 1996.

Watson, F., *Text and Truth: Redefining Biblical Theology*. Edinburgh: T&T Clark, 1997.

Webster, J. and G.P. Schner (eds.), *Theology After Liberalism*. Oxford: Blackwell, 2000,

Weigel, G., *The Cube and the Cathedral: Europe, America, and Politics Without God*. New York, NY: Basic Books, 2005.

Wellman, S., *David Livingstone: Missionary and Explorer.* Uhrichsville, OH: Barbour, 1995.

Westermann, C., *Genesis, An Introduction.* Minneapolis, MI: Augsburg Fortress, 1992.

White, J.R., *Scripture Alone: Exploring the Bible's Accuracy, Authority and Authenticity.* Bloomington, MN: Bethany House, 2004.

Wilder, A.N., "Story and Story-World." *Interpretation* 37 (1983): 353–64.

Williams, R., *Lost Icons: Reflections on Cultural Bereavement.* London: Continuum, 2002.

Wilson, R.R., *Prophecy and Society in Ancient Israel.* New edn. Minneapolis, MI: Fortress Press, 1980.

Wink, W., *The Bible in Human Transformation: Toward a New Paradigm for Biblical Study.* Philadelphia, PA: Fortress Press, 1973.

—, *The Powers That Be: Theology for a New Millennium.* New York, NY: Doubleday, 1998.

Wittgenstein, L., *Philosophical Investigations.* 3rd edn. London: Prentice Hall, 1999.

—, *The Blue and Brown Books.* Oxford: Basil Blackwell, 1958.

—, *Tractatus Logico-Philosophicus.* London: Routledge & Kegan Paul, 1961.

Wolterstorff, N., *Divine Discourse: Philosophical Reflections on the Claim that God Speaks.* Cambridge: Cambridge University, 1995

Woodhead, L., "The turn to life in contemporary religion and spirituality." In Ursula King (ed.), *Spirituality and Society in the New Millennium.* Brighton: Sussex Academic Press, 2001.

Work, T., *Living and Active: Scripture in the Economy of Salvation.* Grand Rapids, MI: Eerdmans, 2001.

Worrall, B.G., *The Making of the Modern Church: Christianity in England since 1800.* 3rd edn. London: SPCK, 2003.

Wright, N.T., *The Last Word: Beyond the Bible Wars to a New Understanding of the Authority of Scripture.* New York, NY: HarperCollins, 2005.

—, *The New Testament and the People of God.* London: SPCK, 1992.

—, *Paul: In Fresh Perspectives.* Minneapolis, MI: Fortress Press, 2005.

—, *Scripture and the Authority of God.* London: SPCK; 2005.

Wuthnow, R., *Christianity in the 21st Century: Reflections on the Challenges Ahead*. Oxford: Oxford University Press, 1993.

Yoder, J.H., *The Christian Witness to the State*. Newton, KS: Faith and Life Press, 1964.

—, "The Otherness of the Church." In M. Cartwright (ed.), *The Royal Priesthood: Essays Ecclesiological and Ecumenical*. Grand Rapids, MI: Eerdmans, 1994.

—, *The Politics of Jesus*. 2nd edn. Carlisle: Paternoster Press, 1994.

—, *The Priestly Kingdom: Social Ethics as Gospel*. Notre Dame, IN: Notre Dame University Press, 1984.

Young, R.J.C. *Postcolonialism: An Historical Introduction*.Oxford: Blackwells Publishing, 2001.

Zimmerman, M., *Heidegger's Confrontation with Modernity: Technology, Politics and Art*. Indiana, IN: University Press, 1991.

Series Titles Currently Available

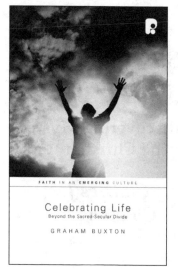

Celebrating Life

Beyond the Sacred-Secular Divide

Graham Buxton

As Christians, our engagement with the world and with culture is often impoverished as a result of unbiblical dualisms. More than we realise, the divide between sacred and secular is reinforced in our minds, contributing to an unhealthy and, at times, narrow super-spirituality. Seeking a more postmodern, holistic and, ultimately, more *Christian* approach to culture, Graham Buxton leads us on a journey towards the celebration of life in *all* its dimensions.

The first part of the book examines the roots of our dualistic thinking and its implications for culture. Part Two draws us from dualism to holism in a number of chapters that consider our engagement with literature, the creative arts, science, politics and business. Part Three draws the threads together by setting out the dimensions of a more holistic theology of the church's engagement with, and participation in, contemporary society that will lead us 'beyond the sacred-secular divide'.

'This is incarnational theology at its best!' – **Ray S. Anderson**, Senior Professor of Theology and Ministry, Fuller Theological Seminary, California.

Graham Buxton is Director of Postgraduate Studies in Ministry and Theology, Tabor College, Adelaide, Australia. He is author of Dancing in the Dark and The Trinity, Creation and Pastoral Ministry.

978-1-84227-507-1

Soaring in the Spirit

Rediscovering Mystery in the Christian Life

Charles J. Conniry, Jr.

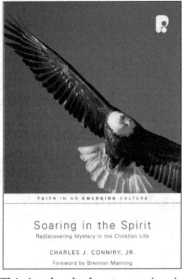

This is a book about experiencing the presence of Jesus Christ in the moment-by-moment 'nows' of daily life. James McClendon, Jr. observed that the first task of theology is to locate our place in the story. Like finding directions at a shopping mall with the brightly coloured words, 'you are here,' the author invites us into an encounter with the 'we-are-here' place in God's Great Story. The claim of this book is that the experience of Christ's presence in the 'right-here' of our daily walk – *Christian soaring* – is the birthright of every follower of Jesus Christ. This is a thoughtful, stirring, and ground-breaking book on the neglected topic of *Christian soaring through discerning discipleship.*

> 'This book is a *tour de force* . . . and can be read with profit by believers and unbelievers, philosophers and theologians, pastors and lay people, and anyone who longs to soar in the Spirit . . . It not only blessed me but drew me to prayer.' – **Brennan Manning**, author of *The Ragamuffin Gospel.*

Charles J. Conniry, Jr. is Associate Professor of Pastoral Ministry and Director of the Doctor of Ministry Program at George Fox Evangelical Seminary, Portland.

978-1-84227-508-5

Chrysalis

The Hidden Transformation in the Journey of Faith

Alan Jamieson

Increasing numbers of Christian people find their faith metamorphos-ing. Substantial and essential change seems to beckon them beyond the standard images and forms of Christian faith but questions about where this may lead remain. Is this the death of personal faith or the emergence of something new? Could it be a journey that is Spirit-led?

Chrysalis uses the life-cycle of butterflies as a metaphor for the faith jour-ney that many contemporary people are experiencing. Drawing on the three main phases of a butterfly's life and the transformations between these, the book suggests subtle similarities with the zones of Christian faith that many encounter. For butterflies and Christians change between these *'phases'* or *'zones'* is substantial, life-changing and irreversible.

This book accompanies ordinary people in the midst of substantive faith change. It is an excellent resource for those who choose to support others through faith transformations. *Chrysalis* is primarily pastoral and practical drawing on the author's experience of accom-panying people in the midst of difficult personal faith changes.

Alan Jamieson is a minister in New Zealand and a trained sociolo-gist. His internationally acclaimed first book, *A Churchless Faith*, researched why people leave their churches to continue their walk of faith outside the church.

978-1-84227-544-3

Re:Mission

Biblical Mission for a Post-Biblical Church

Andrew Perriman

In this innovative and radical book postmodern mission and New Testament studies collide. Andrew Perriman examines the mission of the earliest church in its historical context and argues that our context is very different and *so our mission cannot simply be a matter of doing exactly what the earliest church did*. The key question at the heart of the book is, 'How do we shape a *biblical* theology of mission for a *post-biblical* church?'

> '*Re:Mission* distinguishes Perriman as a scholar who must be reckoned with in this time of rethinking and transition. A great piece of work!' – **Brian D. McLaren**, author (brianmclaren.net)

> 'Andrew Perriman has addressed one of the most challenging facets of New Testament teaching and he does so with remarkable insight and creativity. This fascinating book makes for urgent reading.' – **Craig A. Evans**, Payzant Distinguished Professor of New Testament, Acadia Divinity College, Canada

Andrew Perriman lives in Holland and works with Christian Associates seeking to develop open, creative communities of faith for the emerging culture in Europe. He is author of *Speaking of Women* about Paul's teaching on women, *Faith, Health and Prosperity*, and, *The Coming of the Son of Man: New Testament Eschatology for an Emerging Church*.

978-1-84227-545-0